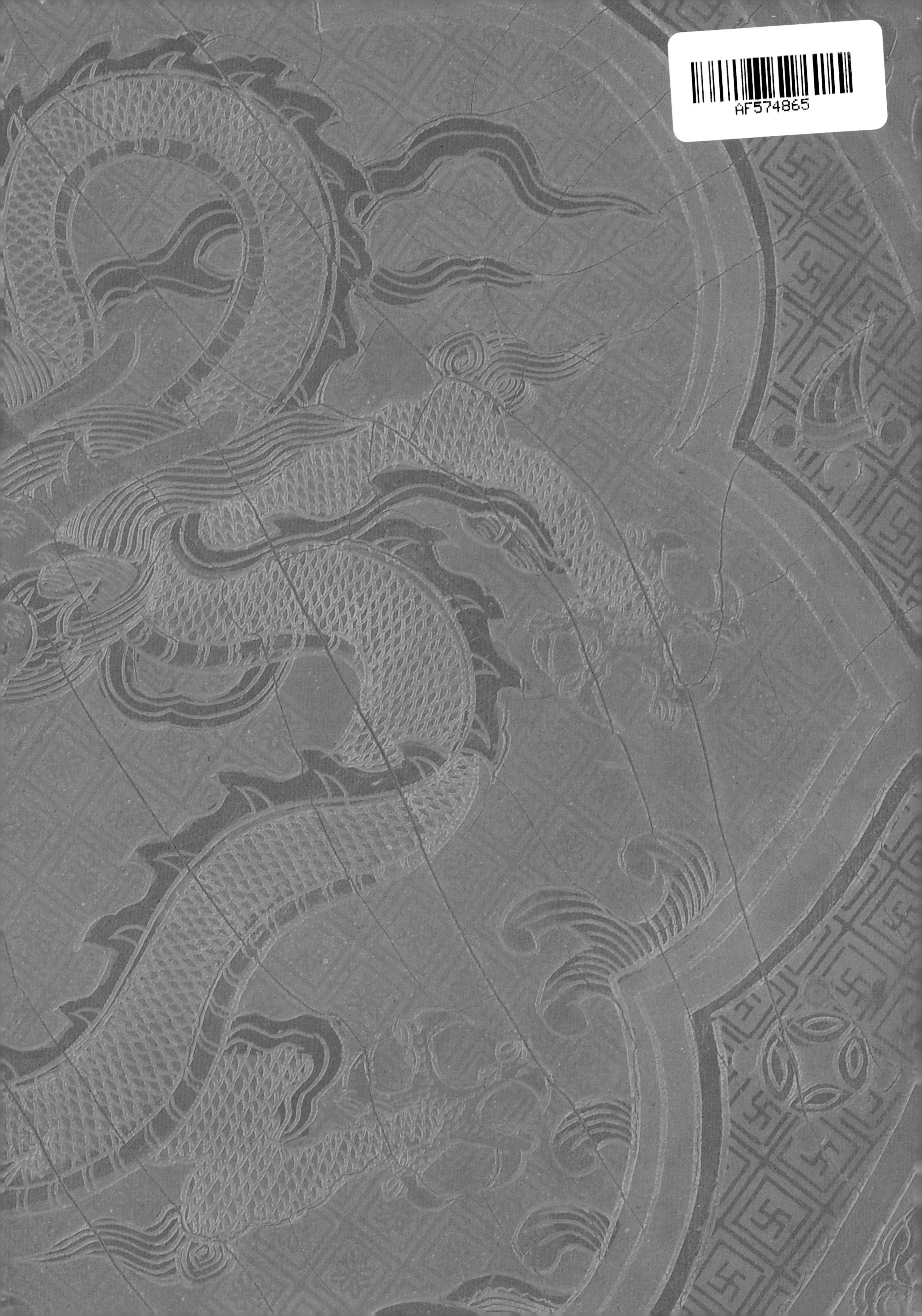

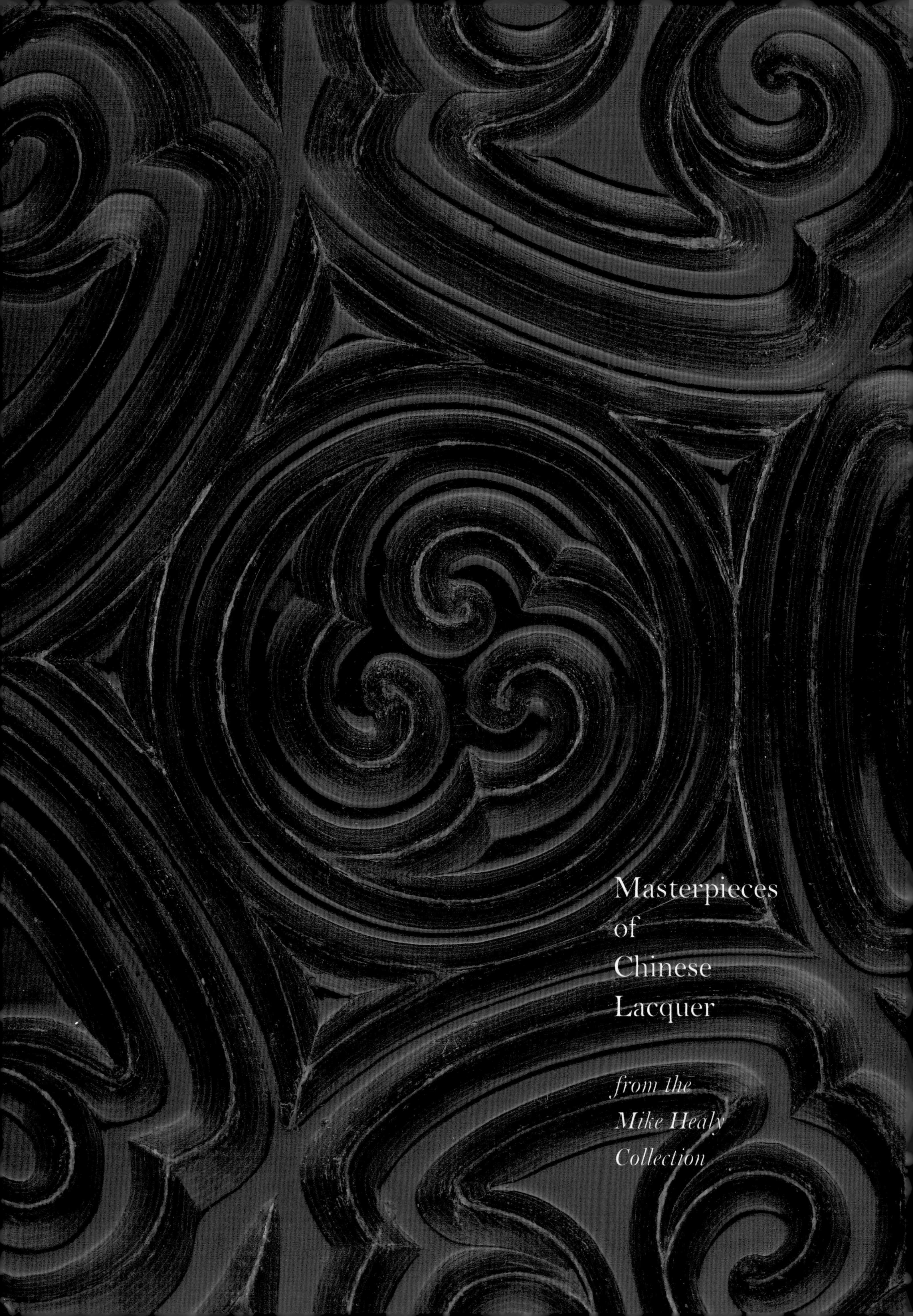

Masterpieces of Chinese Lacquer

from the Mike Healy Collection

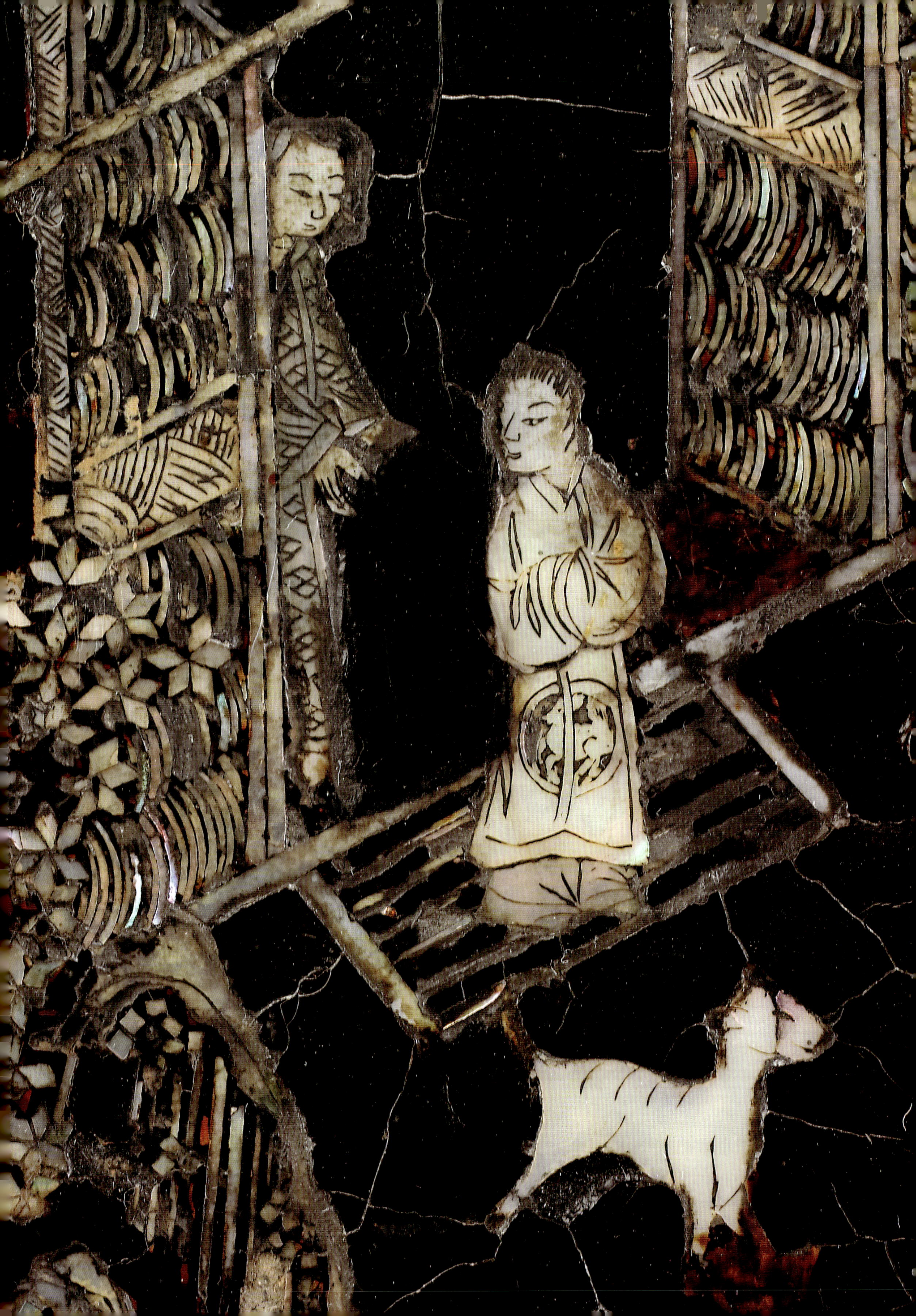

An exhibition organized by the
Honolulu Academy of Arts

Julia M. White
Curator of Asian Art
Honolulu Academy of Arts

With a contribution by
Bao Yanli
Associate Director and Researcher
for the Artistic Techniques
Research Department
Shanghai Museum

Honolulu Academy of Arts

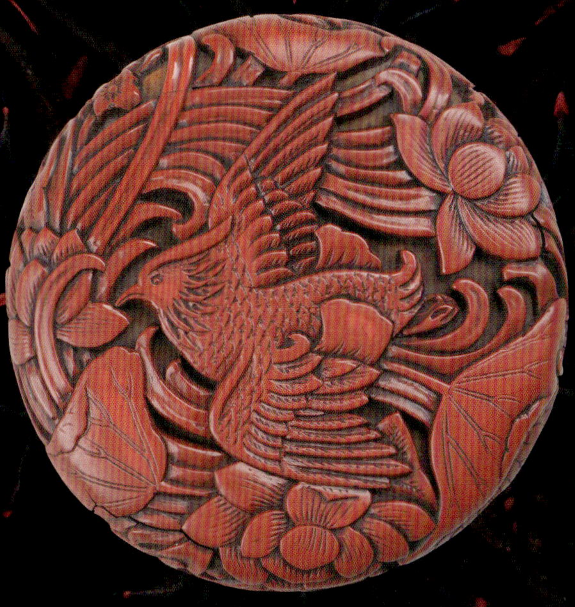

Masterpieces of Chinese Lacquer

from the Mike Healy Collection

Exhibition venues

Honolulu Academy of Arts
December 19, 2002–
April 27, 2003

China Institute of America
September 15–
December 3, 2005

Santa Barbara Museum of Art
January 14–April 16, 2006

Library of Congress Cataloging-in-Publication Data
White, Julia M.
Masterpieces of Chinese lacquer from the Mike Healy collection : an exhibition organized by the Honolulu Academy of Arts / Julia M. White ; with a contribution by Bao Yanli.
p. cm.
Catalog of the exhibition held at the Honolulu Academy of Arts, Dec. 19, 2002–Apr. 27, 2003, at the China Institute of America, Sept. 15–Dec. 3, 2005, and at the Santa Barbara Museum of Art, Jan.14–Apr. 16, 2006.
Includes bibliographical references and index.
ISBN 0-937426-66-0 (hardcover : alk. paper)
1. Lacquer and lacquering—China—Exhibitions. 2. Art objects, Chinese—Exhibitions. 3. Healy, Mike, 1943– —Art collections—Exhibitions. 4. Art objects—Private collections—United States—Exhibitions. I. Bao, Yanli. II. Honolulu Academy of Arts. III. Title.
NK9900.7.C6W55 2005
745.'26'095107496931—dc22
2005010366

Distributed by
University of Washington Press
PO Box 50096
Seattle, WA 98145-5096 U.S.A.
www.washington.edu/uwpress

Designed by John Hubbard
Edited by Lorna Price and Suzanne Kotz
Proofread by Laura Iwasaki
Photography by Shuzo Uemoto
Color separations by iocolor, Seattle
Produced by Marquand Books, Inc., Seattle www.marquand.com
Printed and bound in China by
C&C Offset Printing Co., Ltd.

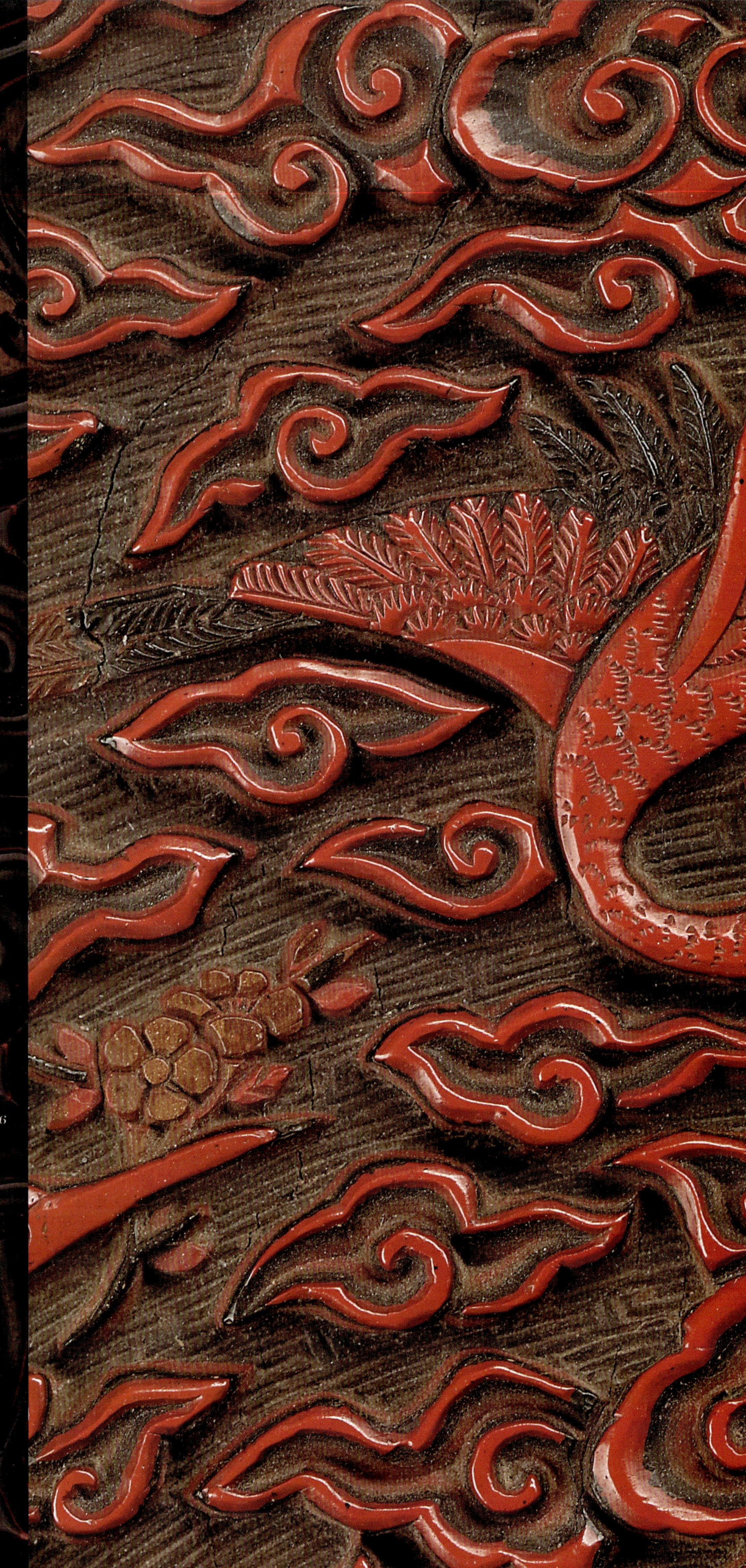

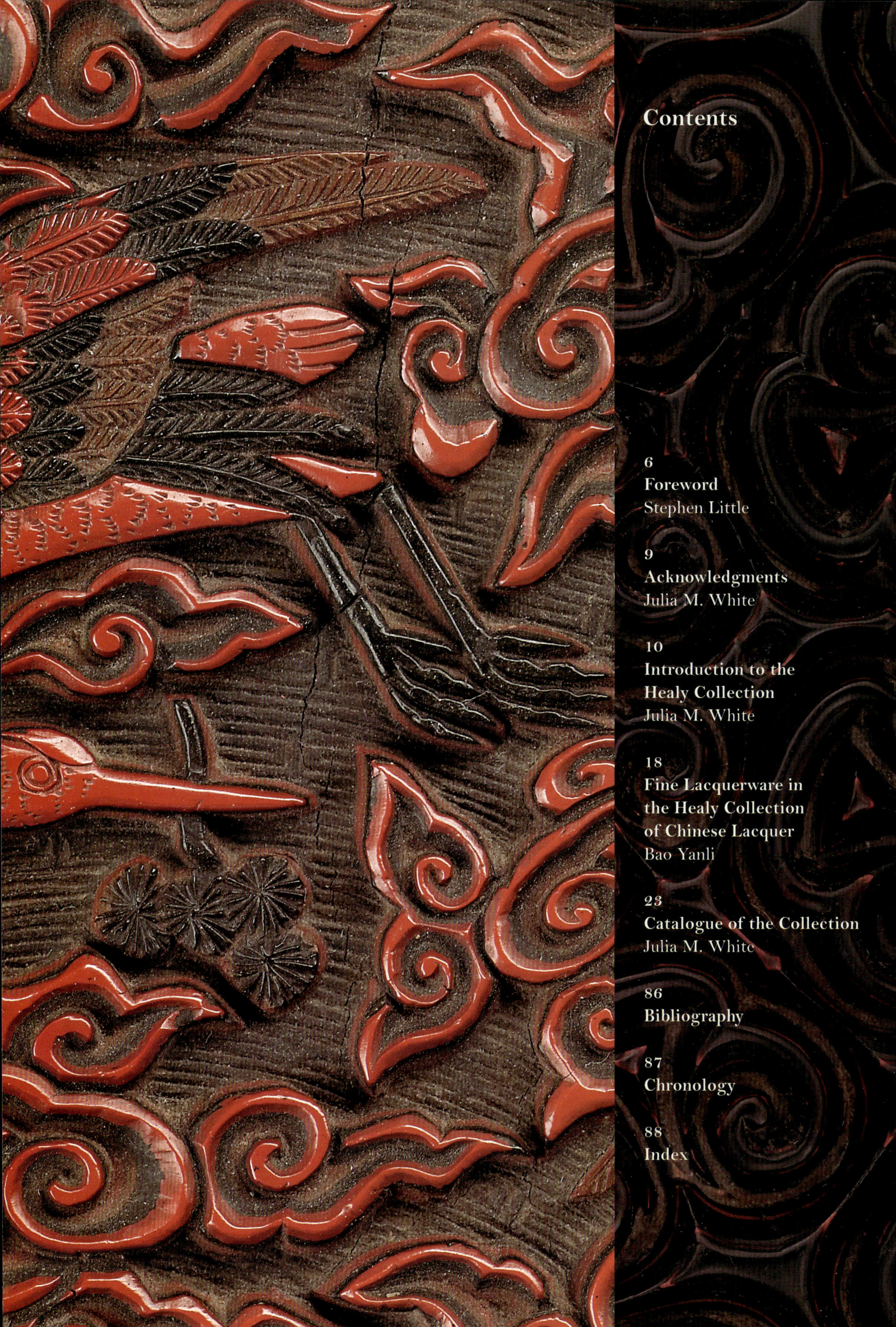

Contents

Foreword

This exhibition presents a stunning group of Chinese lacquers, ranging in date from the Han dynasty (206 BCE–220 CE) to the Ming (1368–1644). Chinese lacquer art existed as early as the Neolithic period, but very few examples survive from before the late Zhou dynasty (5th–3rd century BCE). We are deeply grateful to Mike Healy for sharing his magnificent collection with the people of Hawai'i and the world. These marvelous lacquers present one of China's most ancient and dynamic artistic traditions at its highest level. In this exhibition one sees works that are essentially utilitarian in function yet embody the most extraordinary and subtle beauty.

The Healy Collection is remarkable for several reasons. First, it is unusual to see a collection of this caliber in the West. Early Chinese lacquers of the type seen here, the majority dating to the Yuan (1260–1368) and Ming dynasties, rarely appear on the art market. Second, the Healy Collection presents a superb introduction to a wide range of Chinese lacquer techniques. This collection offers neophytes and experts alike a wonderful opportunity to learn from some of the finest examples known in the world. Third, the Healy Collection is fascinating for the ways in which it reveals the history of collecting Chinese lacquers in Japan. Many of the works in the collection have been in Japan for centuries, and as such they speak as much to Japanese as to Chinese aesthetics and taste. Many of these objects have intact their original Japanese wooden storage boxes, some of which preserve old documentary notations in ink. Such works speak to the deep cultural relationship between China and Japan.

I would like to thank both Mike Healy and Tim Walsh for making this delightful exhibition possible. I am also grateful to Julia M. White, Curator of Asian Art, for creating the exhibition's superb installation, and to both Julia M. White and Bao Yanli for writing the text of the beautiful catalogue that accompanies and documents this exhibition.

Stephen Little
Director
Honolulu Academy of Arts

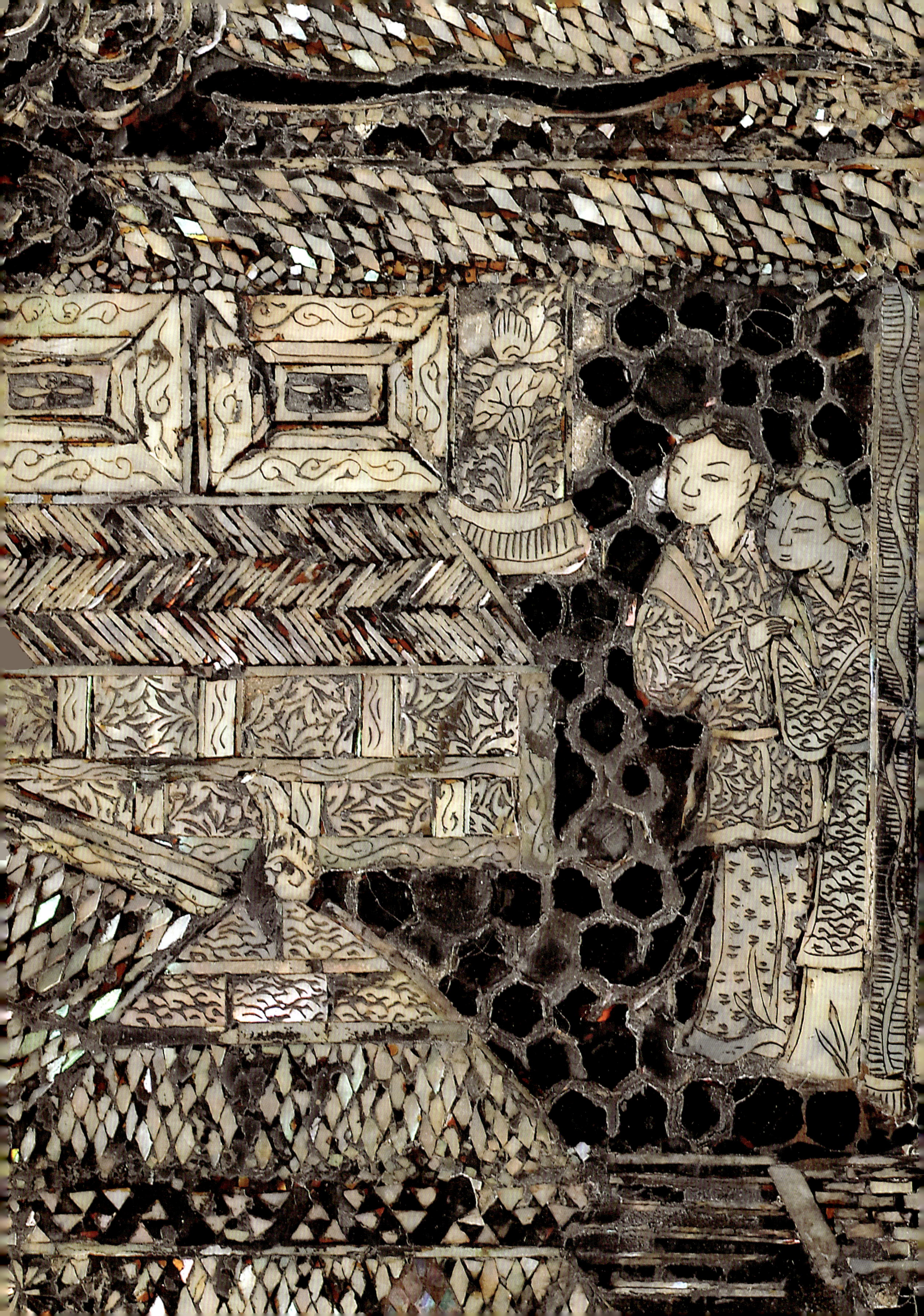

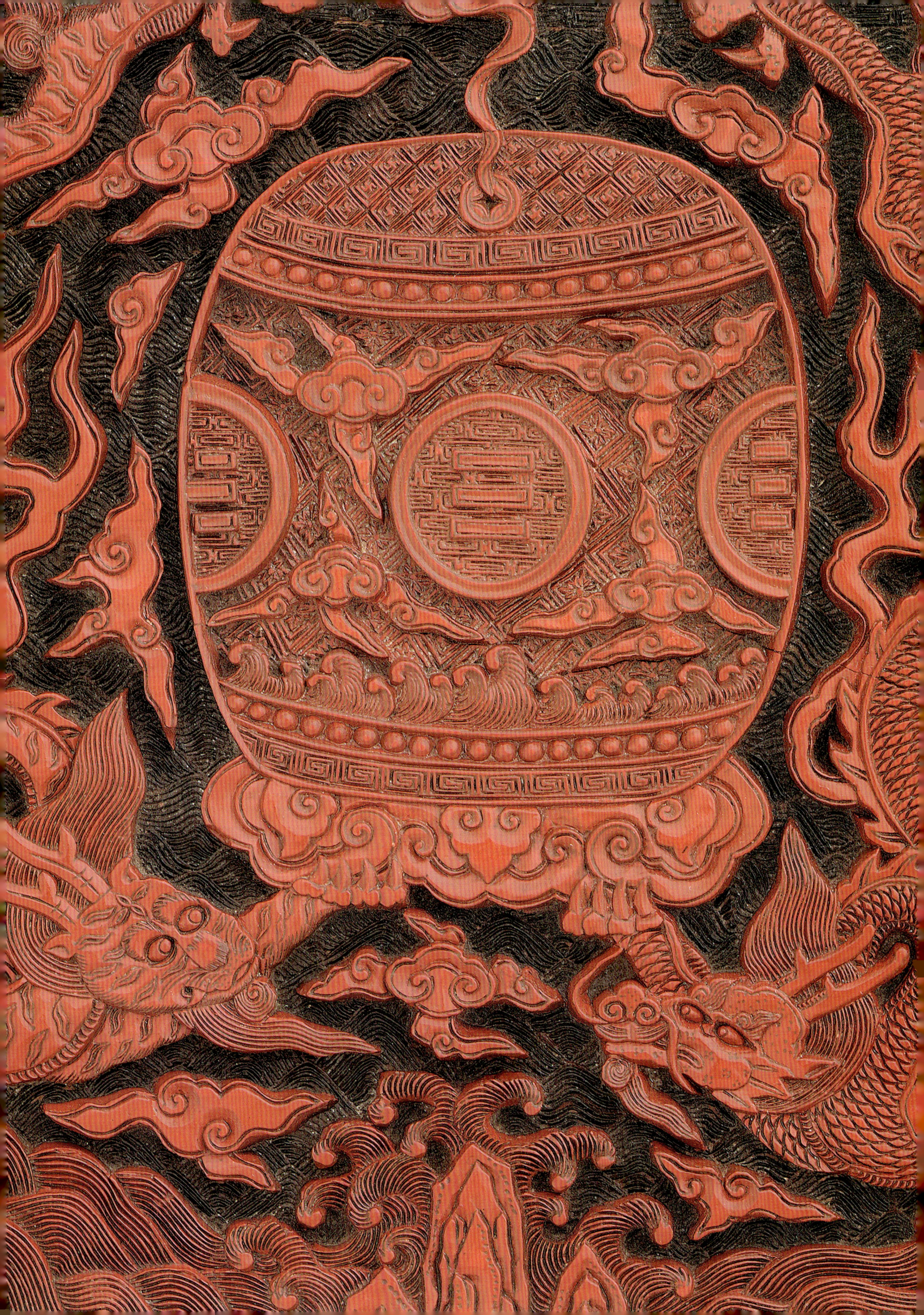

Acknowledgments

The most important element in the success of this project has been the generosity of Mike Healy, who entrusted the Honolulu Academy of Arts with his unique collection of Chinese lacquer. The opportunity to show this collection at the Academy came partly as a result of Mike's decision to live part-time in Honolulu and his immediate involvement in the arts community here. Mike and Tim Walsh have made many contributions to the islands, and I am grateful to them for their generosity and friendship.

I would also like to thank Anthony Carter, who kindly introduced me to Mike. Tony played a major role in assembling Mike's collection, offering or helping to locate many of the lacquers. He recently wrote the following about Mike's collecting:

> In creating his remarkable collection of Chinese lacquer, Michael Healy did not seek to own representative pieces from each period, to possess the quirky or the mercifully rare or the oddity which excites only the intellect. His choice was informed by a real enthusiasm for the medium, the invention and craft, which, combined well, create a remarkable object: the superb, minutely decorated Han dynasty cosmetic box so like the famous one in the British Museum, the small but beautifully robust Yuan dynasty dish decorated with peonies, or the mother-of-pearl octagonal box and cover, spotted by him in an auction catalogue as the one illustrated by Sir Harry Garner in his seminal book on Chinese lacquer—the auction house had failed to note this important detail!

The Honolulu Academy of Arts was pleased to present the collection in the spring of 2003 in a special exhibition. The success of that exhibition convinced us that a catalogue and a tour of the material would be well received. Many people at the Academy have had a role in bringing this to reality.

I am most grateful to Director Stephen Little and former director George Ellis for recognizing the value of this project and for their support in bringing it about. Thanks also to Registrar Sanna Deutsch and to Assistant Registrar Pauline Sugino, who managed the insurance, shipping, and tracking of the collection. The stunning photographs in this catalogue are all by staff photographer Shuzo Uemoto. Librarian Ron Chapman and Assistant Librarian Marybeth Weber provided valuable help in locating research materials, and I appreciate their support. Fujio Kaneko and his staff were instrumental in designing the gallery and the installation here as well as preparing the objects for shipping to the other venues. Independent Objects Conservator Laura Gorman spent many hours professionally cleaning the lacquers and preparing them for exhibition.

In the Asian department, my thanks go to Curatorial Assistant Sati Benes for carefully reading the texts and offering editorial advice and for organizing the many layers of preparation necessary for this project. Thanks also to Art Technician Megan Callan, who took care of the details necessary for storing the objects and preparing them for photography. Sawako Chang, Chenshan Tian, Grace Kohatsu, and Dr. Valdo Viglielmo assisted with translation. Dr. Viglielmo offered valuable editorial advice as well.

My thanks and appreciation go to Bao Yanli, Associate Director and Researcher for the Artistic Techniques Research Department at the Shanghai Museum, for her contribution to this catalogue. At the China Institute of America in New York, I would like to thank Gallery Director Willow Chang for including this exhibition in an already busy schedule. Thanks also to John and Julia Curtis for embracing the idea of a special exhibition on Chinese lacquer. I am also grateful to colleague and fellow traveler Susan Tai at the Santa Barbara Museum of Art for introducing the collection to a West Coast audience. My thanks to colleagues Terese Tse Bartholomew of the Asian Art Museum in San Francisco and to Kung-shin Chou of Fu Jen Catholic University for their comments and suggestions.

At Marquand Books, I would like to thank Ed Marquand for enthusiastically taking on this project and John Hubbard for his unique and stunning design. Thanks also to Marie Weiler for her consistent patience as we prepared the catalogue and for bringing in Lorna Price and Suzanne Kotz, who polished the text with their meticulous editing.

Julia M. White
Curator of Asian Art
Honolulu Academy of Arts
January 2005

Introduction to the Healy Collection

Julia M. White

It is with great pleasure that the Honolulu Academy of Arts presents the Healy Collection, one of the few Chinese lacquer collections in America, in either institutional or private hands. Of consistently high quality, the material presents a broad chronological range, from the Han period (206 BCE–220 CE) through the later Ming (1368–1644). Thus, through the thirty-one objects shown here, it is possible to see the development of one of China's richest decorative arts traditions. Lacquered objects began to appear as early as the Neolithic period (10,000–ca. 2100 BCE), but it is the later vessels, plates, and boxes that we generally associate with fine Chinese lacquers, such as those comprising the Healy Collection.

This collection reflects the major trends in lacquer production in China. It includes early painted lacquers of the Han period as well as the restrained and refined monochrome lacquers of the Song dynasty (960–1279). One of the great strengths of the collection is the range of mother-of-pearl inlaid lacquers, with examples from the Yuan (1260–1368) to the Ming dynasties.

Likewise, carved lacquers of cloud collar and sword-pommel *(ruyi)* decoration from the same time define the essence of the tradition known as *tixi* carved lacquers. Carved red lacquer of the Yuan and Ming dynasties, with its strong pictorial design, is also well represented in the collection. Floral motifs of the earlier Yuan period are matched by the strong narrative patterns of early and middle Ming period examples. Also found in the collection are several imperial marked pieces from the Jiajing (1522–1566) and Wanli (1573–1620) periods. The collection is focused on pre-Qing wares and does not extend beyond this period.

Chinese Lacquer in Japan

The survival of many fine examples of Chinese lacquer must be credited to their popularity over many centuries in Japan, where they have been treasured as items of great rarity. Documentation of the first official gifts of lacquers from China to Japan occurred in the late fourteenth and early part of the fifteenth centuries.[1] Earlier trade between Tang China and Japan of the Nara period certainly made Japan aware of Chinese lacquer, as evidenced by the Chinese material in the Shōsōin, Japan's Imperial Repository. It was, however, the renewed interaction of Buddhist pilgrims during the thirteenth and fourteenth centuries that reinvigorated trade with China and prompted the importation of the elegant polished lacquers of the Song and Yuan. This led to the incorporation of Chinese lacquer into areas of Japanese life and culture, and their rarity contributed to their value and preciousness. Eventually the early lacquers found a role within the budding tea culture that was to become the formal tea ceremony.[2]

Japan's tea culture began in the ninth century and saw expanded interest in the twelfth, when tea drinking was seen as having a positive health effect. The Zen priest Eisai (1141–1215) brought the beneficial properties of tea to light in his *Kisai yōjōki* (Book on improving health by drinking tea),[3] and he is credited with reintroducing tea consumption to Japan after a hiatus of several hundred years. At its reintroduction, tea was associated and aligned with Zen Buddhism, but tea drinking and tea games quickly spread to the

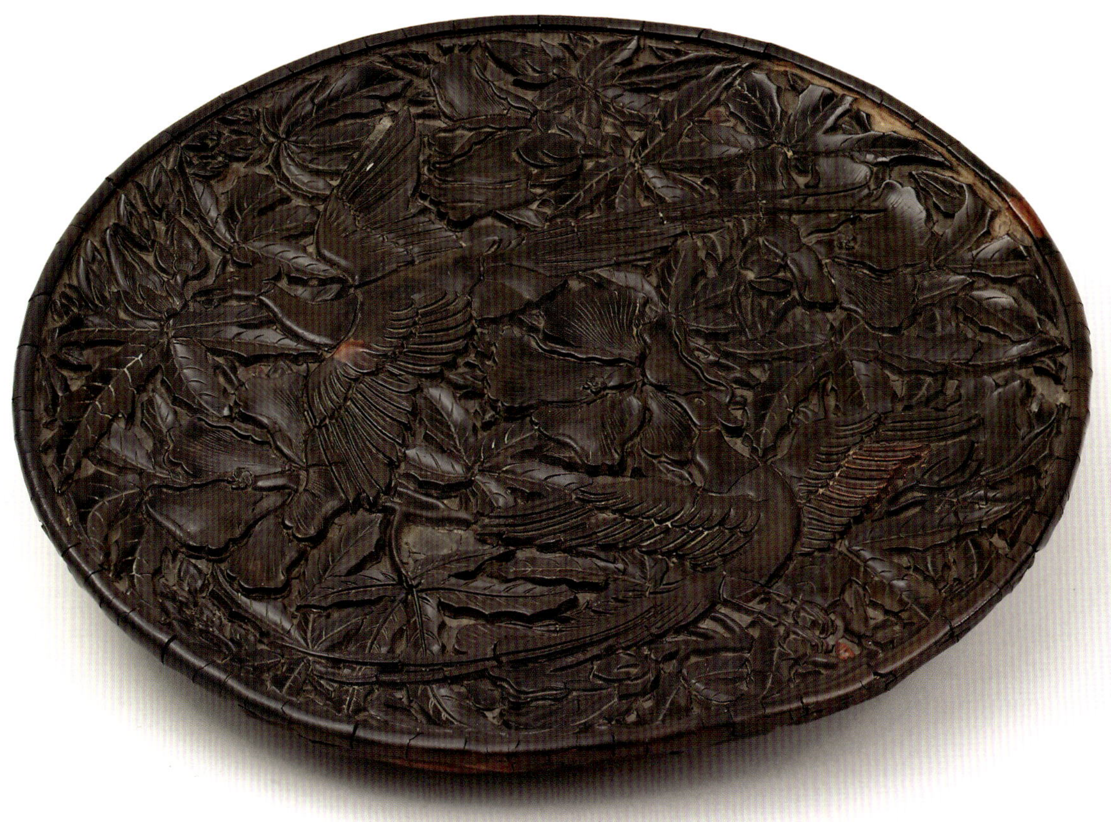

Fig. 1 Plate China, Yuan dynasty (1260–1368), lacquered wood, diam. 12½ in., Honolulu Academy of Arts, Purchase, 1955 (2118.1)

general populace. Tea has been consumed throughout Japan ever since.

It is important to our understanding of the preservation of Chinese lacquers in Japan to recognize the close link between lacquer and the introduction and evolution of Japanese tea culture. The rise in popularity of tea took tea enthusiasts to new heights of ardor for collecting things Chinese. Thus, even before the official gifts of the Ming emperor Yongle to the Japanese shogun Yoshimitsu (1358–1408), high-ranking Japanese were already keenly aware of and interested in collecting Chinese artworks, including painting, silks, and lacquers. The late fourteenth and fifteenth centuries saw the quick expansion of Chinese collections among the samurai population.

The shogunal collections of Chinese material were assessed under the guidance of the eighth Ashikaga shogun, Yoshimasa (1436–1490), who in the Higashiyama period created a group known as the *dōbōshū*, or "cultural advisers." These three generations of respected and trusted men, Nōami (1397–1471), Geiami (1431–1485), and Sōami (d. 1525), surveyed and catalogued the art and antiquities that had been collected by powerful samurai over the preceding years.[4] Influential as painters as well as connoisseurs, the *dōbōshū* helped to establish the foundations of Japanese connoisseurship. Their important contributions included the 1476 compilation *Kundaikan sō chōki*, a book about Chinese painters, interior decoration, and the tea ceremony.[5]

By the Ming period, lacquer was counted among the tribute items sent from China and was specifically listed along with many other gifts. The 1388 *Ge gu yao lun*, a commentary by the Yuan antiquarian Cao Zhao which describes every aspect of art and antiquity known at the time, includes a section on ancient lacquer. In it, the author relates that "carved red lacquer is greatly favored by peoples of Japan."[6] The text is valuable both for describing the preferences of the Japanese and for noting the places and types of manufacture of pre-Ming lacquer.

In 1403 the Yongle emperor sent fifty-eight pieces of red carved lacquer to the shogun Yoshimitsu. The record of this gift is one of the most complete listings of lacquer sent to Japan. This important document, which describes in some detail the types and styles of lacquer comprising the gift, including dimensions, is now held in the Myōchi-in Temple in Kyoto.[7] (A copy of the list and a translation of it, as well as a commentary on lacquers of the period, can be found in an article by Harry Garner.[8]) Gifts from the Yongle emperor from 1406 and 1407 also contained lacquer, but they are not described to the same degree as the 1403 group.[9]

Carved lacquer listed in the 1403 group included plates bearing two-bird designs similar to one in the collection of the Honolulu Academy of Arts (fig. 1). This large black lacquer plate with a two-bird design on the surface and a *xiang cao* (fragrant grass) spiral on the border was purchased in Japan in 1955.[10] The plate has the deeply carved surface of other late Yuan pieces and also exhibits the typical instability of the adherence of the thick lacquer to the core. Two other examples of Yuan two-bird plates can be seen in the collection of the National Museums of Scotland, both acquired from the Sammy Lee Collection.[11]

The current dispersal of lacquers that entered Japan both officially and unofficially is not certain, but temples, museums, and private collectors (among them tea connoisseurs) certainly preserve some from both categories. Many of the finest lacquer items in the Healy Collection arrived via Japanese collections, and some of the storage boxes, which are of Japanese origin and bear inscriptions indicating Japanese ownership, still remain with the lacquers. Some lacquers in the collection show remarkable similarities to the type exported to Japan in the late fourteenth and early fifteenth centuries, very close to the time of manufacture.

The 1403 list describes an oval tray, carved inside with tree peony and on the back with *xiang cao*, that is slightly smaller than the round plate in the Healy Collection (fig. 2, cat. no. 17).[12] This peony plate is a fine example of the same density of design seen in the two-bird plate (see fig. 1) as well as in other examples determined to be from the late Yuan or early Ming period. The sharply carved, deep design is characteristic of these early pieces. The border on the back of the plate has the distinctive *xiang cao* pattern.

Likewise the large plate with chrysanthemum pattern (fig. 3, cat. no. 16) shares some design elements that are expressed in the objects from the 1403 list. A floral pattern covers the entire surface of the plate, which is without a border except for its plain rim. The border on the back is of the same flower as seen on the front, a linked and continuous chrysanthemum scroll. The carving on this plate is considerably deeper than that seen on the earlier peony plate.

Lists of official gifts include a number of carved red lacquers that are decorated with narrative compositions. The Healy Collection contains three plates and two spectacular boxes with narratives. The figural examples are clearly intended to be narratives of life among literati scholars and officials. In the literature of the time, these narratives are described as *renwu gushi* (stories of men), in which landscape serves as a backdrop for interaction and

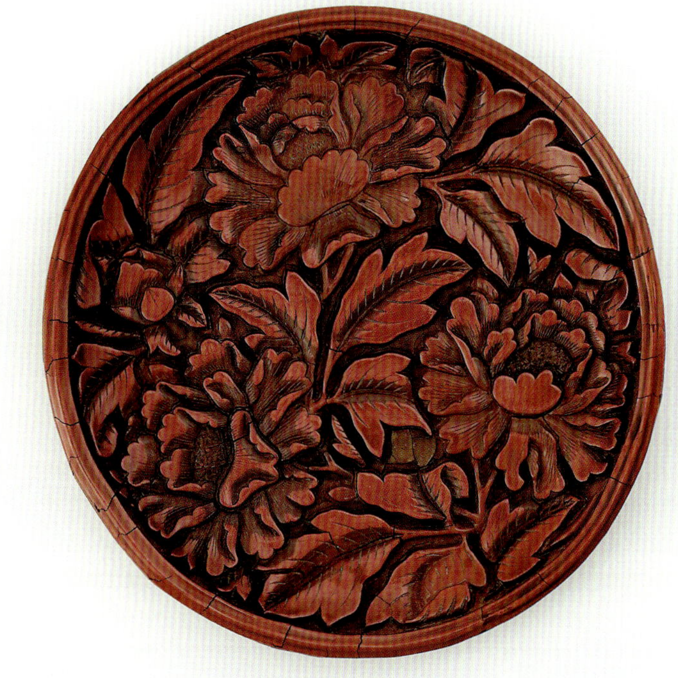

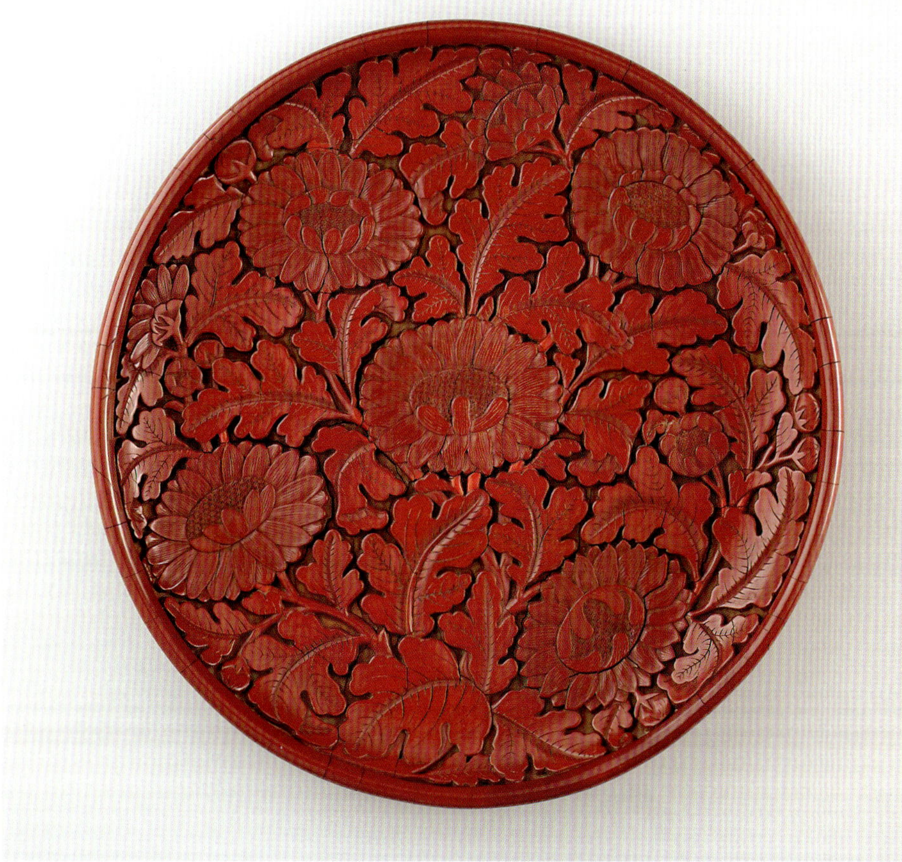

Fig. 2 **Peony Plate** Yuan or early Ming dynasty, 14th century, carved red lacquer (cat. no. 17)

Fig. 3 **Plate with Chrysanthemum Pattern** Ming dynasty, 14th–15th century; possibly late Yuan dynasty (1260–1368), carved red lacquer (cat. no. 16)

storytelling with figures walking, riding on horseback, seated in pavilions, or gazing into the landscape.

The small round plate of carved red lacquer (fig. 4, cat. no. 18) and the small lobed plate (fig. 5, cat. no. 22) are both decorated with charming narrative compositions. The round plate depicts an elderly, bearded man with a staff who, accompanied by a young boy, approaches a teahouse. In the teahouse, the viewer can see the details of furnishings and a waiting attendant. Many aspects of the water, land, and air appear very similar to those found in a fourteenth-century lobed dish from the Victoria and Albert Museum.[13]

The small lobed plate from the Healy Collection shows a gentleman on a terrace gazing toward a lotus pond with an open pavilion to one side. The 1403 list does not provide us with detailed descriptions of narrative scenes, but given what we know of the Japanese wish to collect Chinese objects displaying Chinese themes, these two plates would have been most desirable. A third plate (fig. 6, cat. no. 23) is much larger and depicts a departure scene.

The narrative themes with figures that appear on two carved red lacquer boxes (cat. nos. 19 and 26) also adhere to *renwu gushi* themes. The frequency of these themes and their appearance on at least some of the items sent to Japan indicate that the Japanese appreciated and understood the illustrative nature of the designs. Because of the great appeal these narrative designs held for the Japanese, items decorated with them were kept and treasured.

Some of the most delightful renditions of narrative designs can be found on inlaid mother-of-pearl lacquer. The Healy Collection contains two Yuan boxes that depict virtually the same scene, with only minor variation. One is a square box (fig. 7, cat. no. 5) and the other (fig. 8, cat. no. 6) is octagonal. Both are inlaid across the top with a scene of rural domesticity. This close adherence to a thematic composition, also seen in the red carved narrative boxes and plates mentioned above, points to the likely use of templates for the creation of certain themes, particularly narrative designs. The *Ge gu yao lun* mentions mother-of-pearl inlay lacquers being made within the buyer's own home during the Yuan period in order to control the quality.[14] They are also mentioned as being heavily

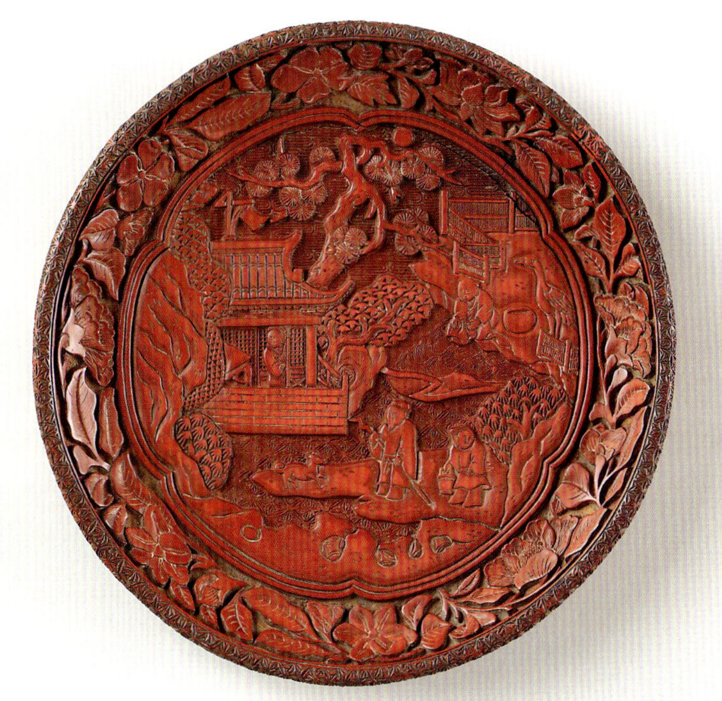

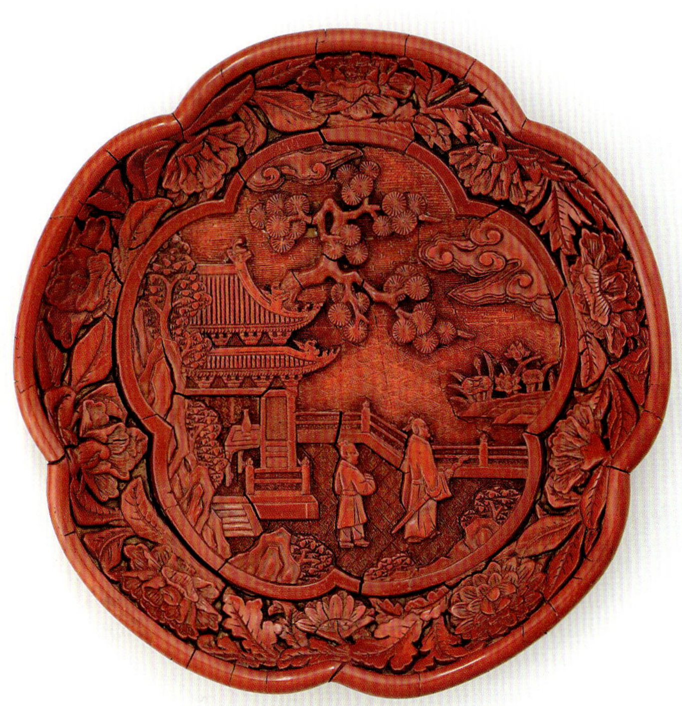

Fig. 4 **Round Plate** Late Yuan or early Ming dynasty, 14th–15th century, carved red lacquer (cat. no. 18)

Fig. 5 **Lobed Plate** Late Yuan or early Ming dynasty, 14th–15th century, carved red lacquer (cat. no. 22)

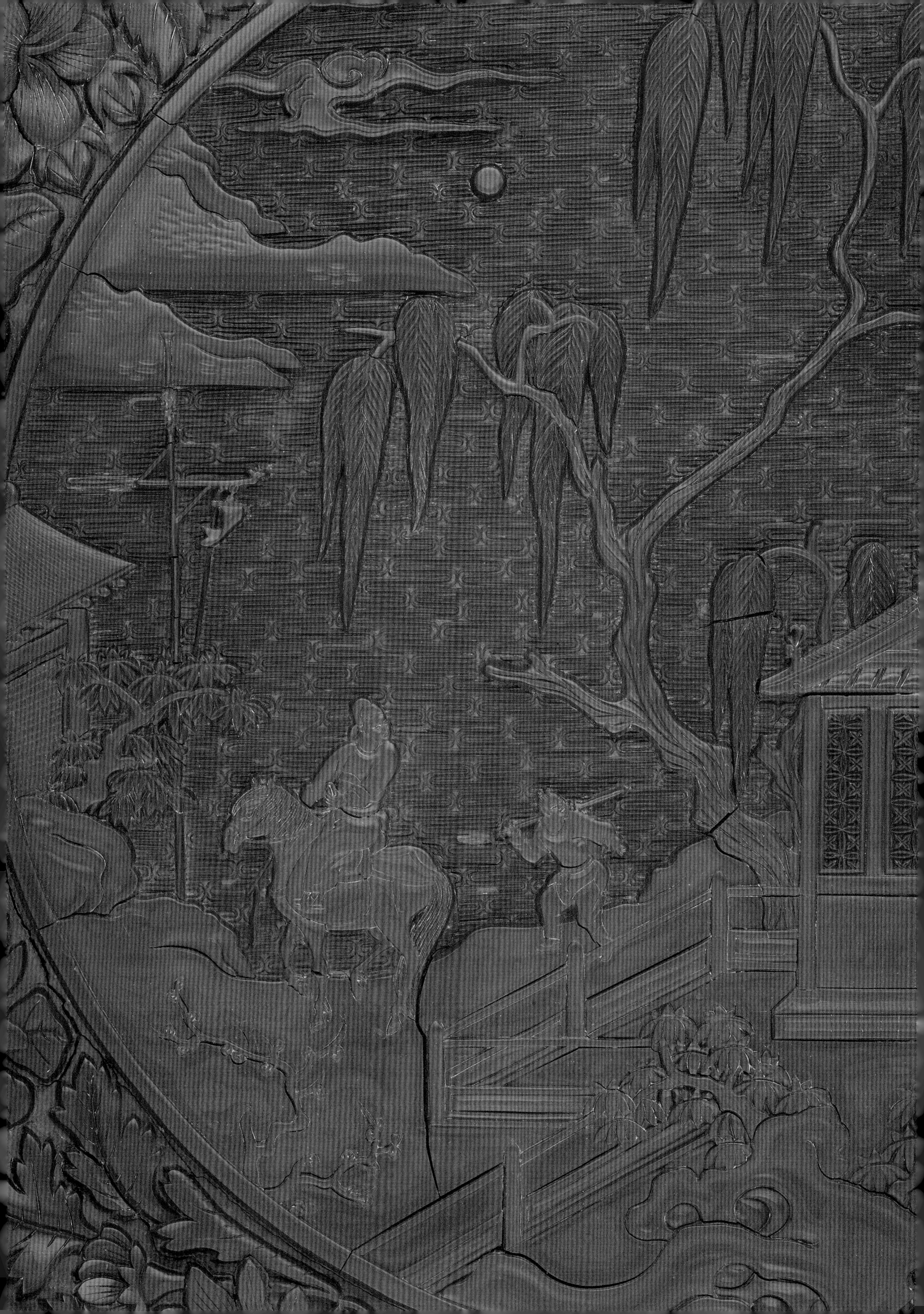

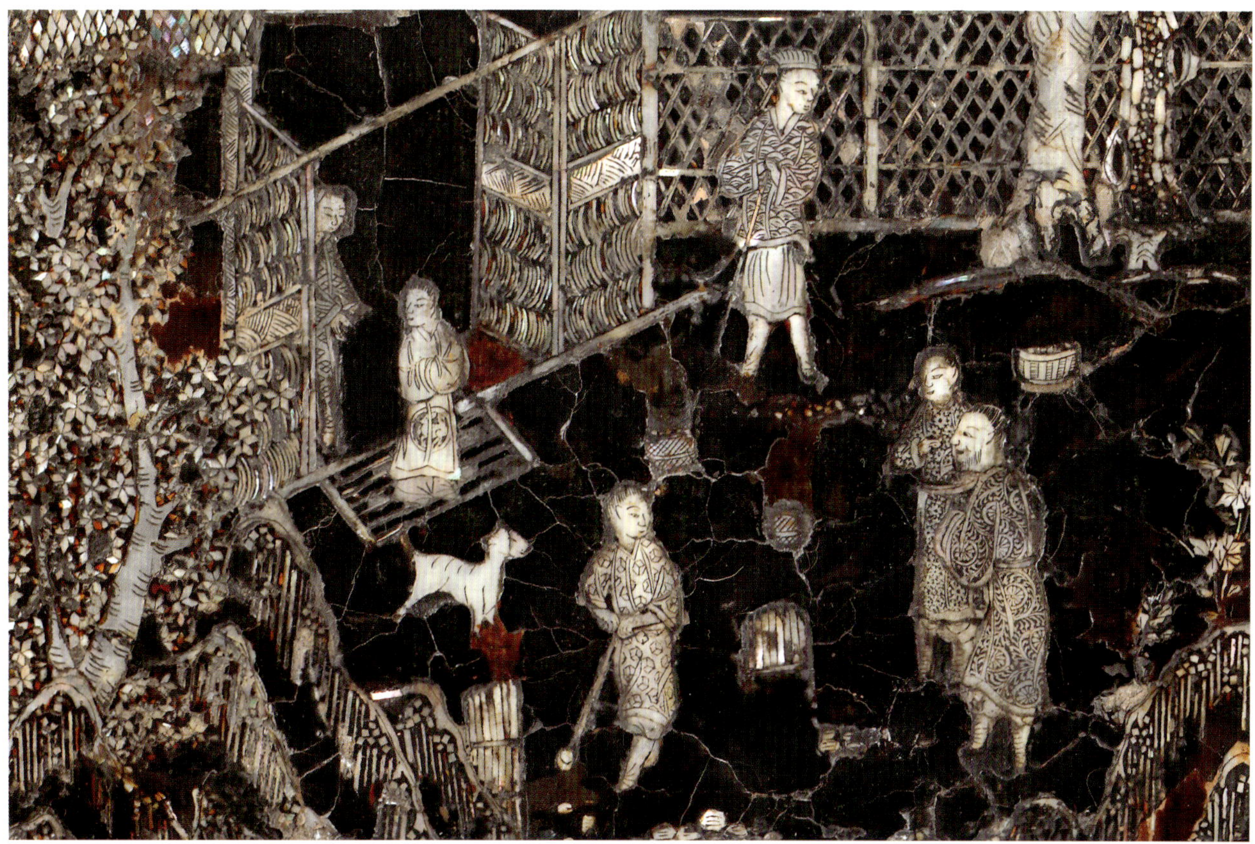

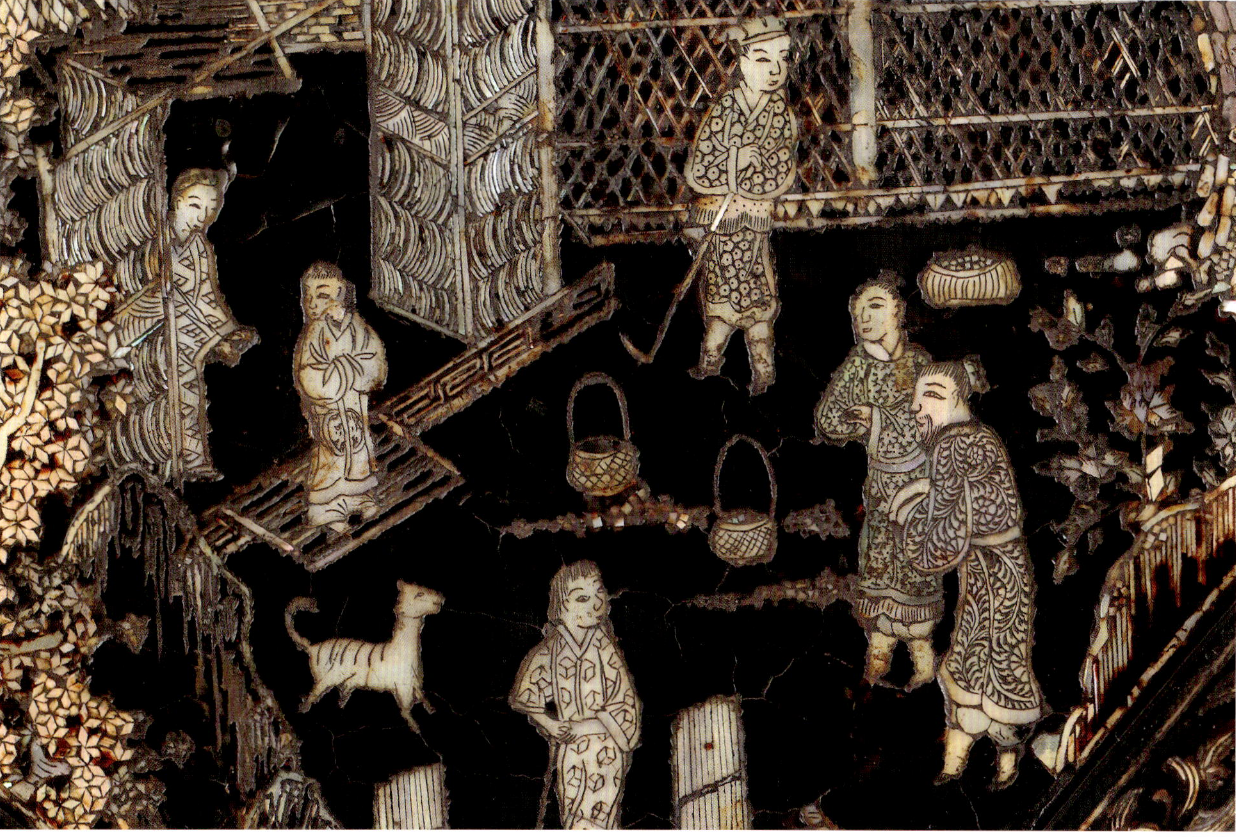

Fig. 6 Plate with Horse and Rider Late Yuan or early Ming dynasty, 15th century, carved red lacquer (detail; cat. no. 23)

Fig. 7 Box Yuan dynasty (1260–1368), black lacquer with inlaid mother-of-pearl (detail; cat. no. 5)

Fig. 8 Octagonal Box Yuan dynasty (1260–1368), black lacquer inlaid with mother-of-pearl (detail; cat. no. 6)

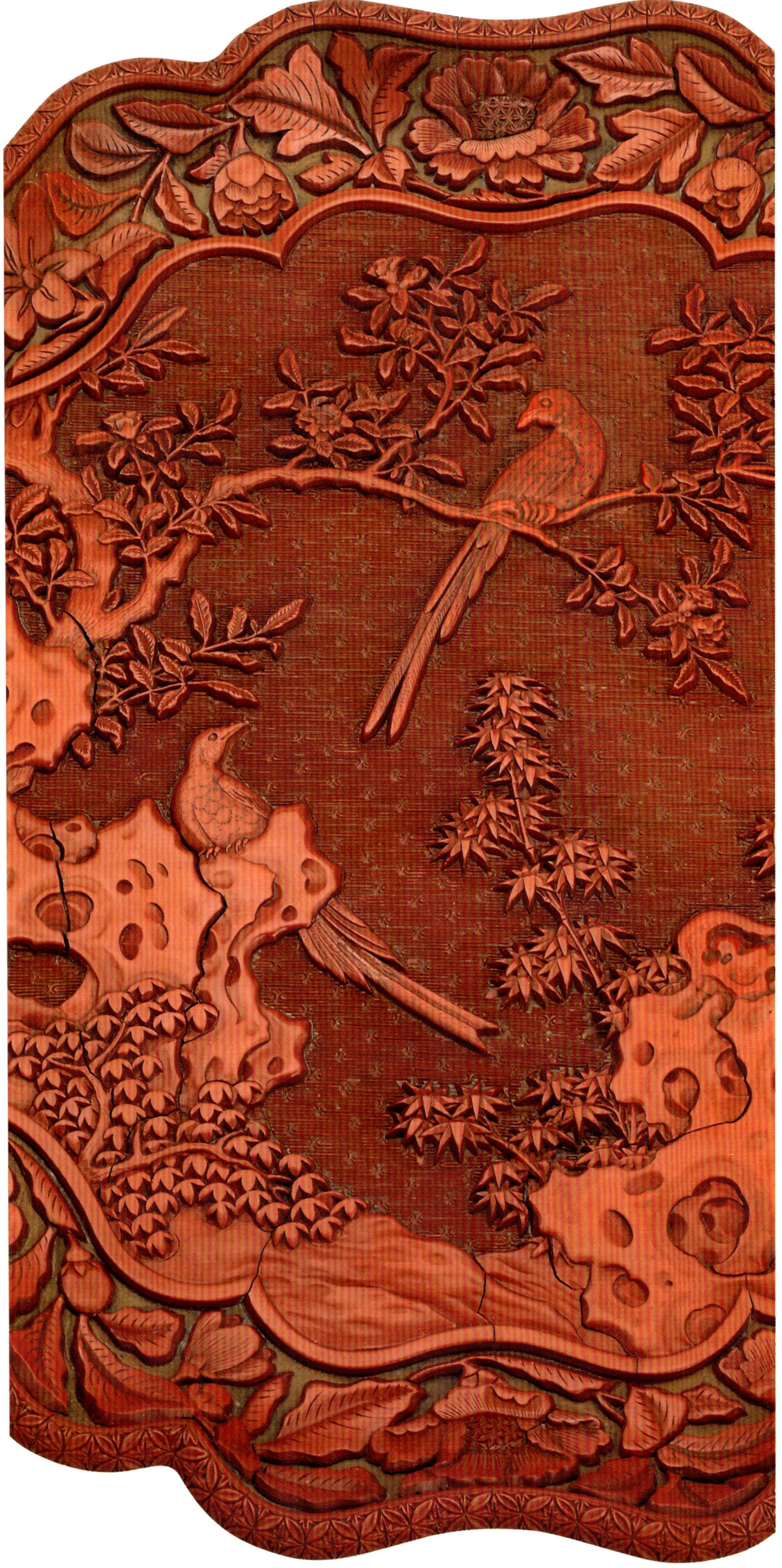

favored by the early Ming court and are said to have been confiscated from a collector "early in the Hongwu reign period."[15]

One petal-shaped plate with a landscape dominated by two birds (fig. 9, cat. no. 15) is reminiscent of fan and album paintings of the Song and Yuan periods. It is remarkably similar to one described in the 1403 list as *mu di zhu mei* (tree, earth, bamboo, plum) and by Garner as a "prunus-shaped" dish.[16] Garner describes this depiction as being much more specific and unique an expression than the more common landscape theme. The Healy plate incorporates elements of fine late Yuan and early Ming production, including broad, highly polished surfaces on the foreground rock and a typical "air diaper" pattern that sets off the bamboo, prunus, and leaf patterns. The whole scene is outlined by a single band of raised lacquer and surrounded by a border of flowers of the four seasons. The decoration of the back rim, also the flowers of the four seasons, is the only variation in design from the plate described in the 1403 list. Its back carries the *xiang cao* pattern.[17]

The carved *tixi* oblong plate from the late Yuan period (fig. 10, cat. no. 14) is an example of a lacquer type that may have been exported to Japan and over time came to be a treasured item for the tea ceremony. It has many of the characteristics of early Ming pieces, including a very thick lacquer coating that has cracked and separated slightly from the wood core. *Tixi* carved lacquer may have been an early export to Japan, though it is not mentioned in the 1403 list.

The initial gifts and other items imported from China were likely put to use in Japan, where these elegant and refined lacquers were appreciated for their understated beauty. As the tea ceremony changed under the influence of powerful shoguns, the importation of Chinese lacquer expanded, and the large tea ceremonies held by Oda Nobunaga and Toyotomi Hideyoshi no doubt called for greater numbers of lacquers. With the development of Chanoyu (The Way of Tea) in the fifteenth century, codification of the tea ritual included the exclusive use of "Chinese articles" in the

Fig. 9 Octagonal Plate Yuan dynasty, 14th century, carved red lacquer (detail; cat. no. 15)

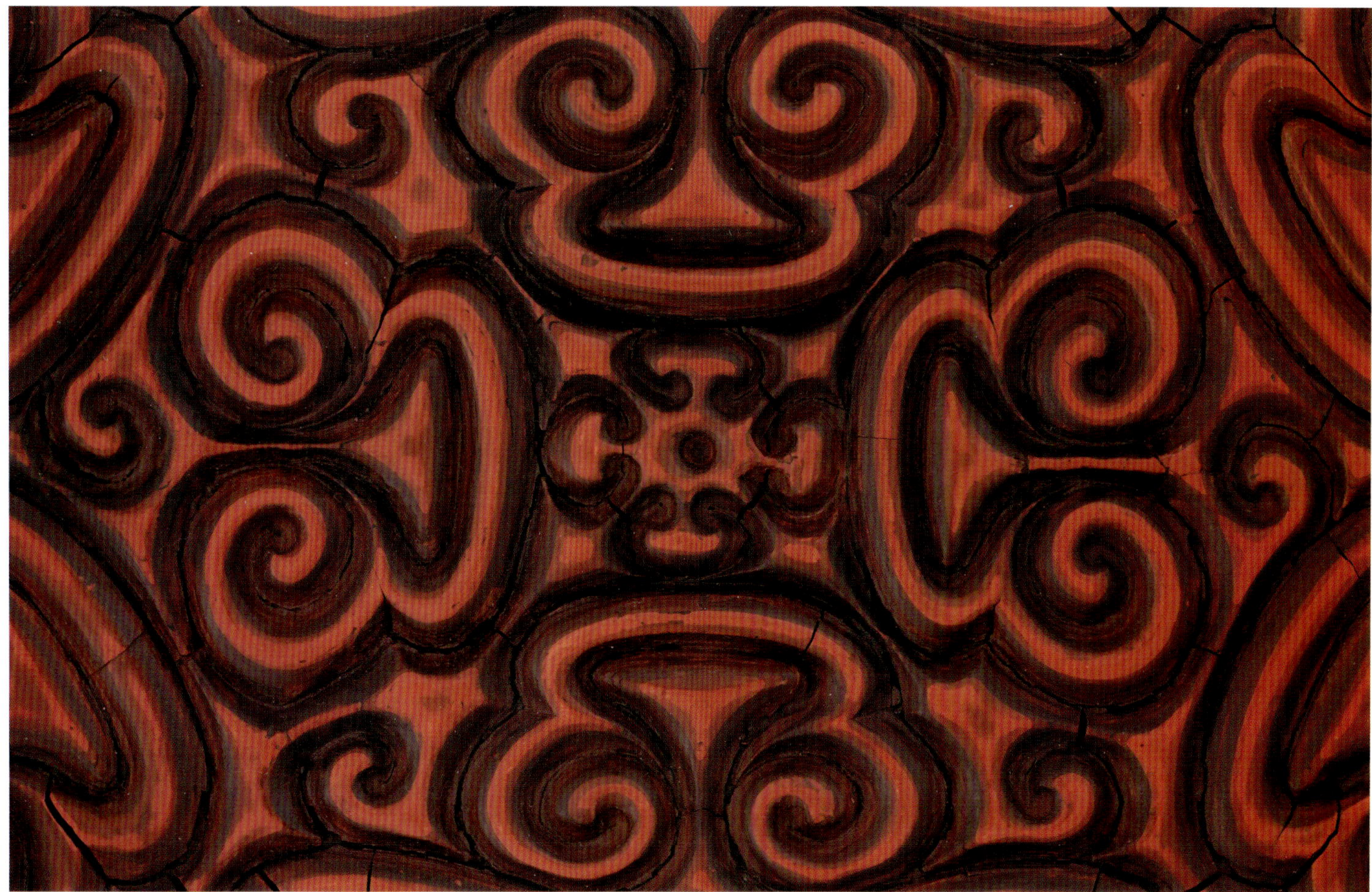

preparation and consumption of tea. By later in the century, the tea ceremony came to include both Japanese and Chinese items, thanks to a hybrid taste promoted by the Zen Buddhist adherent Murata Shūkō (d. 1502) and followed by the great master Sen no Rikyū (1521–1591).

The rich, polished surface of these lacquers contrasted nicely with the rougher natural forms of many other items used in the tea ceremony, such as naturally glazed ceramics. Chinese lacquerware became a treasured part of many high-ranking tea connoisseurs' collections. Without this level of passion for Chinese lacquer among the Japanese, who treasured and protected the delicate pieces, it is likely that many of the finest would not have lasted. Those pieces that survived in Japanese collections very much reflect Japanese taste for Chinese lacquer. The Healy Collection beautifully demonstrates this preference for the understated and for a restrained elegance of form, surface, and texture.

Fig. 10 Oblong Plate early Ming dynasty (ca. 1400), carved red and black lacquer *(tixi)* (detail; cat. no. 14)

Notes

1. See Harry M. Garner, "The Export of Chinese Lacquer to Japan in the Yuan and Early Ming Dynasties," *Archives of Asian Art* 25 (1972): 7–28. Garner surveys the surviving lists of items sent from China to Japan and the circumstances of the tribute system during the period.

2. This concept is explored by John Figgess in "Ming and Pre-Ming Lacquer in the Japanese Tea Ceremony," *Transactions of the Oriental Ceramic Society* 37 (1967–68, 1968–69): 37–51.

3. Paul Varley, *Japanese Culture*, 4th ed. (Honolulu: University of Hawaii Press, 2000), pp. 124–29, traces the renewed interest in tea in Japan.

4. Ibid., p. 126.

5. *Japan: An Illustrated Encyclopedia* (Tokyo: Kodansha International, 1993), vol. 2, p. 1108.

6. The translation is from Sir Percival David, trans. and ed., *Chinese Connoisseurship: The Ko Ku Yao Lun, The Essential Criteria of Antiquities* (New York: Praeger, 1971), p. 146.

7. Garner, "The Export of Chinese Lacquer to Japan," p. 11.

8. Ibid. A copy of the original list can be found in fig. 10 of the Appendix; a transcription as well as a translation can be seen in figs. 11, 12, and 13.

9. John Figgess, "A Letter from the Court of Yong Lo," *Transactions of the Oriental Ceramic Society* 34 (1962–63): 97–101, translates a letter detailing the official shipment of fifty red lacquers as part of the 1407 gift. No details of design or other specifics are included.

10. The plate is illustrated in Garner, "The Export of Chinese Lacquer to Japan," figs. 1a and 1b, p. 14.

11. Hu Shih-chang and Jane Wilkinson, *Chinese Lacquer* (Edinburgh: National Museums of Scotland, 1998), pls. 8 and 9. One is black and the other is red; both have the *xiang cao* pattern on the back.

12. Garner, "The Export of Chinese Lacquer to Japan," Appendix, p. 26, 9c.

13. Ibid., figs. 3a and 3b, p. 16.

14. David, *Chinese Connoisseurship*, p. 148.

15. David, *Chinese Connoisseurship*, pp. 148–49.

16. Garner, "The Export of Chinese Lacquer to Japan," p. 15.

17. Derek Clifford, *Chinese Carved Lacquer* (London: Bamboo Publishing, 1992), pl. 39, p. 65, illustrates a similar lobed plate of black lacquer with birds, prunus, and bamboo that is in the British Museum collection.

Fine Lacquerware in the Healy Collection of Chinese Lacquer

Bao Yanli

China's extensive history in the lacquer arts extends as far back as the Neolithic period (10,000–ca. 2100 BCE), when artisans used lacquer to protect and beautify everyday utensils. Unfortunately, few lacquer objects from this time are extant. The earliest example, a red lacquer wooden bowl, dates to about seven thousand years ago. It was discovered at the old Mudu ferry pier of the Yuyao River in Zhejiang Province. In large part because of excavations conducted over the past thirty years, we know that lacquer was part of the earliest decorative arts in China, used not only on everyday vessels but also on musical instruments and bronze objects.

Lacquer production reached its peak during the Warring States (476–221 BCE), Qin (221–206 BCE), and Han (206 BCE–220 CE) periods. Demand reached unprecedented heights as people began to use lacquered objects in their daily lives. Lacquer products were designed in large and colorful varieties, and for many different purposes. Production techniques improved remarkably, and the lacquer production business became extremely professional. During this time, lacquer decoration encompassed as many as ten different techniques, including colored painting, print patterns, needle motifs, gold foil, heavy lacquer, engraved lacquer, floral attachments, and inlaid work. Lacquer workers adorned their products with richly patterned motifs, including clouds, animals, plants, geometric designs, mythological creatures, historical figures, and illustrations of stories that reflected all aspects of life. More than ten thousand examples of such Han dynasty lacquer have been excavated.

The Healy Collection includes two early pieces that date to the Han dynasty: a cosmetic box (cat. no. 1) and a wine cup with two handles (cat. no. 2). These two examples were constructed with fine wood-core bodies, covered with multiple layers of lacquer, and decorated with swirling painted designs. The cosmetic box is covered with a brownish-black lacquer base, over which a swirling red lacquer design is painted. Appliquéd patterns of animals and birds executed in silver further embellish the surface. Similar early lacquers have been found at tomb sites in the state of Chu in the south.

After the Han dynasty, with the rise of ceramic production, lacquered tableware was gradually replaced by ceramics. Perhaps for this reason, lacquer products became more refined, and many new varieties were created. The remaining Healy lacquers date from after the Han dynasty. Fourteen, or almost half, are red carved lacquer, one of the most popular types. Most of the objects in this collection are fine examples from the early Ming period, accomplished by skilled artisans and considered highly valuable.

Carved lacquerware, its techniques handed down from generation to generation, constitutes a large proportion of the finest pieces in the collection. Artisans painstakingly applied lacquer layer upon layer, very often as many as dozens, or even more than a hundred. With a knife they carved different patterns into the lacquer, which comes in a multitude of colors: red *(tihong)*, yellow *(tihuang)*, black *(tihei)*, multicolor *(ticai)*, and layered color *(tixi)*. Carved red lacquer originated in the Tang dynasty (618–907), became popular in the Song (960–1279), and reached its highest point during the late Yuan

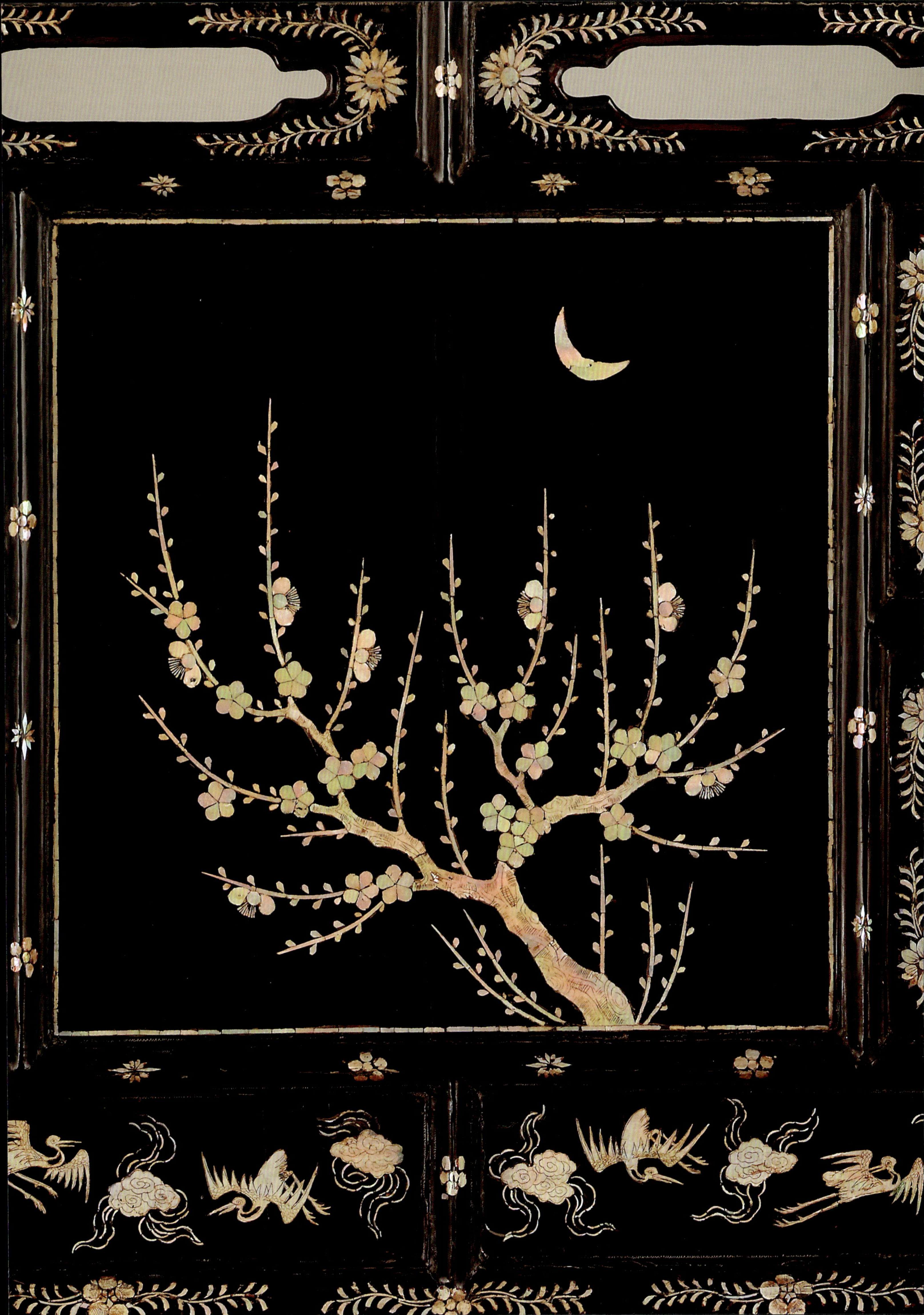

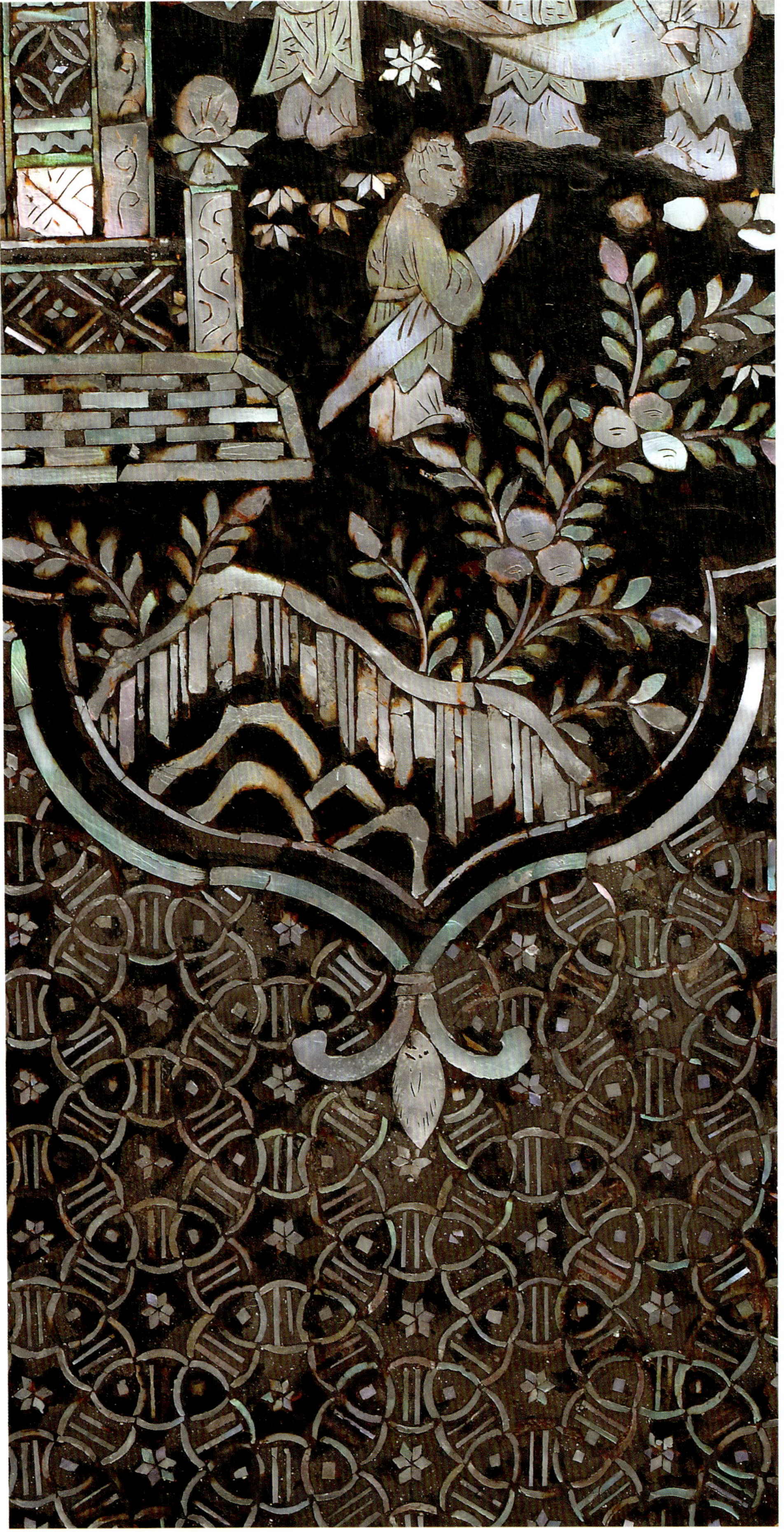

(1260–1368) and early Ming (1368–1644) dynasties. It continued to flourish and be produced in different styles during the Ming and Qing (1644–1911) dynasties.

The methods for producing red carved lacquer designs are among the most straightforward. Carving through multiple layers of lacquer, colored red with cinnabar, the artisan created landscapes, birds and flowers, dragons, and garden scenes. In a number of Yuan lacquers, a yellow background is seen in the secondary areas of the design, as in the flower scroll surrounding the main design on an octagonal plate (cat. no. 15). The backgrounds are rendered in diaper patterns, a design convention that helped differentiate the planes of ground, water, and sky.

Yuan-dynasty carved red lacquer featured inconspicuous knife traces, smooth surfaces, and fine, detailed pattern work. The heavy lacquer *(duiqi)* of the early Ming dynasty had broad, thick layers of lacquer, a darker color, and close and abundant pattern work that demonstrated the sophisticated skills of the lacquer artist. Particularly famous pieces include those manufactured in the government ateliers in the Yongle (1403–1424) and Xuande (1426–1435) periods. Lacquer work of the Jiajing period (1522–1566) and later often demonstrates conspicuous knife traces and, therefore, sharper angles. Many new designs were created in this period. After the Wanli reign period (1573–1620), however, knife work on lacquer became restrained and spare.

The charming design of the octagonal plate (cat. no. 15) demonstrates fine workmanship dating from the pre- or early Hongwu period (1368–1398). It is similar in shape and theme to an octagonal plate in Japan as well as a Yuan-dynasty black lacquer plate from the British Museum. The large circular box with figures and landscape (cat. no. 19) has a story theme and intricate details, and its circular stand is well decorated. It is a standard piece of Yuan or Ming dynasty lacquer. The red color of the circular peony plate (cat. no. 17) is rather dark. The lively peony flowers have straight, thin leaf veins; brocade is used to symbolize the pistil. The carving resembles that of the circular plate with figures (cat. no. 18), whose natural and energetic patterns were rendered with sophisticated craftsmanship. The back border surface of the peony plate (cat. no. 17) has designs of *xiang cao* (fragrant grass), as does the plate with horse and rider (cat. no. 23). These examples are all representative of standard-quality lacquer work of the Yuan dynasty.

The peony box (cat. no. 20) has a flat top and vertical walls; in the center is a peony blossom in full bloom, its petals curling naturalistically. Its entire composition is dense and embedded in heavy, solid-layered lacquer. Both shape and design demonstrate the most popular style of early Ming work. The cup stand (cat. no. 27) has designs of seasonal flowers on its body, plate, and feet. The inner surface of its foot is vertically engraved with six Chinese characters reading "Made in the Yongle period of the great Ming dynasty." This piece appears overwhelmingly similar to one preserved in the Palace Museum in Beijing. It was likely crafted during the Yongle or Hongwu periods.

The carved design of the lobed plate (cat. no. 22) depicts an elderly man enjoying lotus flowers outdoors, with a young servant in attendance. The setting includes houses, trees, and large rocks. Diaper patterns represent clouds and waves, and a rhombus pattern symbolizes sky, water, and ground. The plate's edges and exterior are fully engraved with flower patterns. The left side of its bottom surface has six vertically engraved Chinese characters reading "Made in the Yongle period of the great Ming dynasty," indicating that it is a standard work of the Yongle reign.

The plate with chrysanthemum pattern (cat. no. 16) is decorated both inside and out with an extremely neat and detailed design of chrysanthemums in full bloom. It appears identical to a circular box with a chrysanthemum pattern in Beijing's Palace Museum which also has the same six Chinese characters mentioned above. The plate also exhibits the craftsmanship of the Yongle period.

The large lidded box (cat. no. 26) has, on one side, a figural design and, on the other, a display of phoenixes and peony flowers. The edges are decorated with a variety of floral designs. It was very probably manufactured in the mid- or late Ming dynasty. Although it might not have a very long history, the box is a masterwork for its large size, charming decorative patterns, and exquisite craftsmanship.

The technique of multicolor carving *(ticai)* was accomplished on pieces that had been covered in layers of lacquer in different colors according to a set design. As the artist carved the decoration, the variety of colors became evident. On the *ticai* box in the Healy Collection (cat. no. 25), eight cranes surrounded by clouds fly toward the Chinese character for longevity *(shou)*, suggesting that this item commemorated a birthday celebration. The crane was a popular auspicious motif of the mid- and late Ming dynasty.

Another multicolor technique is *tixi*, or carving layered colors. The lacquerer applied more than two lacquer colors, one on top of the other, layer by layer, before using a knife to carve geometric and floral patterns. Available *tixi* objects, both those unearthed archaeologically and those handed down from generation to generation, indicate that this style of lacquer was very popular by the Song dynasty. *Tixi* lacquers often have red, black, or purple surfaces with other colors in between. The most popular include designs of clouds, square sword-pommels, and circular rings. There are five Healy *tixi* pieces, most of which exhibit Ming-style cloud patterns. Judging from its decorative patterns, the oblong plate (cat. no. 14) might have been produced as early as the Yuan dynasty or early Ming dynasty.

Luodian, or lacquer inlaid with mother-of-pearl, has been used for thousands of years. Ancient Chinese began decorating lacquer with clam and mussel shells as early as the Shang dynasty (ca. 1600–1100 BCE). A bronze mirror with dragon pattern and shell decoration unearthed in the Sanmen Gorge and a mirror with figure, flower, and bird patterns found in Luoyang, Henan Province, demonstrate the sophisticated shell decoration of the Tang dynasty. This decorative effect, achieved with thick shells, is known simply as "thick-shell inlaying."

Another type of inlay, called "soft-shell," originated in the Yuan dynasty and soon became the preferred technique. Here the *luodian* craftsman soaked shells in water to soften them before grinding them into a fine thin sheet. He then divided the shells based on their natural colors and cut, classifying them for production purposes. To ready an article for the application of lacquer, the worker carved the design into the wood with very fine tools, making the appropriate shaped or patterned spots for inlaying the shell. Cloth pattern templates helped guide the carver's hand. Raw lacquer paste was applied to the inlay spot as well as to the back of the shell. While inlaying the shell, the worker took care to set it flush with the lacquer surface. To avoid leaving any visible crevice, a mixture of lacquer and wax was applied to the inlaid shell and smoothed out.

During the late Ming and early Qing dynasties, soft-shell inlaying reached its peak. Because of its sensitivity to temperature changes, shell-inlaid lacquer work was very difficult to preserve, and pieces from the early period are scarce, even in the collections of large museums. It is truly a rarity that the Healy Collection has preserved five pieces of *luodian* lacquer, all products of the Yuan and Ming dynasties.

In *tianqi*, or lacquer filling, after cutting an inlaid pattern, the craftsman applied and then smoothed out a thick, colored lacquer. Although the double-dragon plate (cat. no. 30) and dragon plate (cat. no. 31), with patterns filled by colored lacquers, have been worn down by time, they still demonstrate richly varied hues. One can well imagine how brilliant the colors would have been shortly after the skilled *tianqi* craftsmen fashioned them.

The lacquers in the Healy Collection have a special history and demonstrate a variety of the finest techniques of the lacquer arts. Although in number they represent only a small portion of the entire corpus of Chinese lacquer works, as a group they constitute a significant collection of sophisticated artifacts from an ancient civilization.

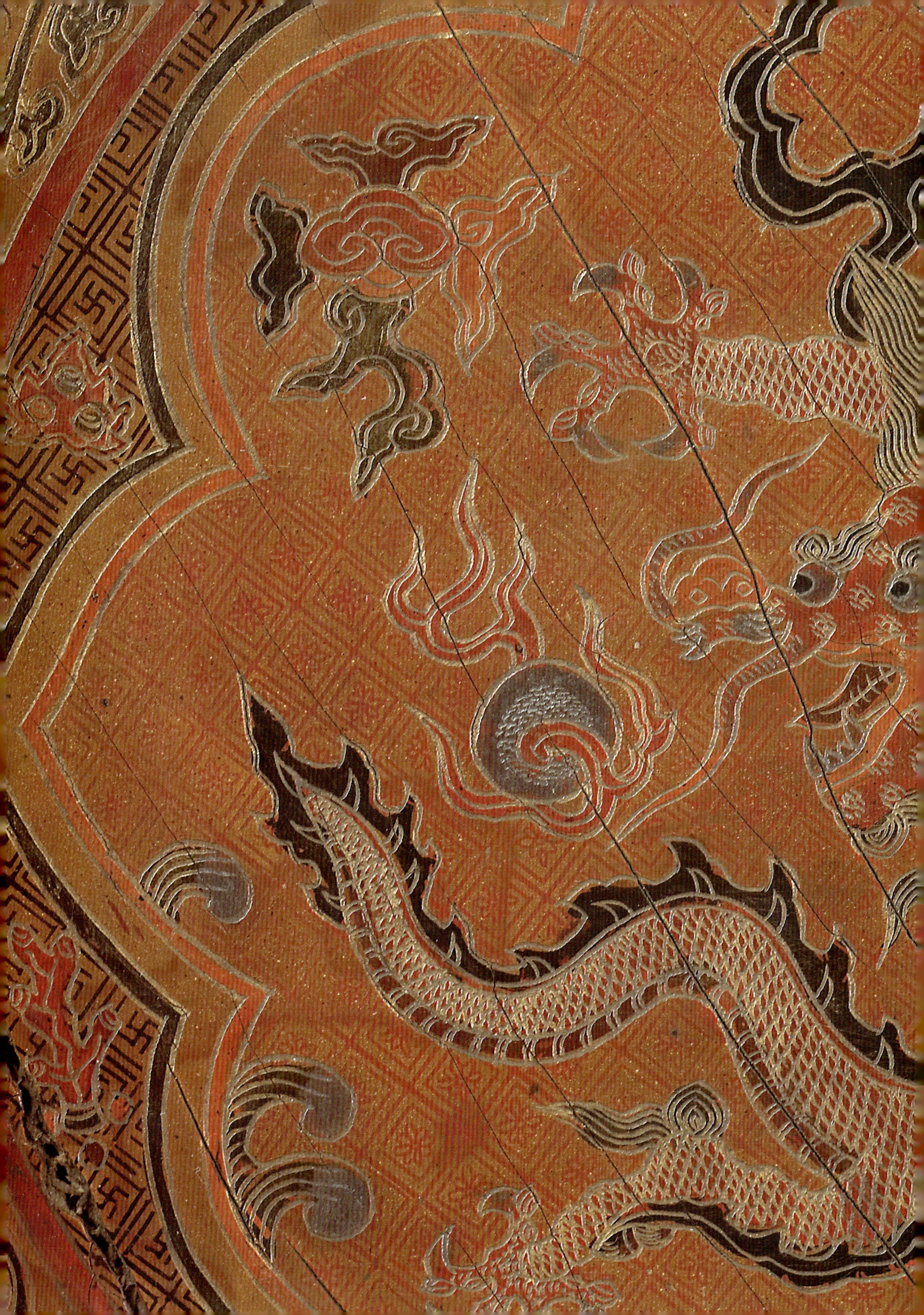

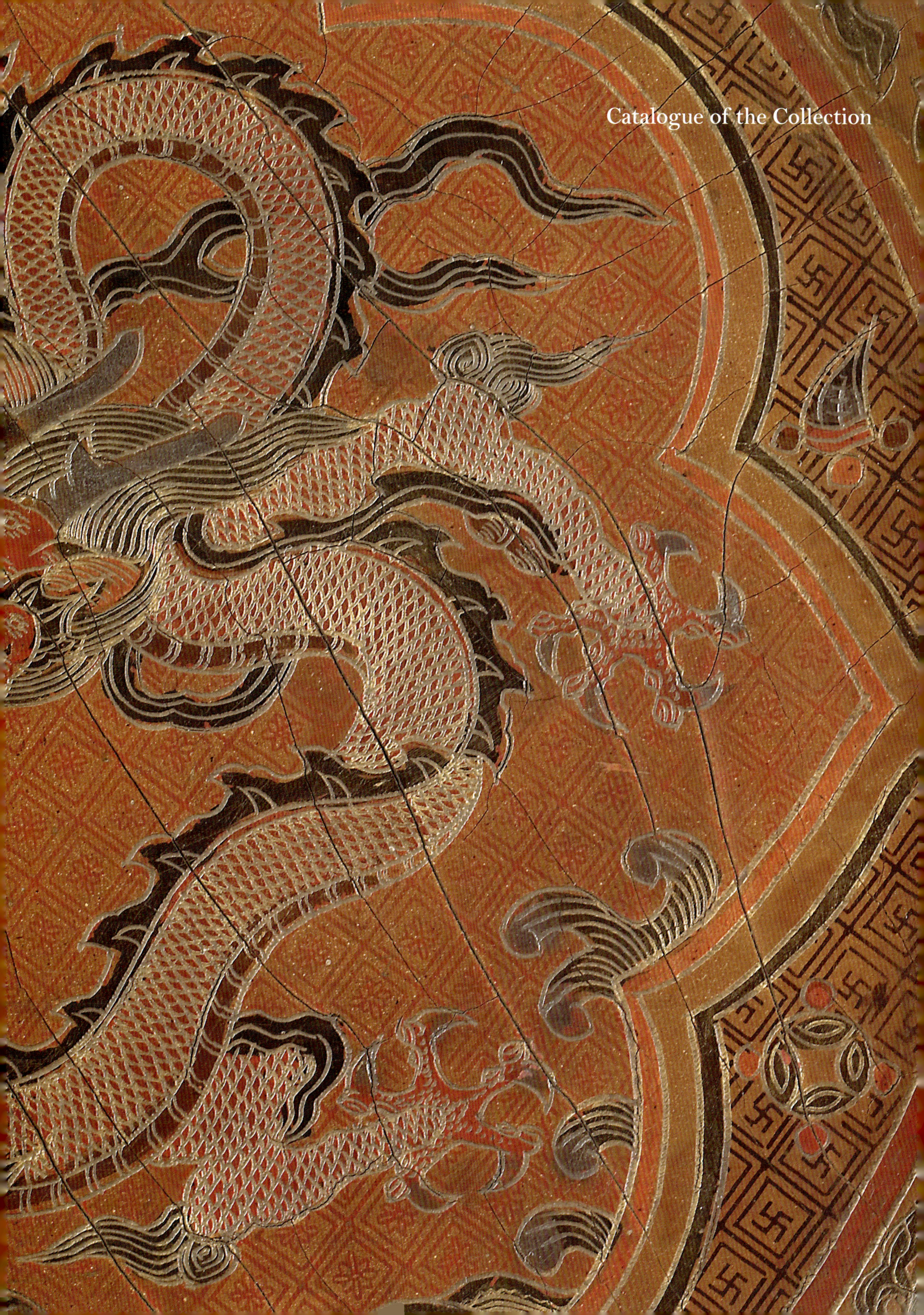

Catalogue of the Collection

1

Cosmetic Box (Lian)

Han dynasty, 1st–2nd century CE
Black and red lacquer with silver fittings
H. 4½ in. DIAM. 6¾ in.
L37,929

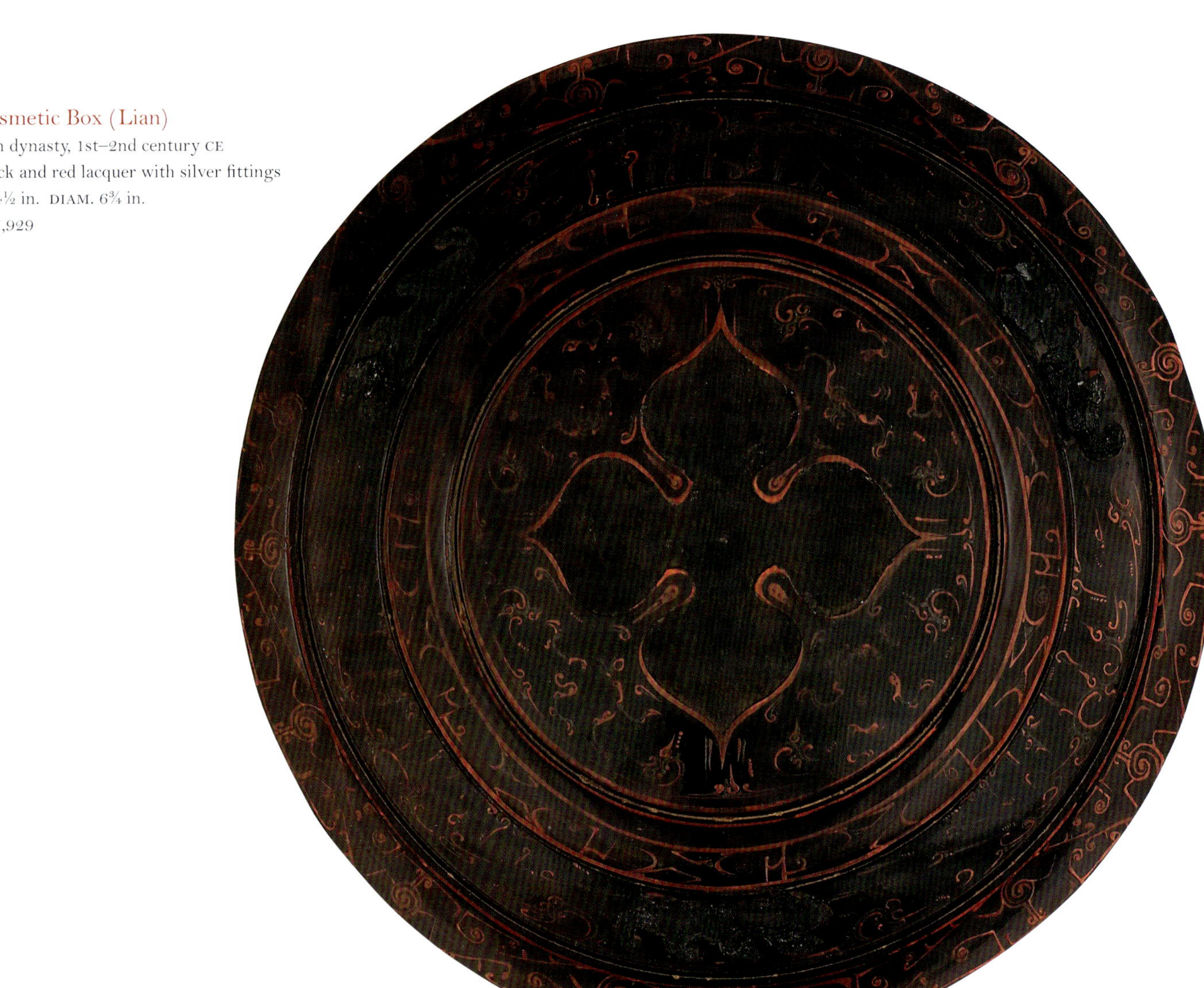

The cover of this tall, round box fits over a deep, round, straight-sided bowl with a fluid decoration of swirling arabesque and geometric patterning. The surface is further embellished with a four-petaled central medallion of silver. Four silver catlike creatures adorn the second band of decoration on the lid, and four more creatures, including birds and four-legged animals, are depicted on the lid's central band. All were added to an already intricate system of bands of red lacquer applied to a dark brown base. A box with similar appliquéd decoration amid scrolling designs can be seen in the British Museum.[1] The body of the vessel is thin, and the interior is red lacquer with a black central roundel with swirling red patterns on the base. This is consistent with decoration on lacquers in burial finds from the state of Chu in southwestern China.

An extensive and complex system of production for painted lacquer existed in imperial China. Its earliest flowering was in the late Warring States (476–221 BCE) and Han (206 BCE–220 CE) periods. The state of Chu produced finely made, painted lacquerware in state-sponsored factories dedicated to the manufacture of elegant household items for use by the nobility. Much of our current understanding of its development comes from the numerous examples found buried in the richly appointed tombs of the aristocracy, which have come to light through the extensive scientific excavations over the last thirty years.

A cosmetic box of this quality of manufacture and design was surely a highly prized item of an upper-class Han-period household. The black surface has been carefully polished to a high sheen, and a red lacquer decoration dances across the top, shoulders, and sides. Cosmetic boxes of this type also belong to a type of *mingqi*, or burial items, which were intended for use by the deceased in the afterlife.

Note

1. Suo Yuming, ed., *Zhongguo wenwu* (Chinese art treasures), vol. 3, *Qipin* (Lacquer) (Taipei: Guangfu Publishing, 1983), no. 14, p. 22. A black-and-white photo is reproduced in Harry M. Garner, *Chinese Lacquer* (London and Boston: Faber and Faber, 1979), illus. 16, p. 47. He describes the box on p. 45 and compares it to the type found at Mawangdui, the rich archaeological site in Changsha. The British Museum box "is said to have come from a tomb in Hai-chou, Kiansu Province, and it is ascribed to the first century B.C."

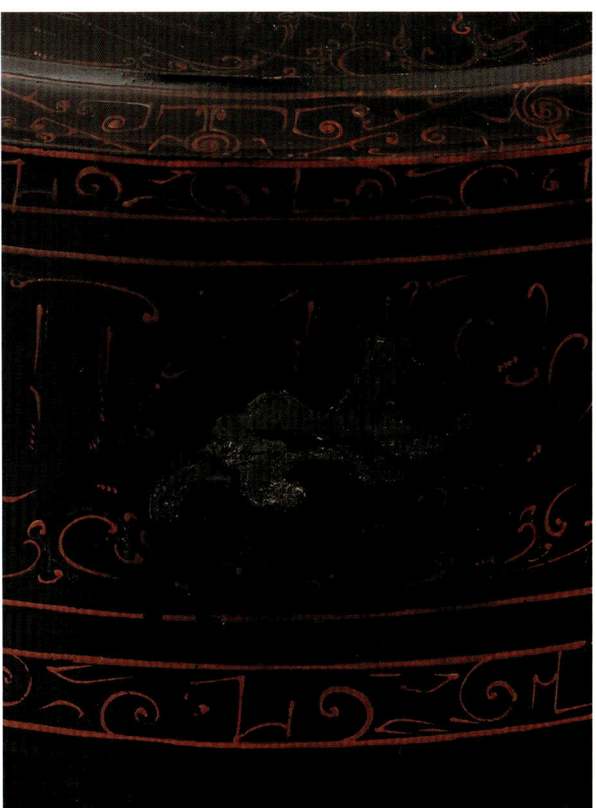

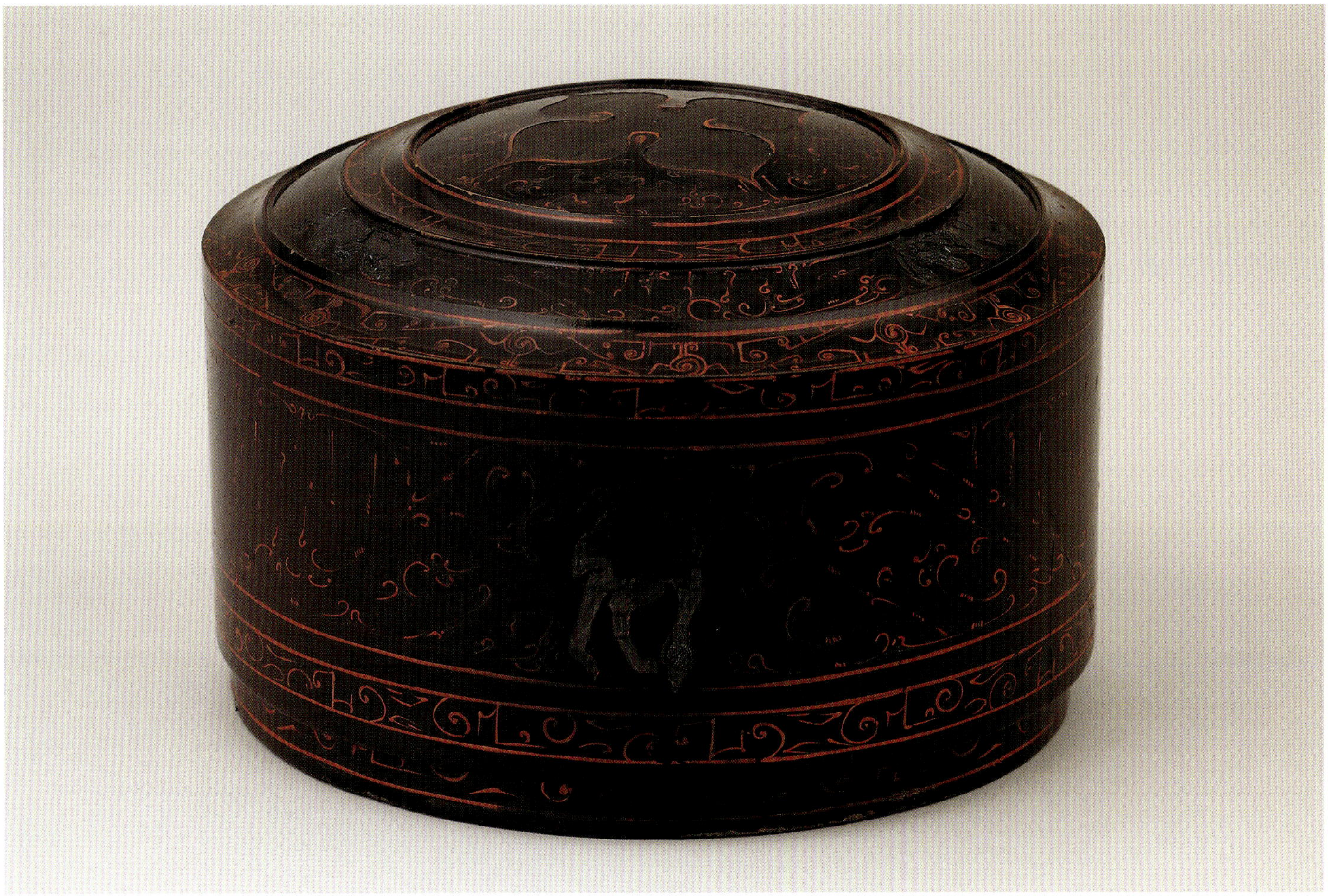

2

Wine Cup with Two Handles

Han dynasty, 1st–2nd century CE
Black and red lacquer
H. 1½ in. L. 5½ in. W. 4¼ in.
L37,930

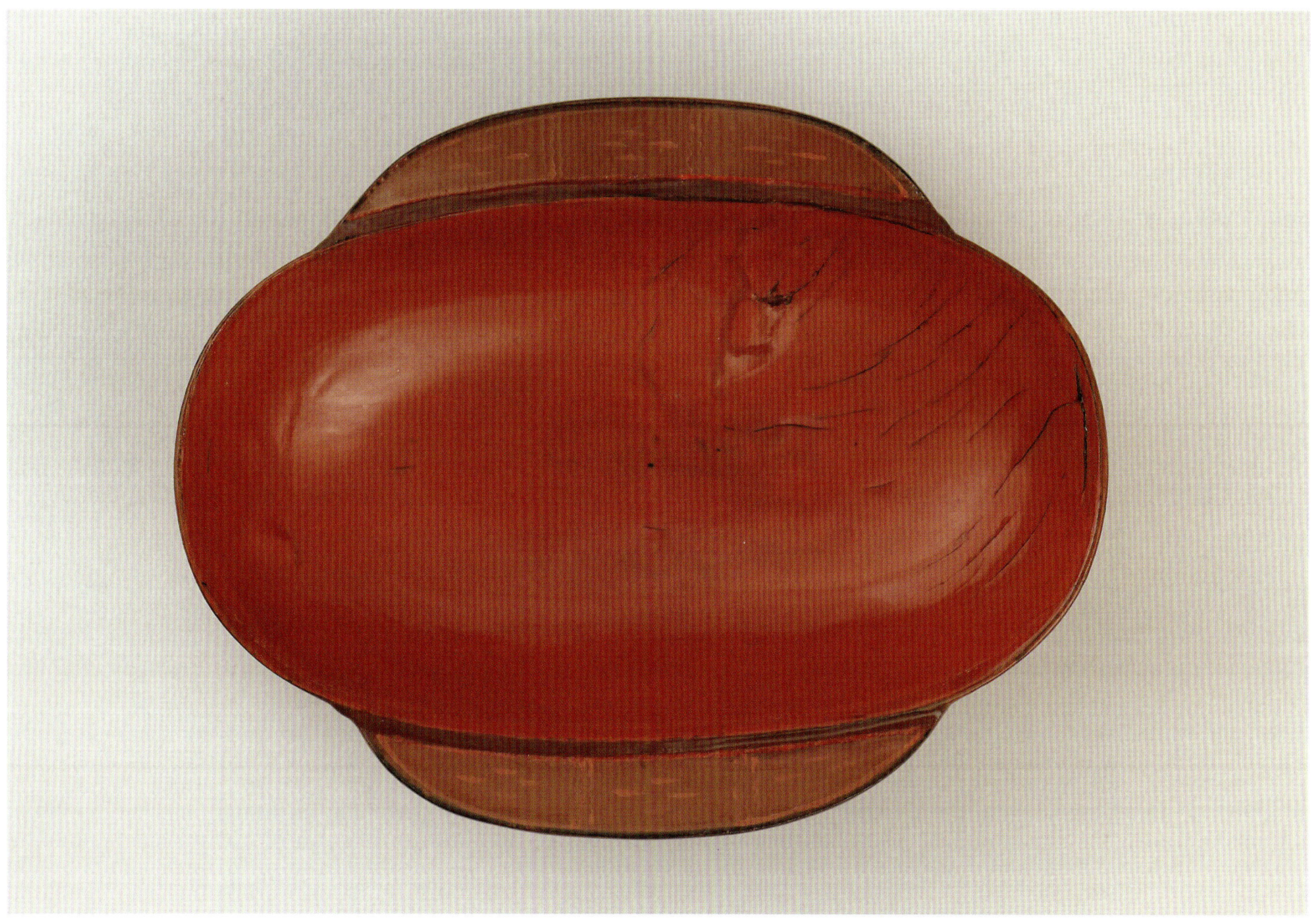

This type of shallow, oblong cup with two opposing flat handles on either side is found in southern Chinese tombs from the fourth century BCE. The interior of this cup is red, whereas the exterior has a combination of red and black designs on the handles and across the body. It is similar to the type found in tombs that date from the Warring States period (476–221 BCE) through the end of the Han period in the third century CE. The decoration on this cup is restrained and highly abstract, arguing for a slightly later date than the more elaborately decorated vessels of the early Han period.

The surface bubbles apparent in this cup's interior indicate problems faced during early lacquer production. One unfortunate trait of early lacquerware is a thin and fragile base material susceptible to humidity and temperature changes. Such stress causes detachment of the lacquer from the base. New methods of preservation have rescued many of these fragile pieces, but perhaps the most important condition of preserving them is to maintain a consistent level of both temperature and humidity.[1]

Note

1. In the past twenty years, much work has been done in China to preserve ancient lacquers. The Hubei Provincial Museum, in conjunction with the Hubei Provincial Institute of Archaeology, and the Art Gallery, The Chinese University of Hong Kong, produced an exhibition and catalogue describing these efforts: Hubei Provincial Museum, *Lacquerware from the Warring States to the Han Periods Excavated in Hubei Province* (Hong Kong: Art Gallery, The Chinese University of Hong Kong, 1994).

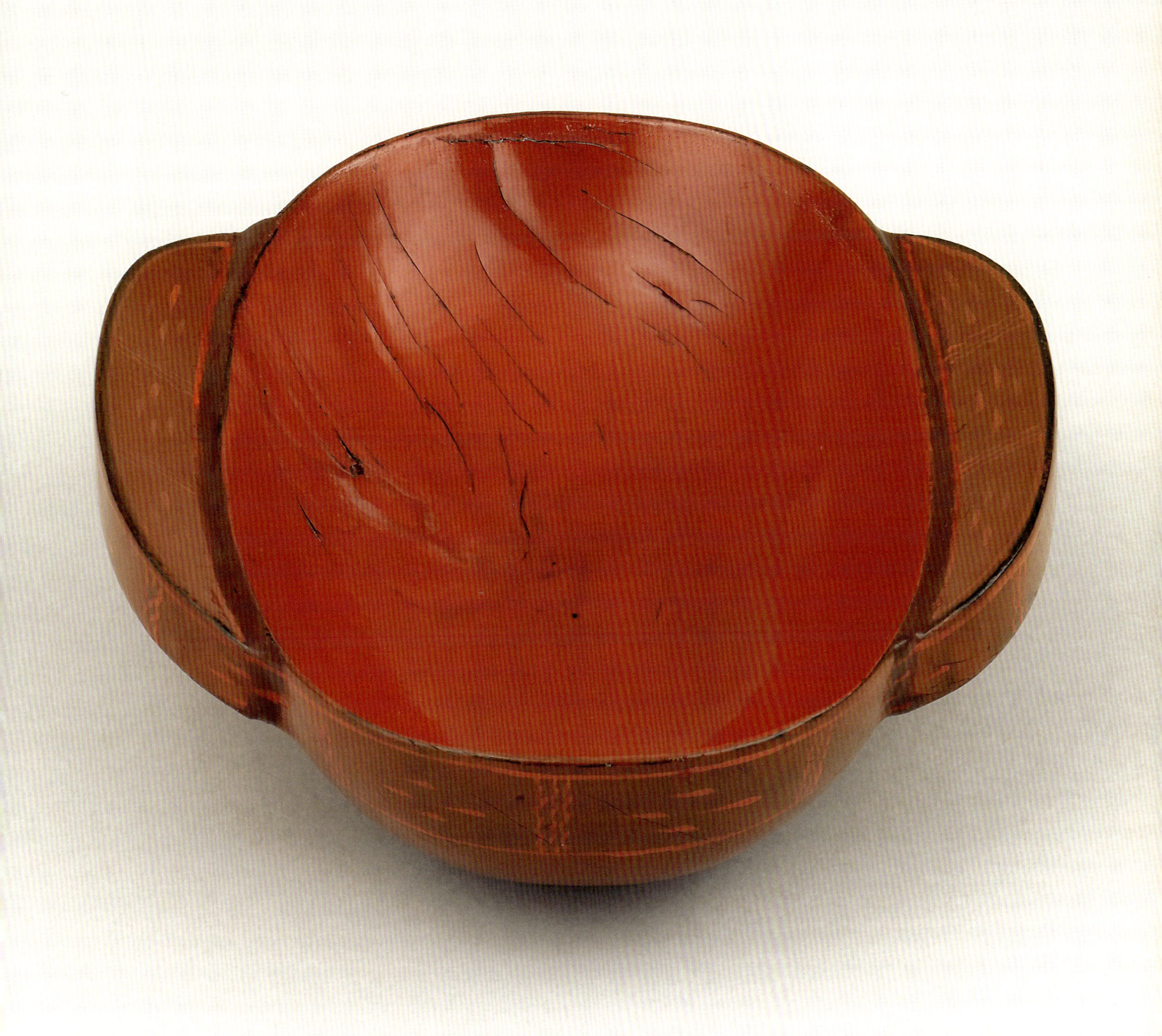

3

Lobed Toiletry Box

Yuan dynasty, 14th century
Dark brown lacquer with pewter
H. 7 in. DIAM. 8¾ in.
L37,931

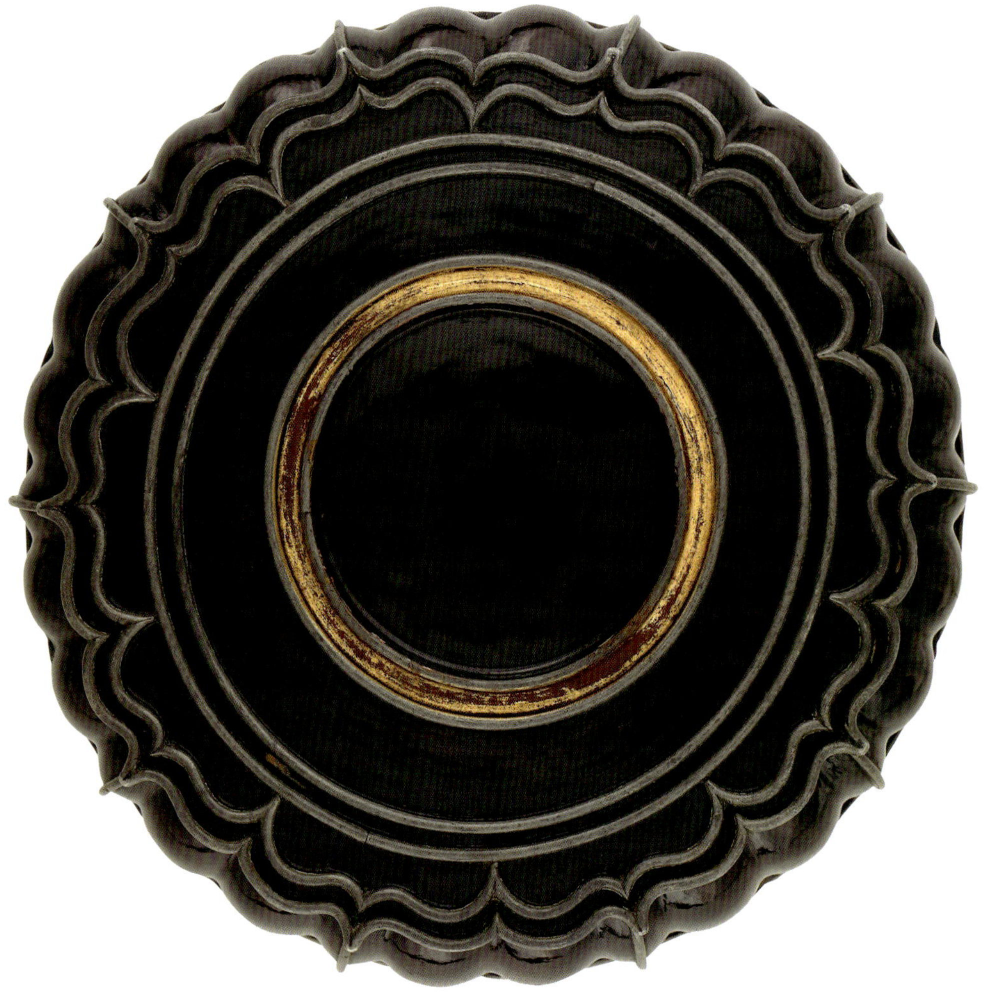

Deceptively simple and elegant in form, this toiletry box is actually a complex arrangement of ten foliated sections encompassing thirty-lobed sections. The top of the box is flat, with a solid gold-washed raised metal disk in the center. Radiating from it is a band of dark lacquer followed by a double band of gold-washed raised metal, followed by yet another lacquer band, and finishing in a foliated rim of metal that connects to a vertical banding down the sides of the box's top.

The metal rim follows the top ridge of one lobe and connects to a foliate design across the base of the top of the box. Emphasizing the overall shape of this elegant box, the trimming is repeated in reverse across its bottom, with pointed foliates meeting in the middle at the opening to the box. The overall form is extremely pleasing, with a high, swelling shoulder and tapering base ending in a slight foliate flare. Evidence of a link between these restrained lacquer shapes and ceramics has been demonstrated in a fine article by Hin-Cheung Lovell.[1] This shape is also seen in the Song period; however, the addition of metal banding is not seen until the Yuan period.[2]

Clearly, the box was created for someone with great appreciation for subtle elegance and restrained beauty. Every aspect (except perhaps for the gold wash on the metal) speaks to an understated aesthetic. This type of box was probably used and cherished by a high-level court lady of considerable wealth and status.

Although it may have been factory made, this box could have been a commissioned piece made by a skilled artisan. We do not know artists' names at this time, although records of ateliers are a part of the history of lacquer manufacture. Similar boxes are in the collection of the Metropolitan Museum of Art, the Freer Gallery in Washington, D.C.,[3] and several other North American museum collections.[4] A very similar box is in the collection of the Tokyo National Museum.[5] An elaborately decorated ten-lobed box with gold dragon designs can be seen in the exhibition catalogue from the Lee Family Collection.[6]

Notes

1. Hin-Cheung Lovell, "Sung and Yuan Monochrome Lacquers in the Freer Gallery," *Ars Orientalis: The Arts of Islam and the East* 9 (1973): 121–30.
2. Ibid., p. 128.
3. The Freer box is well described and interpreted by Lovell; ibid.
4. James C. Y. Watt and Barbara Brennan Ford, *East Asian Lacquer: The Florence and Herbert Irving Collection* (New York: Metropolitan Museum of Art, 1991), cat. no. 3, pp. 44–45.
5. Tokyo National Museum, *Tōyō no shikkōgei: Tokubetsu-ten* (Oriental lacquer arts: Special exhibition), glossary and object list in English (Tokyo: Tokyo National Museum, 1977), illus. no. 484, description p. 249.
6. Lee King Tsi and Hu Shih Chang, *Drache und Phoenix: Lackarbeiten aus China: Sammlung der Familie Lee, Tokyo / Dragon and Phoenix: Chinese Lacquerware: The Lee Family Collection, Tokyo* (Cologne, Germany: Museum of East Asian Art, 1990), no. 25, pp. 76–77.

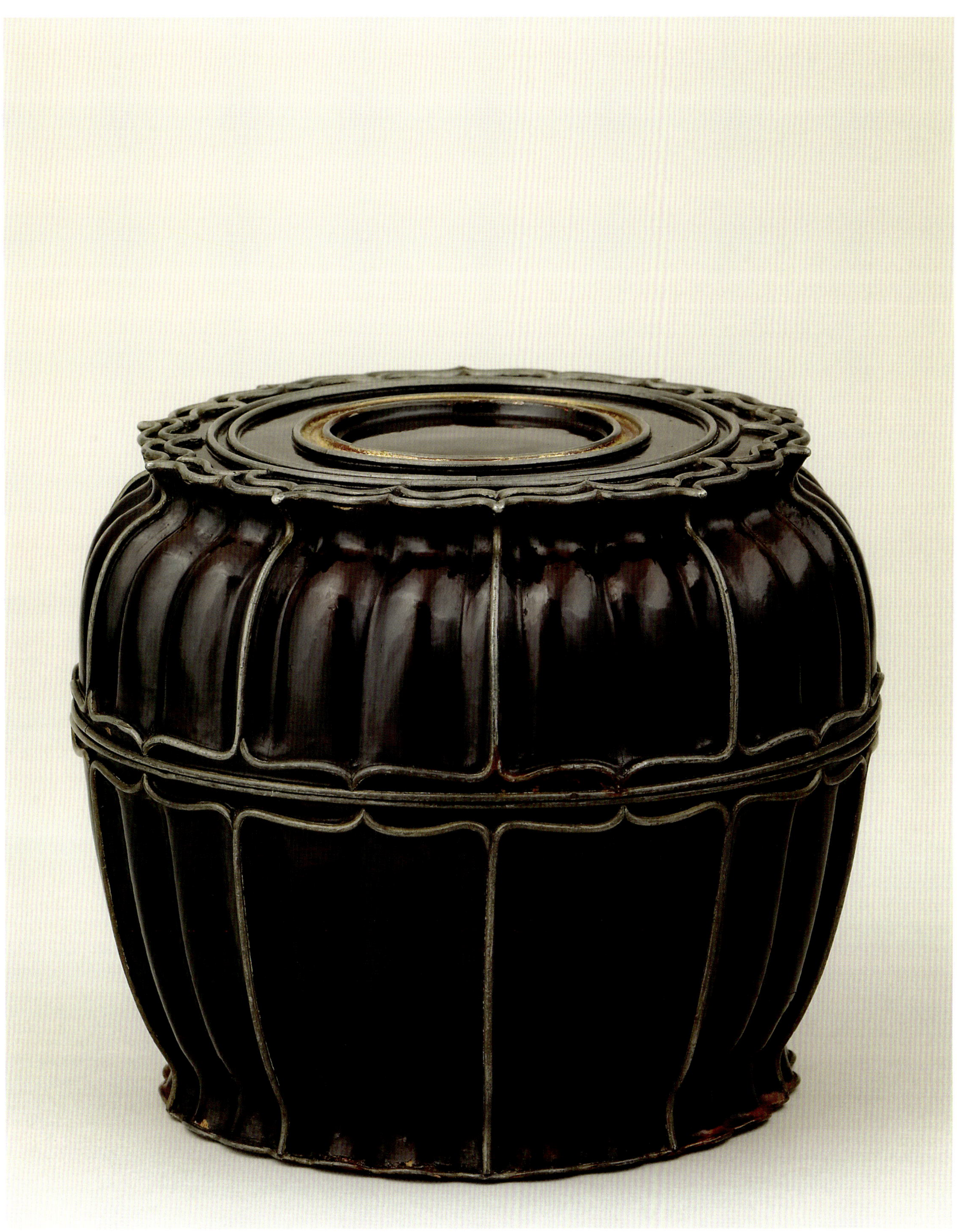

4

Oval Box

Yuan dynasty, 14th century
Dark brown lacquer with pewter trim
H. 4 in. W. 6 in. L. 14½ in.
L37,923

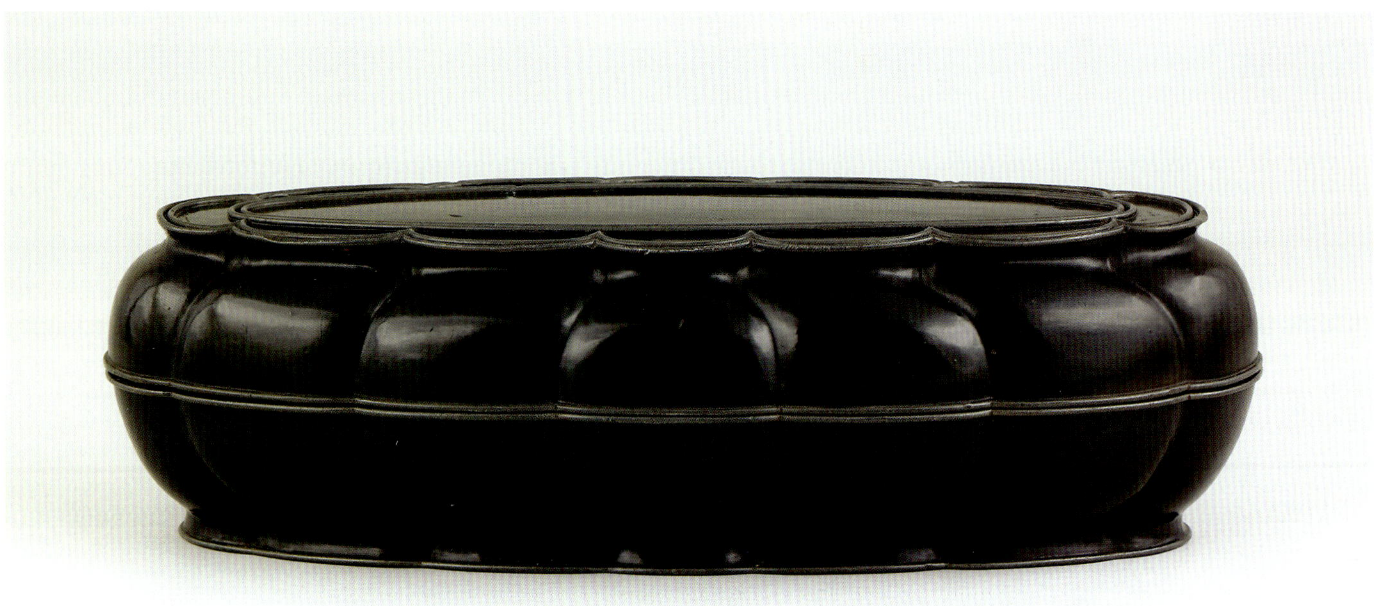

This lacquer box displays an elegant and restrained style that expresses the love of pure form seen in early, uncarved lacquers from China. The dark, mottled brown exterior of the body, with its twelve-lobed shape, speaks to a love of design as well as a simple, restrained order that was greatly appreciated by the Song and Yuan upper classes. An oval tray of red and dark brown lacquer fits into the base.

The red interior and base of the box, closely hidden except to the owner, belie the love of contrast and color within this type of lacquer box. A shallow tray nests inside the base. The interior red lacquer appears to be a relatively recent addition, although its color corresponds with similar examples.[1] The base of the interior tray is black and includes an inscribed mark; the same mark occurs on the base of the box, which is red. It appears that this mark may have been added later and may be that of a collector.[2] The box's form derives from similar ceramic forms of the period, which in turn may have metalwork as their prototype.[3]

The outline of pewter (which defines the overall shape and enhances the box's form) may well have come from a ceramic heritage as well. Song Ding ware ceramics, with their delicate, unglazed lips, were sometimes rimmed in pewter for protection against wear. These lacquers may have relied on the same type of metal protection against rubbing or other damage to the delicate edges of the box.

A similar twelve-lobed, elongated box is illustrated in a 1990 exhibition catalogue of the Samuel Lee Family Collection of Tokyo.[4]

Most of the excavated Song Chinese wares of this type have come from the areas around the Yangzi River valley from as far upriver as Hunan and down into the delta area. It could be that they are the result of the coming together of a lacquer tradition begun in the Han state of Chu farther in the interior. They also spring from an active and progressive ceramic production center around Hangzhou and the lower reaches of the Yangzi River, where a rise in production occurred through the Song period.[5]

High lian, or cosmetic boxes, like cat. no. 3, as well as boxes of this shape have also been found in silver. The lian shape is seen in ivory too.[6] It seems likely from the literature of the period that production was great, and that lacquers of this sort were produced in factories. Even so, lacquer remained a luxury item for the wealthy and well-placed. Evidence of lacquer in use as a domestic and a court item can clearly be seen in contemporaneous and earlier paintings.[7]

Notes

1. A round, lobed box in the Florence and Herbert Irving Collection is lacquered red in the interior dome but black in the base; see James C. Y. Watt and Barbara Brennan Ford, *East Asian Lacquer: The Florence and Herbert Irving Collection* (New York: Metropolitan Museum of Art, 1991), cat. no. 3, pp. 44–45.

2. Hin-Cheung Lovell, "Sung and Yuan Monochrome Lacquers in the Freer Gallery," *Ars Orientalis: The Arts of Islam and the East* 9 (1973), figs. 2 and 3, presents examples of inscriptions on excavated monochrome lacquers, but they are consistently brushed on, not incised.

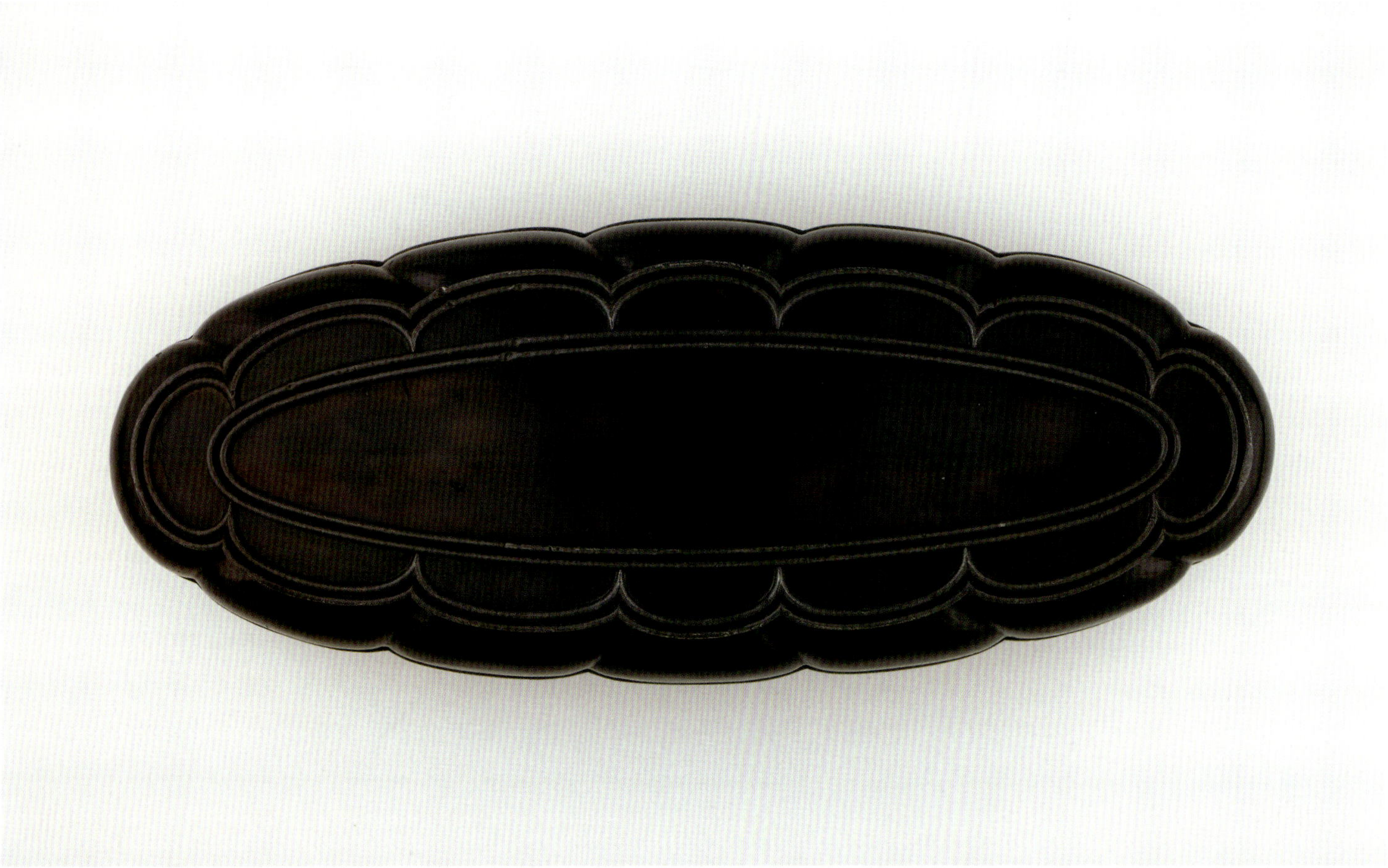

3. Lovell establishes this relationship in "Sung and Yuan Monochrome Lacquers."

4. Lee King Tsi and Hu Shih Chang, *Drache und Phoenix: Lackarbeiten aus China: Sammlung der Familie Lee, Tokyo/Dragon and Phoenix: Chinese Lacquerware: The Lee Family Collection, Tokyo* (Cologne, Germany: Museum of East Asian Art, 1990), no. 24, pp. 74–75.

5. Lovell, "Sung and Yuan Monochrome Lacquers," pp. 121–30, discusses monochrome lacquer production sites.

6. Sherman Lee and Wai-kam Ho, *Chinese Art under the Mongols*, exh. cat. (Cleveland: Cleveland Museum of Art, 1968), cat. no. 299.

7. Ibid. See also Lovell, "Sung and Yuan Monochrome Lacquers," pls. 17 and 18, and Wu Tung, *Masterpieces of Chinese Painting from the Museum of Fine Arts, Boston: Tang through Yuan Dynasties* (Boston: Museum of Fine Arts; Tokyo: Ōtsuka Kōgeisha, 1996), vol. 2: a Southern Song fan painting by Su Hanchen (act. 1120s–1160s) shows a woman at her dressing table on which a stacked lacquer box sits (pl. 20, p. 128), and a detail of a Yuan painting depicts various types of lacquer boxes (pl. 128, p. 311).

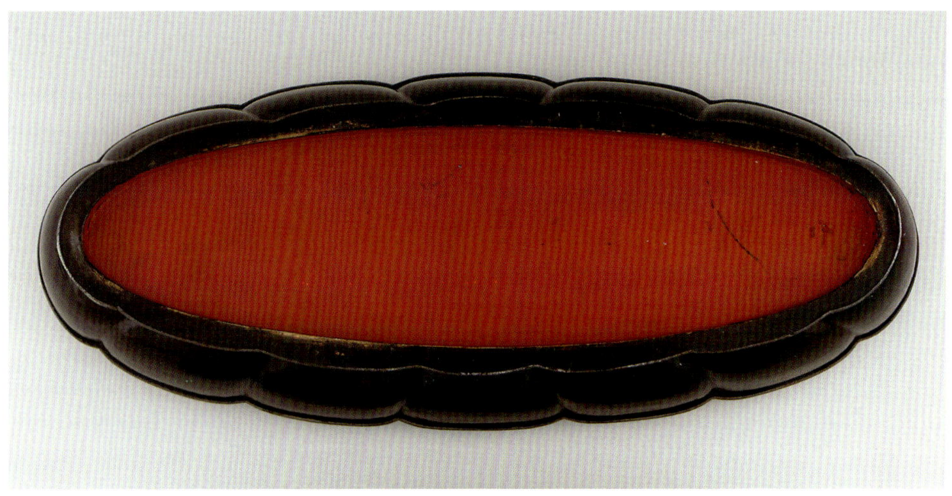

Top: *top of box*. Bottom: *base of box*.

5

Box

Yuan dynasty (1260–1368)
Black lacquer with inlaid mother-of-pearl
H. 3¾ in. W. 7½ in. L. 8½ in.
L37, 933

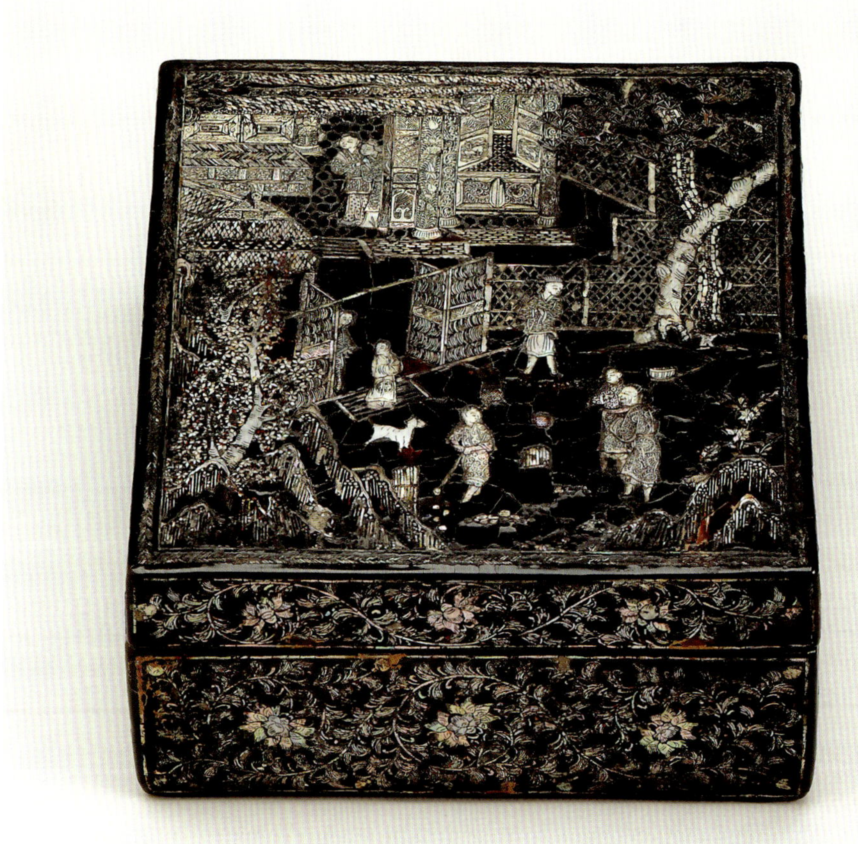

The method of application used in the manufacture of the narrative scene depicted on the lid of this box helps determine its early date. Most of the design is achieved with relatively large blocks of inlay that were incised and made to create lively patterns and natural-looking forms. A group of figures with farm implements stands in the outer courtyard, while a boy and a dog look on at what is either an arrival or a departure scene. At the gate, a woman reaches out to the boy, whose robe is adorned with a rabbit on the lower portions. The two other female figures stand in the doorway of a rural house. Groupings of trees at opposite corners of the box define the natural environment.

The figures at the gate are dressed in beautifully patterned robes, and the two women at the entrance to the house are also shown in clothing that confers a higher status to the scene than one of rural simplicity. The house is also constructed of intricate and fanciful imagery, including the pillars covered with geometric and floral motifs, and the window shutters adorned with images of rabbits. The appearance of rabbits on the boy's robe and the building leads to the speculation that the box was made as a commemoration of the Year of the Rabbit, or as presentation item for someone born in that year.

Inlaid lacquer production is mentioned in the *Ge gu yao lun* as having been made for the Song imperial court. During the Yuan period, wealthy families commissioned inlaid lacquer objects. "In the Yuan dynasty, rich families ordered this type of ware, but left the manufacturers to take their own time in their making. The products are of very solid lacquer, and the designs with human figures on them are delightful to the beholder."[1] The same text notes that mother-of-pearl inlay was produced in Luling xian in Jiangxi.

The sides of the box, both lid and body, are decorated with an elaborate scrolling of leaves around central flower patterns. They are executed in a technique similar to that used in the top of the box—delicately inset mother-of-pearl with incised detail. Each panel of this box is embellished with three-part floral and leaf patterns.

The meaning of the narrative is not clear, and yet the scene is one repeated in two other boxes, one in this collection (see cat. no. 6) and another in the Metropolitan Museum of Art's distinguished Irving Collection of Chinese lacquers.[2] All are exquisitely decorated, with the finest example of mother-of-pearl technique delineating the texture of cloth, tree, fence, window, and gate.

The box was published and exhibited in a Tokyo National Museum exhibition in 1981.[3]

Notes

1. Sir Percival David, trans. and ed., *Chinese Connoisseurship: The Ko Ku Yao Lun, The Essential Criteria of Antiquities* (New York: Praeger, 1971), p. 148.
2. James C. Y. Watt and Barbara Brennan Ford, *East Asian Lacquer: The Florence and Herbert Irving Collection* (New York: Metropolitan Museum of Art, 1991), cat. no. 57, pp. 129–30.
3. Tokyo National Museum, *Chūgoku no raden* (Mother-of-pearl inlay in Chinese lacquer art) (Tokyo: Benridō, 1981).

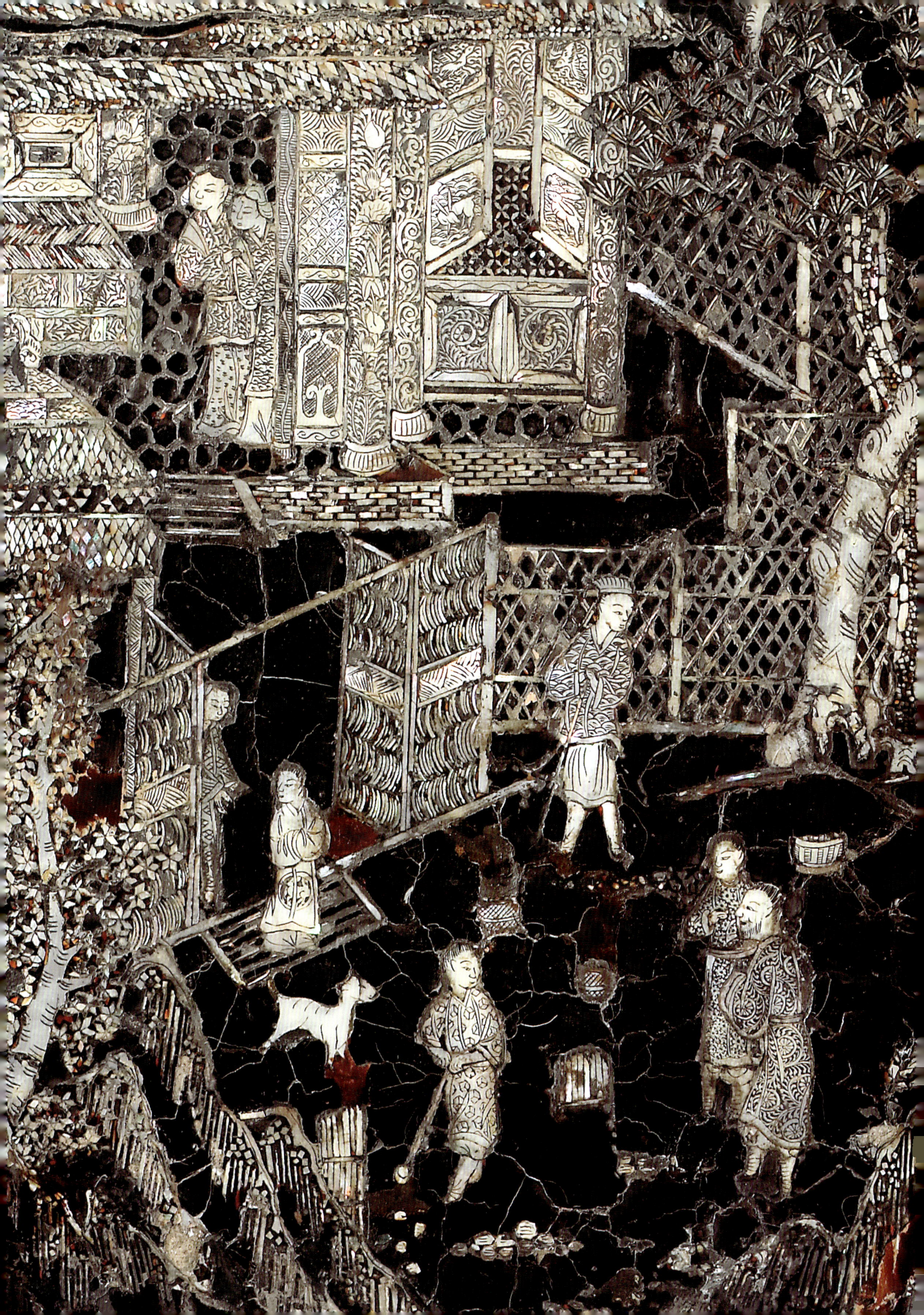

6

Octagonal Box

Yuan dynasty (1260–1368)
Black lacquer inlaid with mother-of-pearl
H. 4¾ in. W. 10¼ in. L. 10¼ in.
L38,156

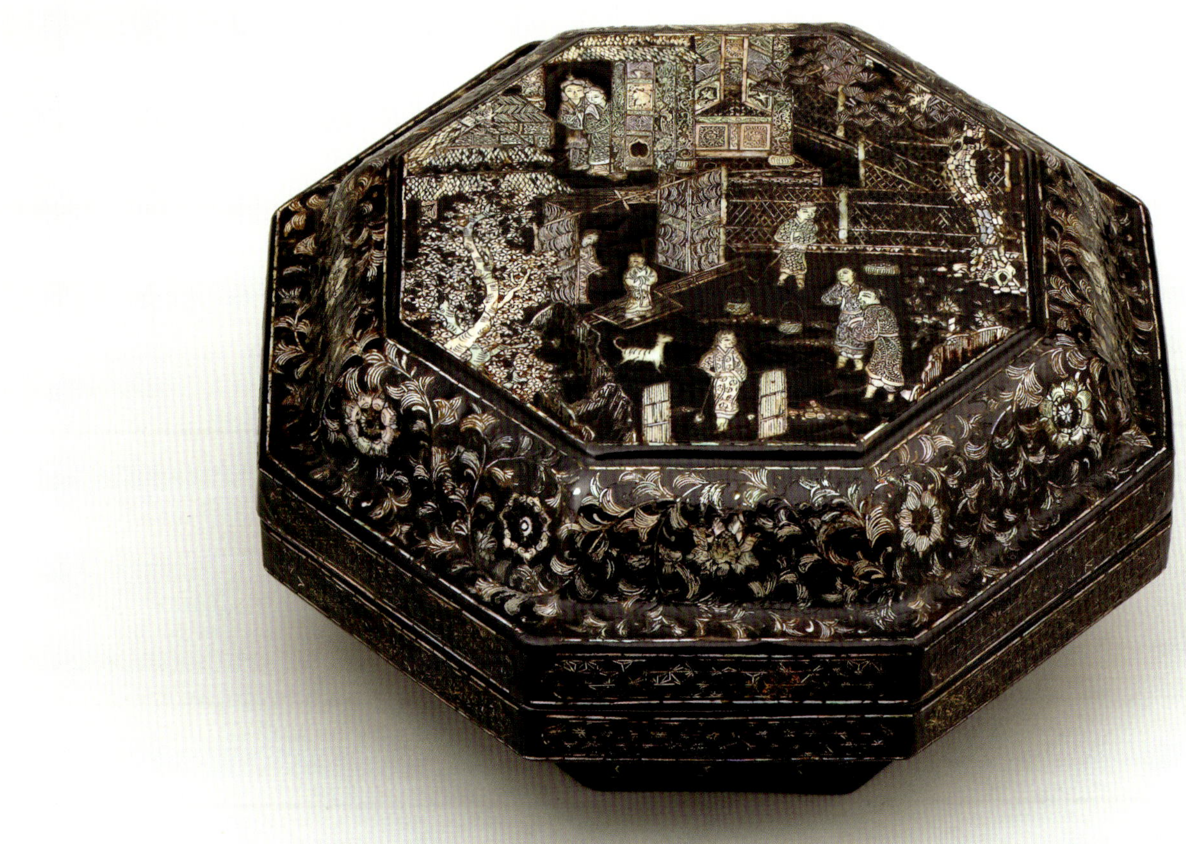

The narrative scene depicted here is nearly identical to that of the inlaid box depicted in cat. no. 5 and is also similar to one in the Irving Collection, now at the Metropolitan Museum of Art in New York.[1] The octagonal shape of this box creates a slightly different framing device for the overall composition, causing a slight attenuation and narrowing of the focus of the scene. Just like the square box, this design is composed around rural Chinese agrarian life. The surface embellishment is extremely intricate, with bits of mother-of-pearl creating surface texture for the entire scene. This inlay technique, which probably originated in Korea, was introduced first to China and later to the Ryukyu Islands and Japan.

A double inlaid line and a slightly swelling shoulder adorned with a scrolling floral motif surround the box top's narrative. The top and base are straight-sided vertical panels adorned with cartouches filled with geometric floral motifs. The base is further enhanced by a similar scrolling floral pattern.

The well-known specialist Sir Harry Garner illustrated this box in an early definitive study, *Chinese Lacquer*. After a lifetime of study, writing, and collecting, he donated his own collection to the British Museum. Garner published this box as one of the finest examples of inlaid lacquer, attesting that it displayed "exceptionally high craftsmanship, hardly surpassed in any of the decorative arts of China."[2]

When published by Garner, the box was in the well-known Figgess Collection of Chinese lacquer. Apparently when the collection was dispersed, this particular box was overlooked, then later discovered at an auction, where it was acquired by the current owner.

Notes

1. James C. Y. Watt and Barbara Brennan Ford, *East Asian Lacquer: The Florence and Herbert Irving Collection* (New York: Metropolitan Museum of Art, 1991), no. 57, pp. 129–30. The entry mentions two boxes from private collections. This box is the one illustrated in Harry M. Garner, *Chinese Lacquer* (London: Faber and Faber, 1979), pls. 162–64.

2. This statement was made in reference to a group of early inlaid Chinese lacquer pieces from a variety of collections. See Garner, *Chinese Lacquer*, pp. 218–21, illus. nos. 163 and 164.

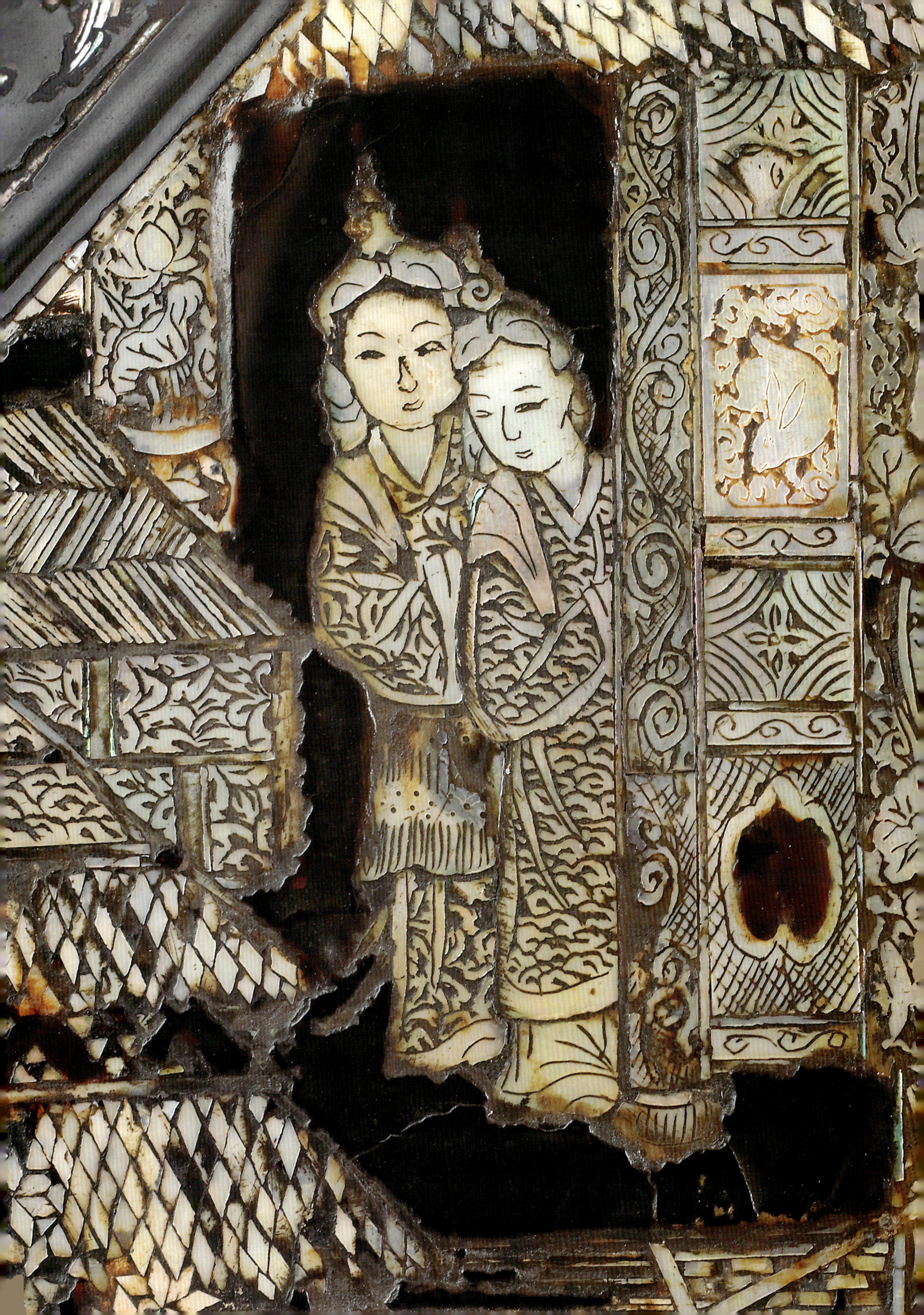

7

Inlaid Box

Yuan dynasty (1260–1368)
Black lacquer with inlaid mother-of-pearl
H. 2½ in. W. 6¾ in. D. 6¾ in.
L37, 912

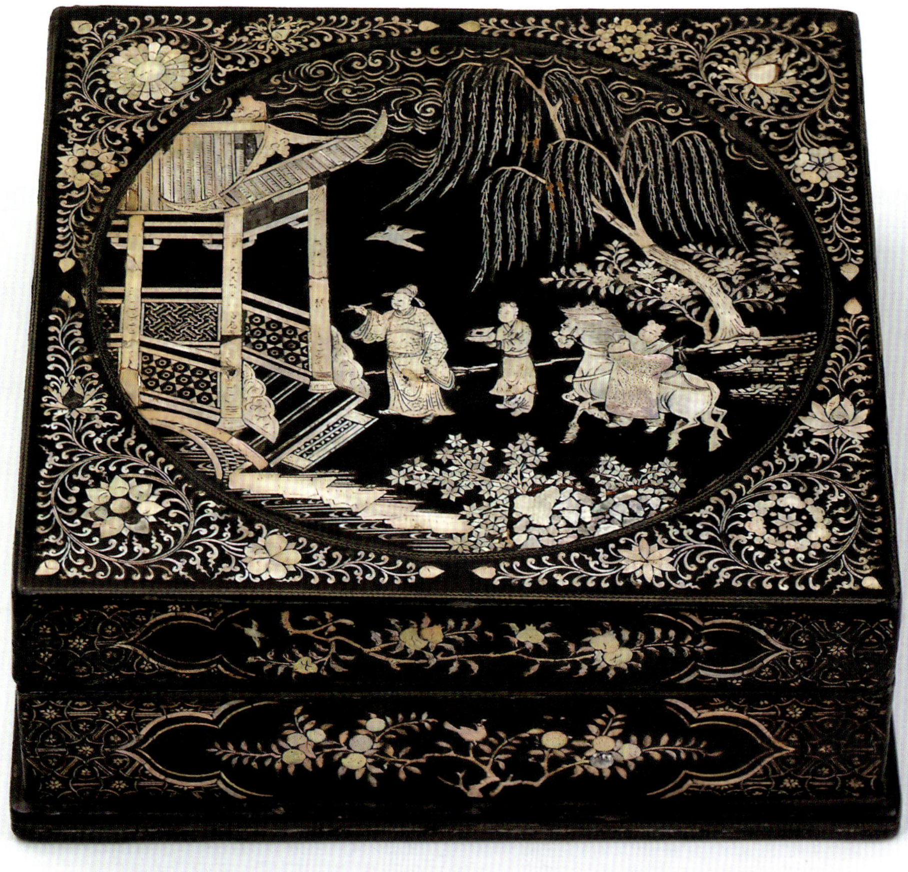

Constructed of solid wood and covered with a thin layer of lacquer, this early square box is decorated in large blocks of mother-of-pearl that are further enhanced with incised designs. The base of the box is stepped out across the bottom to form an unusual foot. The central roundel of a figure by a bridge with his horse and two attendants is encircled by stylized flowers of the four seasons with elaborately linked tendrils of flowers and leaves.

The decoration on this notable and exquisitely inlaid lacquer box is linked to the historical poet Sima Xiangru (179–117 BCE), whose poetic talent was matched by his reputation as an upright Confucian official. The inscription on the pillar of the bridge, "A true gentleman will not cross the bridge again unless he is driving a four-horse chariot," refers to an inscription the poet wrote as a young man.[1]

According to legend, Sima Xiangru vowed that he would not cross the bridge leading to the imperial capital of Chang'an (present-day Xi'an) until he was appointed a scholar-official. During the Yuan period, this decoration took on added meaning: lack of recognition prohibited the overlooked scholar-official from serving his state in proper Confucian fashion.

The inscription on the accompanying Japanese wooden box indicates that the lacquer box is a poetry-paper container made of mother-of-pearl and is also described as a case for an inkstone. Both these uses are possible in Japan for a box of this quality. A paper attached to the side of the storage box bears the number '437' and a stamp of the Yamada Collection. Chinese lacquers began arriving in Japan from the late fourteenth and early part of the fifteenth century as gifts and are well documented.[2] The popularity of Chinese lacquers—carved, inlaid, and *xipi* (*guri*)—continues in Japan, one of the great preservers of this art form.

Notes

1. For a reference to the same theme on Chinese ceramics and a recounting of the legend, see Qianshen Bai, "Inscriptions, Calligraphy, and Seals on Jingdezhen Porcelains from the Shunzhi Era," in *Treasures from an Unknown Reign: Shunzhi Porcelain, 1644–1661*, by Michael Butler, Julia B. Curtis, and Stephen Little (Alexandria, Va.: Art Services International, 2002), pp. 56–67.

2. See Harry M. Garner, "The Export of Chinese Lacquer to Japan in the Yuan and Early Ming Dynasties," *Archives of Asian Art* 25 (1972): 6–28.

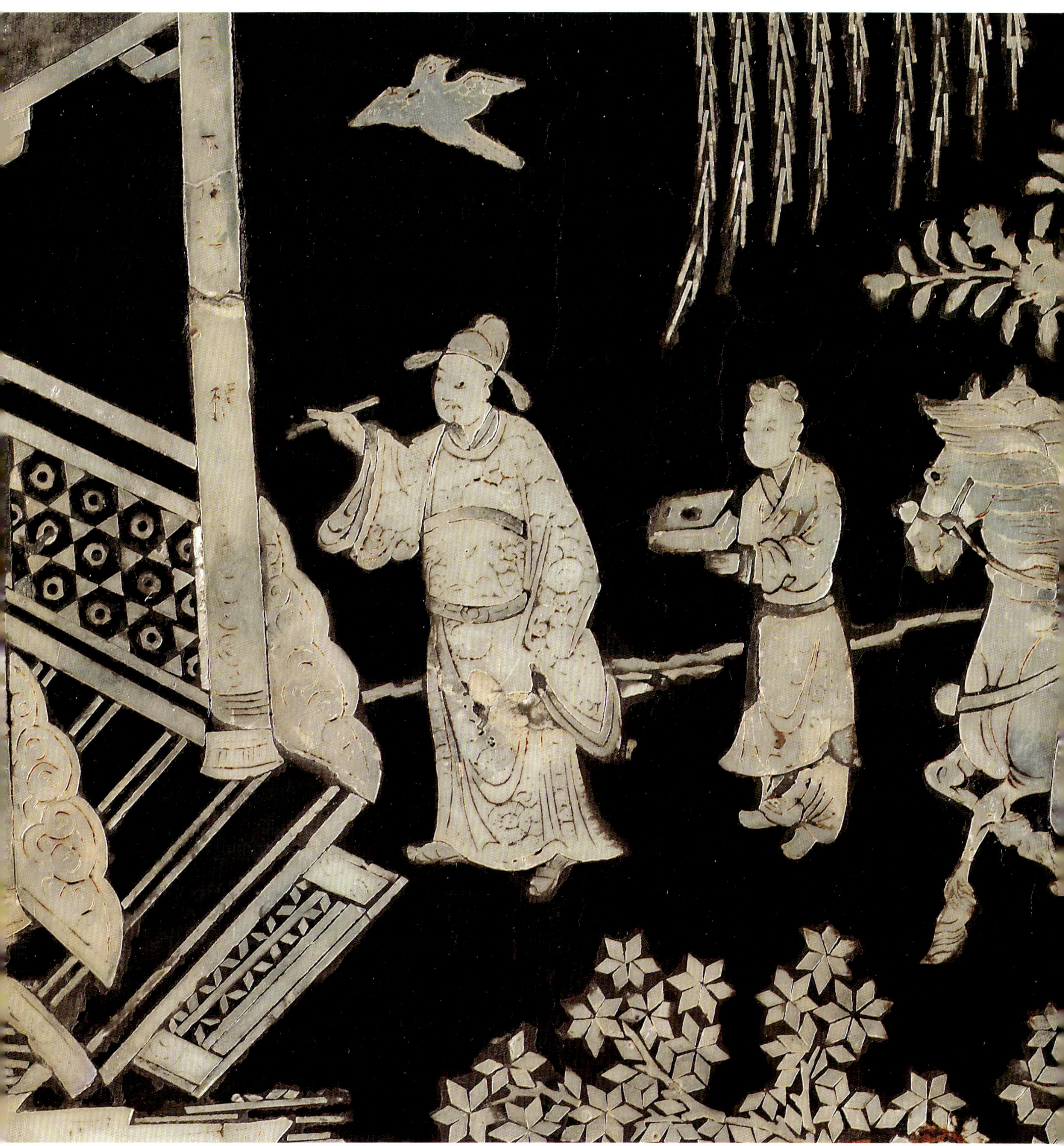

8

Inlaid Tray

Early Ming dynasty, 14th–15th century
Black lacquer inlaid with mother-of-pearl
H. 1⅜ in. W. 5½ in. L. 16¾ in.
L37,916

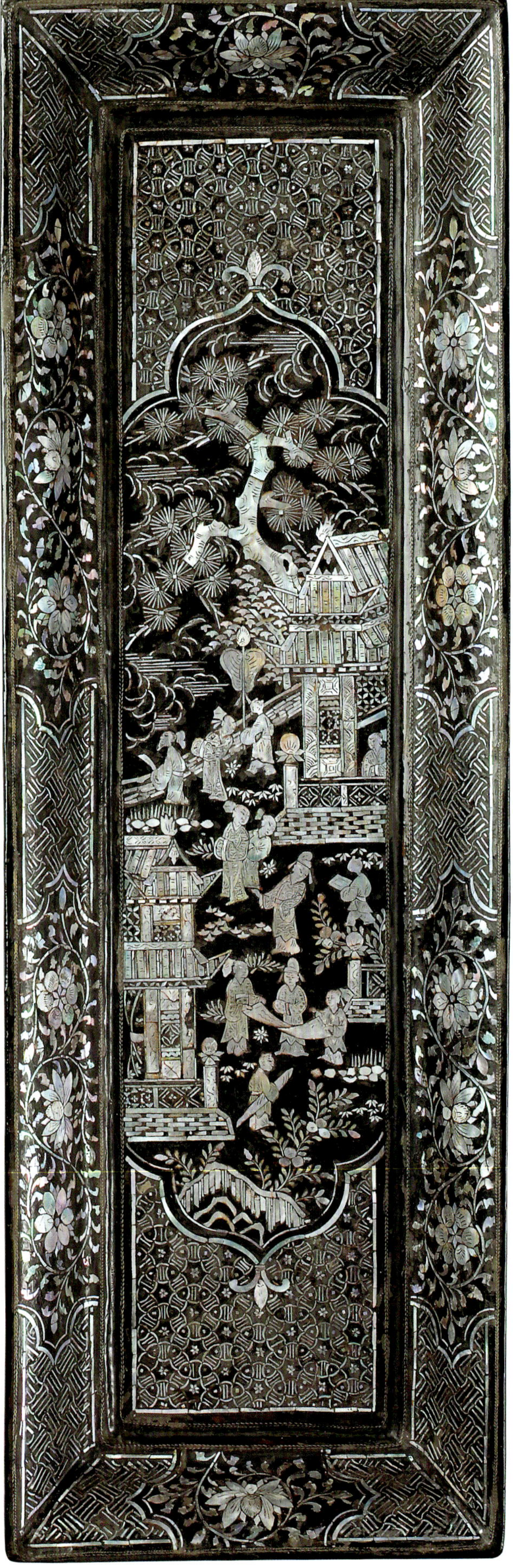

Garden scenes depicting scholars in leisurely pursuits have adorned lacquer trays and boxes since the Yuan dynasty (thirteenth century) and continued to be a popular topic through the Ming period (1368–1644). A long, narrow tray of this type may have been used for scholars' tools such as brushes, scrolls, or ink sticks. The wooden box accompanying the piece indicates it is a scroll tray with mother-of-pearl decoration.

A narrow slice of gentrified life appears in the decoration of this tray, with some hint at the accomplishments of the scholar-literati. At the base of the foliated central panel stands a young boy carrying a musical instrument, a *qin*, or zither, wrapped in a cloth. He faces a group of three figures (two gentlemen and an attendant) looking at an unrolled scroll painting.[1]

Nearer to the middle of the scene, a gentleman with brush in hand awaits a boy bringing writing material, perhaps for the man to practice calligraphy or painting. Standing together, two other figures wait in anticipation for him to begin. At the top of the scene, near the railing, a figure stands facing outward into space holding a *hu*, a rectangular tablet used by court officials during the Ming period. They are also known as "audience boards" because they were carried in the palace and gave access to restricted areas.[2]

The activity is all framed by a double-line border, which is in turn captured by an interlocking ring pattern. The sides of the tray are decorated with flowers of the four seasons in a spiral vine pattern. The details of this border pattern are very similar to those found on the border of the Irving box.[3]

Notes

1. A similar scene is depicted on an octagonal inlaid tray of the fifteenth century in the Irving Collection at the Metropolitan Museum of Art. See James C. Y. Watt and Barbara Brennan Ford, *East Asian Lacquer: The Florence and Herbert Irving Collection* (New York: Metropolitan Museum of Art, 1991), 131–32.

2. Fang Jing Pei, *Symbols and Rebuses in Chinese Art: Figures, Bugs, Beasts, and Flowers* (Berkeley, Calif.: Ten Speed Press, 2004), 99.

3. Watt and Ford, *East Asian Lacquer*, 131–32.

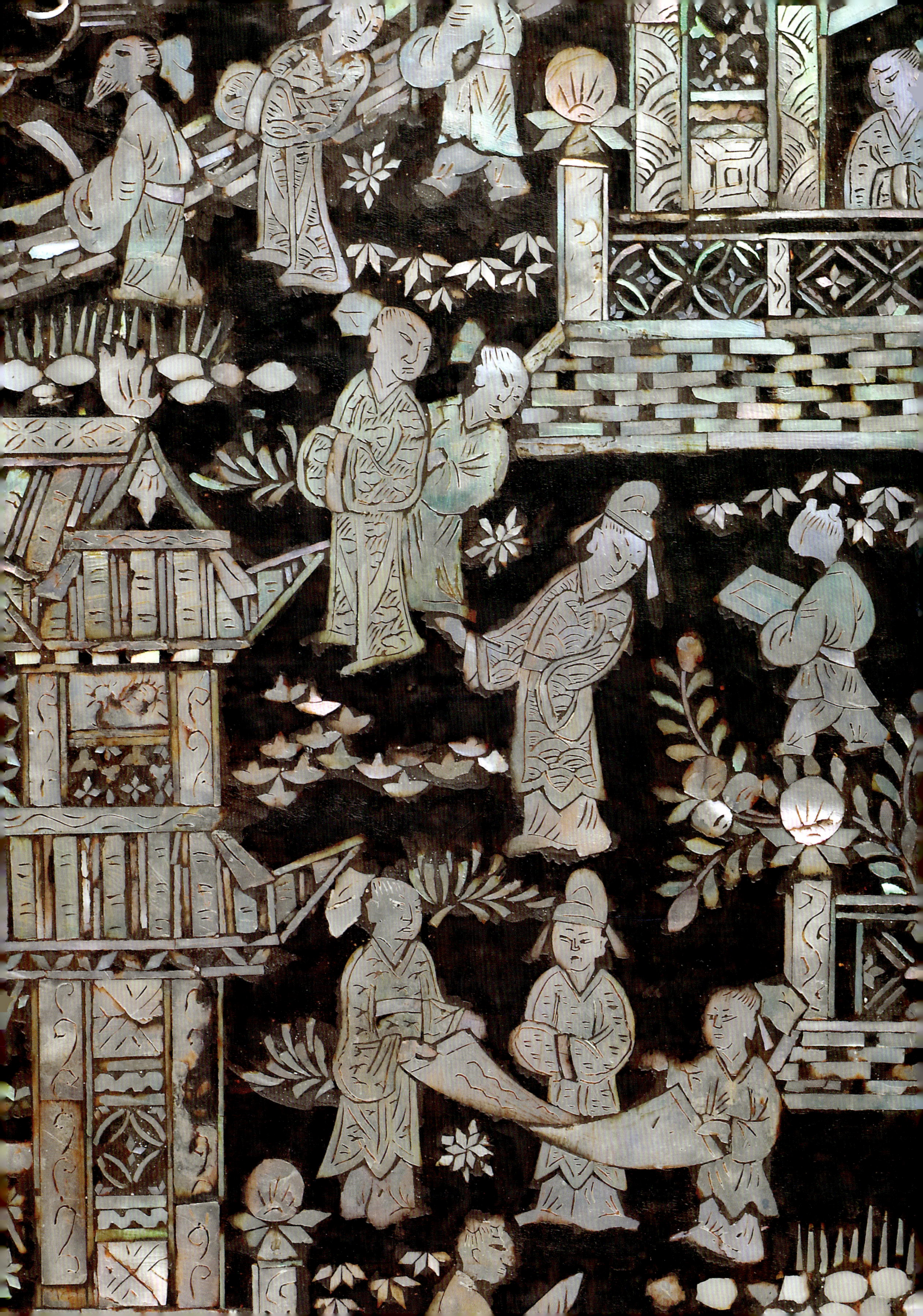

9

Inlaid Screen

Ming dynasty, 15th–16th century
Black lacquer inlaid with mother-of-pearl
H. 18½ in. W. 19½ in.
L37,914

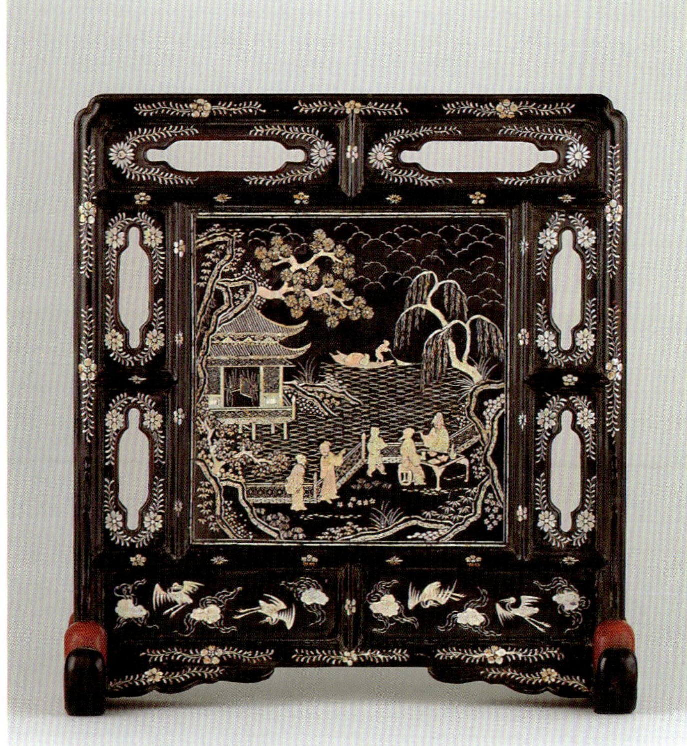

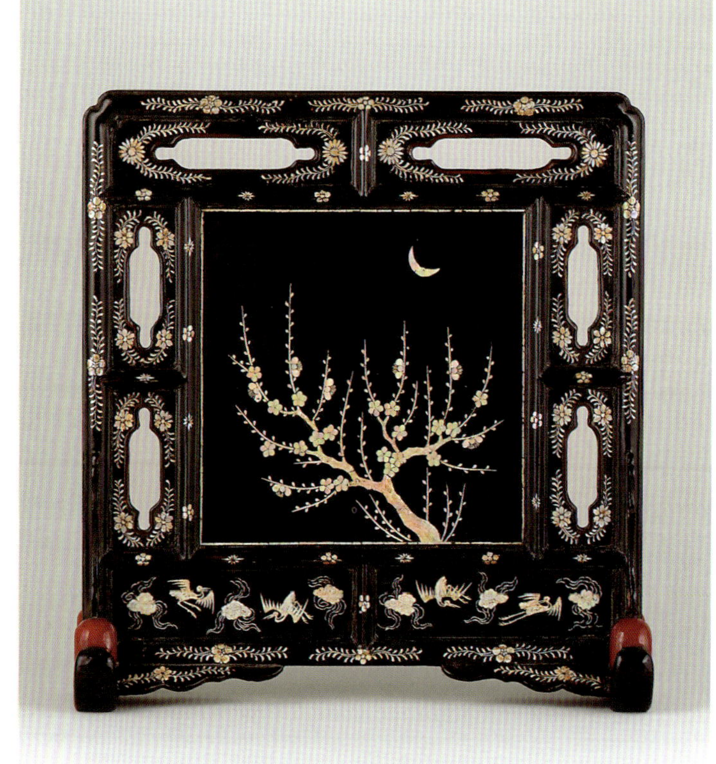

The theme here is most likely a literary gathering, perhaps commissioned as a birthday celebration theme for the screen's owner. Two bearded gentlemen seated under a willow tree share conversation and wine, while an attendant brings dishes to the table. Two other gentlemen move along the lakeside path, with a pine tree above, and waves and fishermen in the distance. The pine tree and the bearded men are frequently associated with old age. The theme of the scene is further enhanced by the presence of flying cranes across the bottom panel, another symbol of longevity.

The stylized cloud forms in the upper right corner are similar to those found on fifteenth-century lacquer. The attention to the details of the figures' clothing and expressions, and the skill with which the scene is constructed, indicate an early to mid-Ming date.

A border pierced by oblong openings decorated with scrolling flower motifs can be seen on both sides of the screen. Red lacquer at the feet of this otherwise black inlaid screen is an unusual feature that may have been added later.

The reverse side of the screen is decorated with flowering plum blossoms under the new moon, a reference to age and renewal. The flowering plum is also a symbol of an upright gentleman.

Large table screens of this type were used in the wealthy households of well-educated men of letters. The most famous table, or dais, screen is one illustrating filial piety and now at the Shanxi Provincial Museum. It was excavated from the tomb of Sima Jinlong (d. 484), proving that lacquered screens have a long history in China.[1] At the end of the Ming period (seventeenth century), lacquer decoration was frequently symbolic and was often drawn from other sources, including painting, woodblock, and ceramic decoration. The themes used would resonate even with viewers lacking much formal education, but the screens typically were owned by the elite.

Note

1. Recently illustrated in James C. Y. Watt, *China: Dawn of a Golden Age, 200–750 A.D.* (New York: Metropolitan Museum of Art, 2004), cat. no. 69, pp. 158–60.

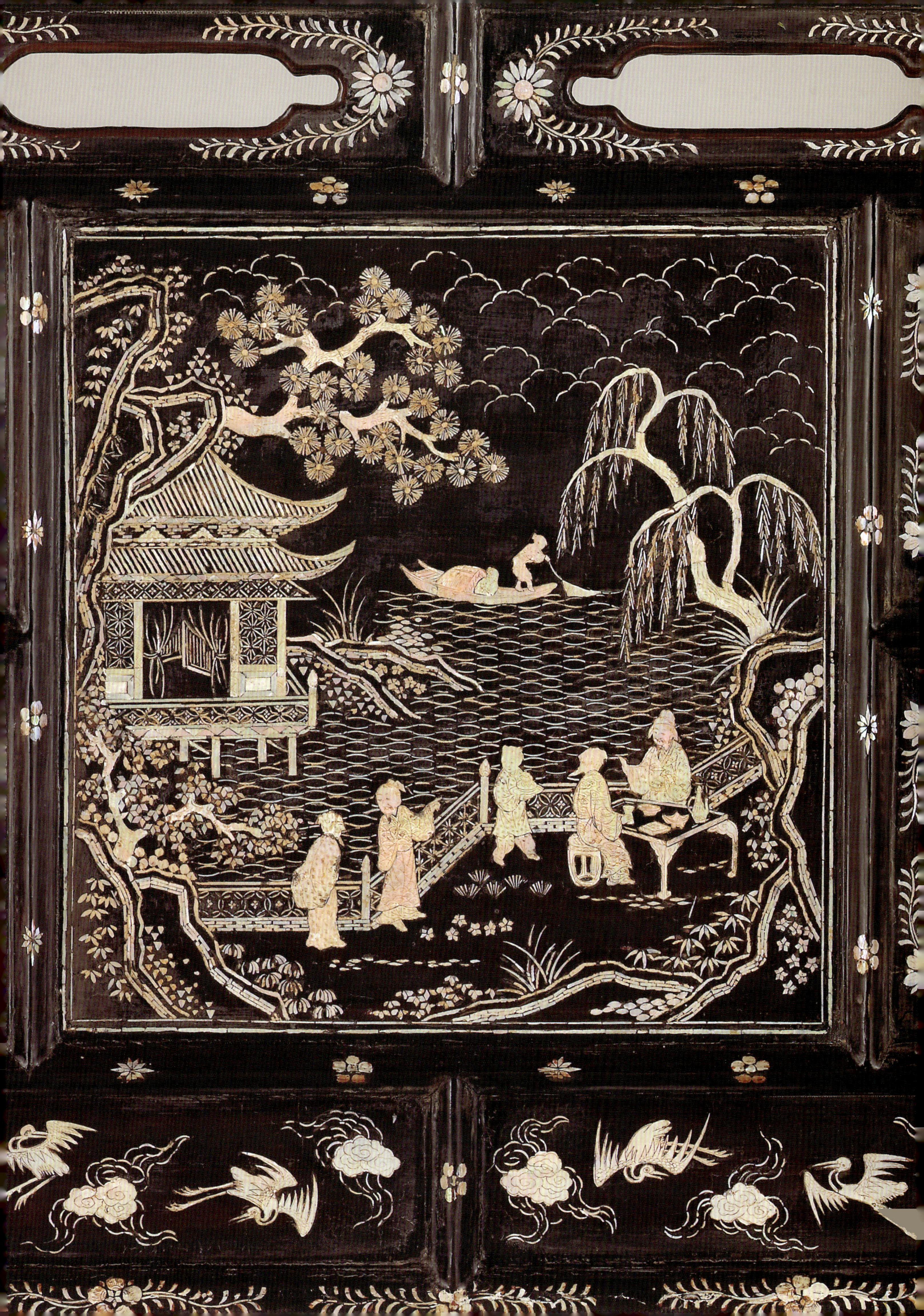

10

Round Box

Yuan dynasty, late 13th–14th century
Carved red and black lacquer *(tixi)*
H. 4¼ in. DIAM. 10½ in.
L37,922

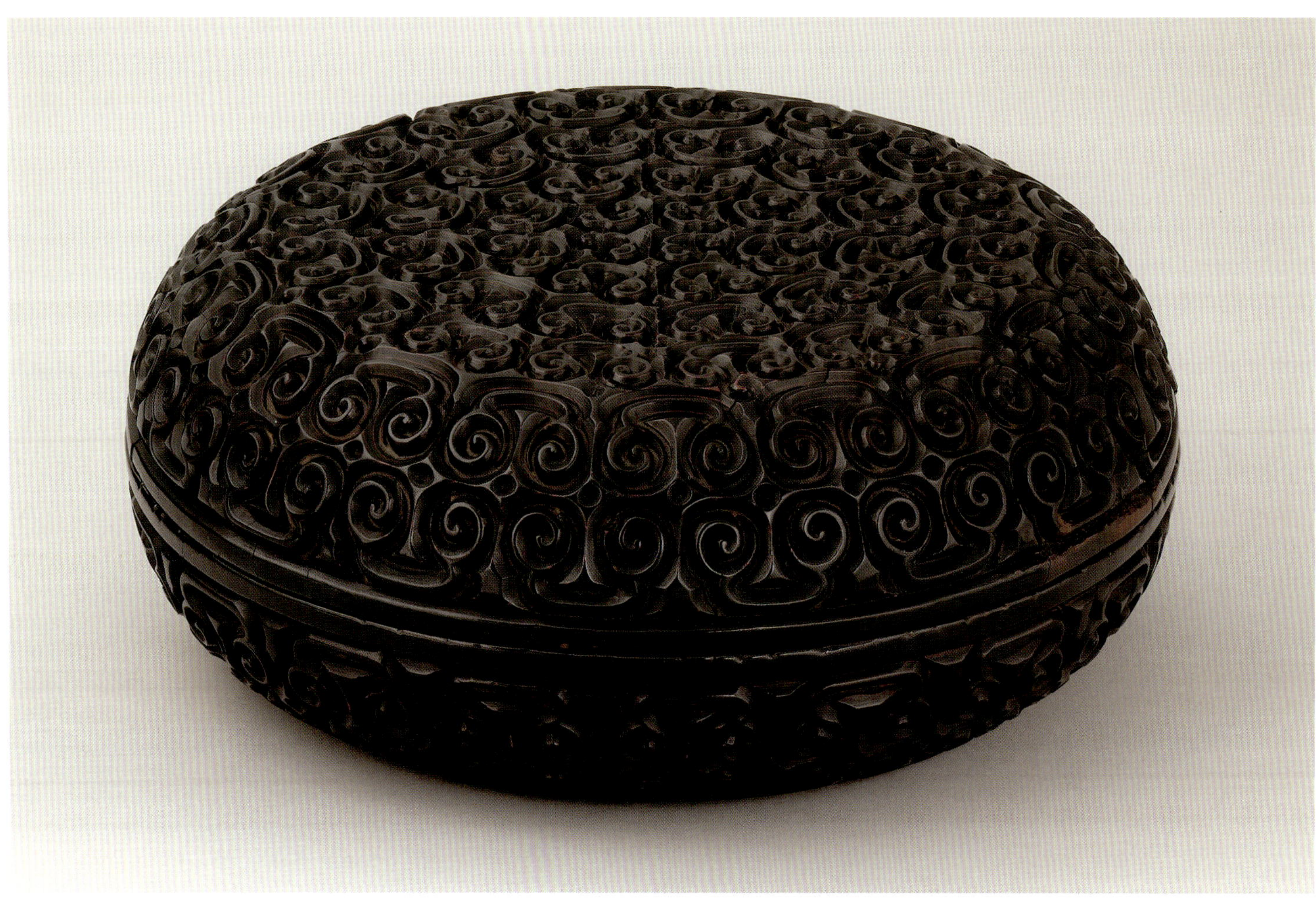

The lid of this large, round box has gently sloping sides. The pommel-scroll design on the top spreads from a center of four out to eighteen elements, all evenly placed to meet with an upside-down pommel-scroll shape on the edge of the box. The exterior of the box's bottom is also covered with a similar pattern. At first glance, it appears to be predominantly black, and yet red and black bands of thin lacquer are clearly visible when the cut-away edges are carefully examined. This technique is referred to in the Chinese context as *tixi*, the carved form of a layered lacquer also known as *xibi*. This piece and others in this collection serve as fine examples of the layered lacquer technique, which developed in China and spread to Japan, where it is sometimes referred to as *guri*.[1]

The decoration on this box, with its pronounced symmetry, the density of the scrolled devices at the end of the sword-pommel shape, and the relatively high ridge of the shapes define it as an early piece, possibly from the Yuan period (1260–1368).[2]

Notes

1. Sir Percival David, trans. and ed., *Chinese Connoisseurship: The Ko Ku Yao Lun, The Essential Criteria of Antiquities* (New York and Washington, D.C.: Praeger, 1971), 145–46 n. 1, traces the history of the interpretation of *xipi*, *tixi*, and other variants and their definitions.

2. Tokyo National Museum, *Tōyō no shikkōgei: Tokubetsu-ten* (Oriental lacquer arts: Special exhibition), glossary and object list in English (Tokyo: Tokyo National Museum, 1977), cat. no. 466, p. 249. The plate is in the Yamato Bunkakan Museum, Nara.

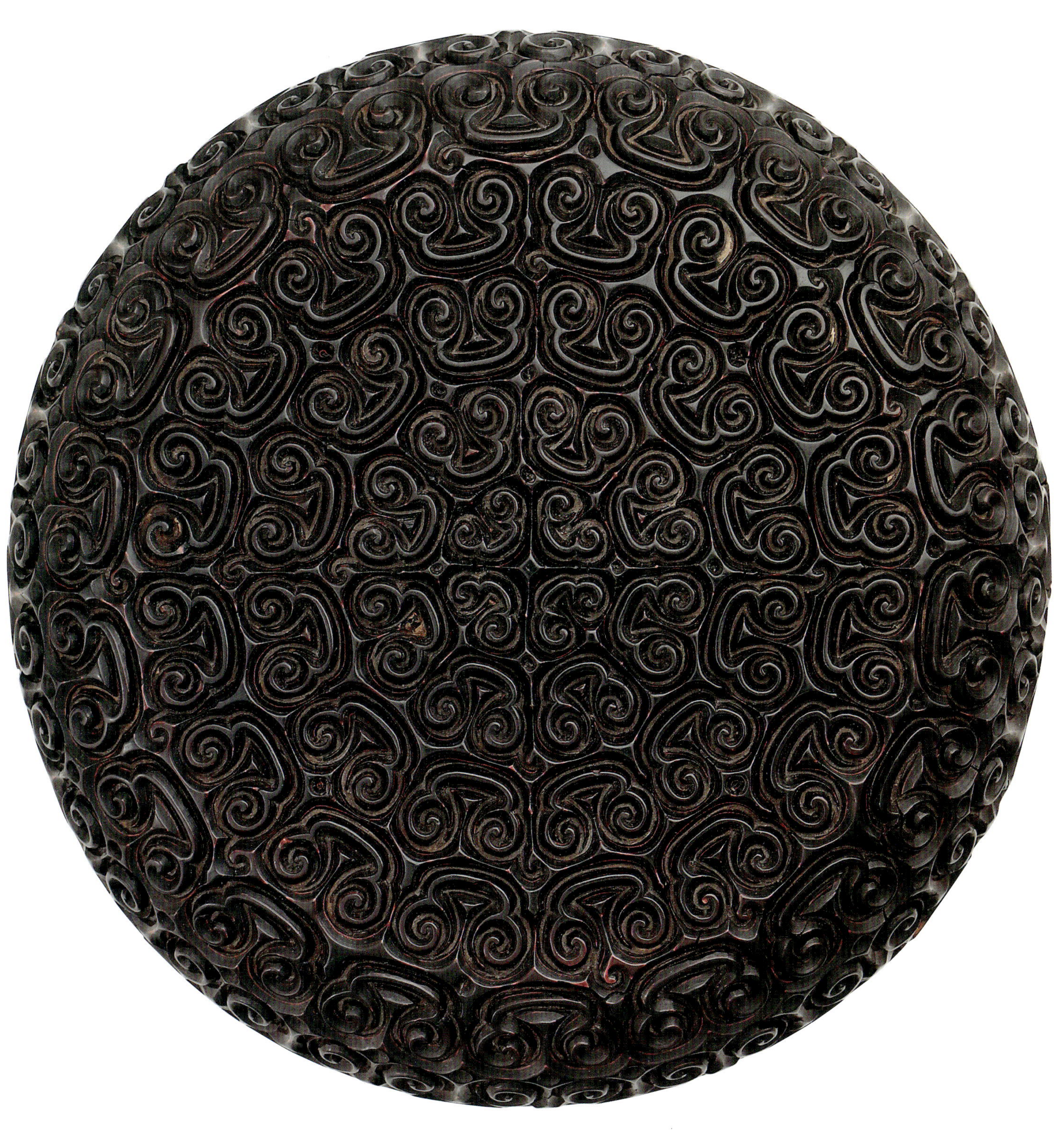

11

Three-Tiered Covered Box

Early Ming dynasty, 15th century
Carved red and black lacquer *(tixi)*
H. 4¼ in. DIAM. 7¾ in.
L38,155

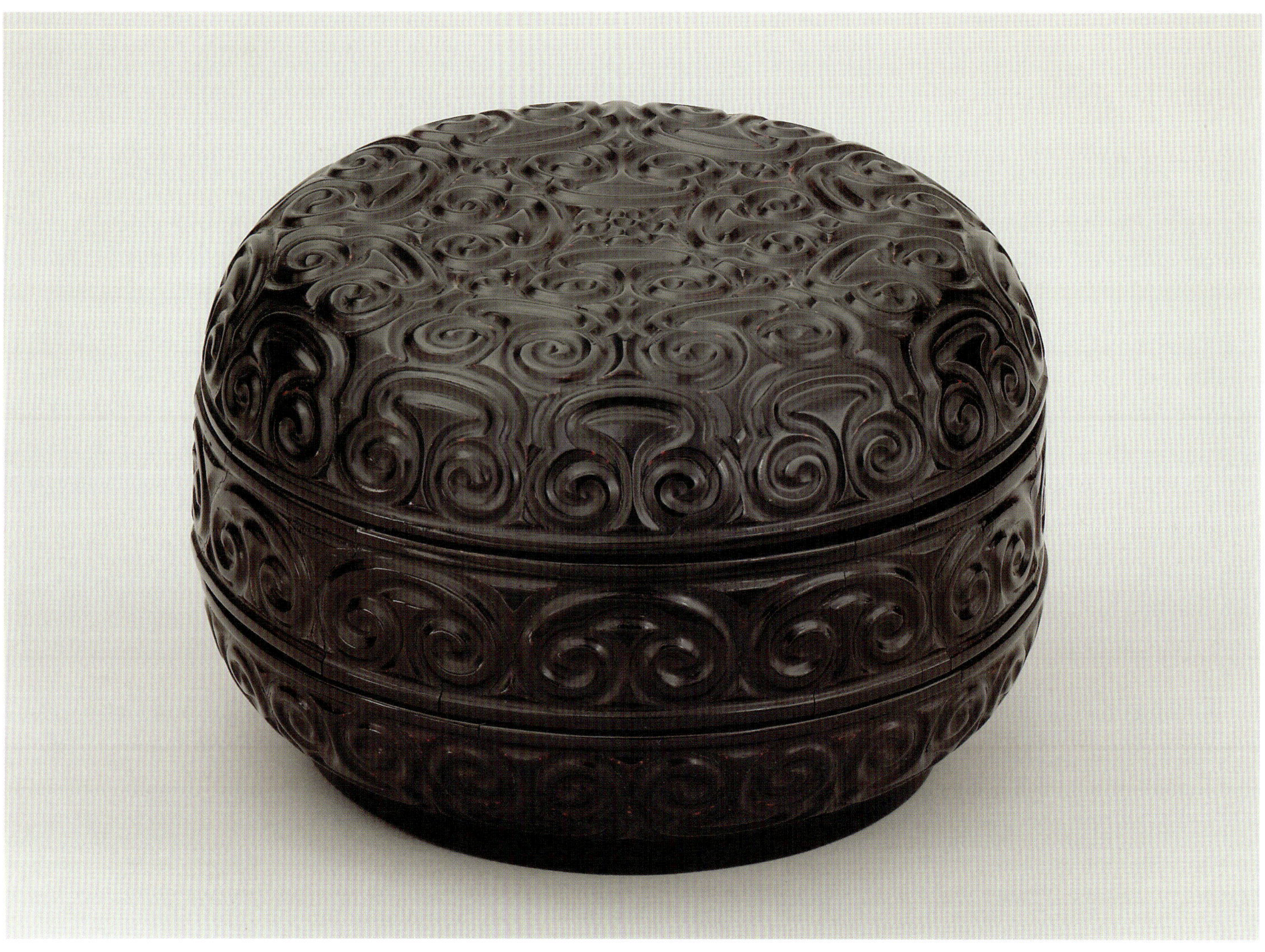

This food box has a domed lid of layered red and black lacquer with a straight-sided middle section and a curved and footed base. The middle tray is divided into four compartments; the lower portion is an open tray. Stacked boxes of this type would have been used to transport and serve food.

The sword-pommel design is evenly distributed across the top of the slightly domed box and along the sides as well. At the center of the top is a radiant star pattern. There are two layers of red lacquer on this otherwise black box. The final coat of black lacquer has been polished to a high sheen. The strongly rounded sword-pommel design is reminiscent of other early Ming lacquers, including two such pieces in the Irving Collection: a *tixi* carved dish and an octagonal food box.[1]

Note

1. James C. Y. Watt and Barbara Brennan Ford, *East Asian Lacquer: The Florence and Herbert Irving Collection* (New York: Metropolitan Museum of Art, 1991), no. 9, p. 53, and cat. no. 12, p. 57.

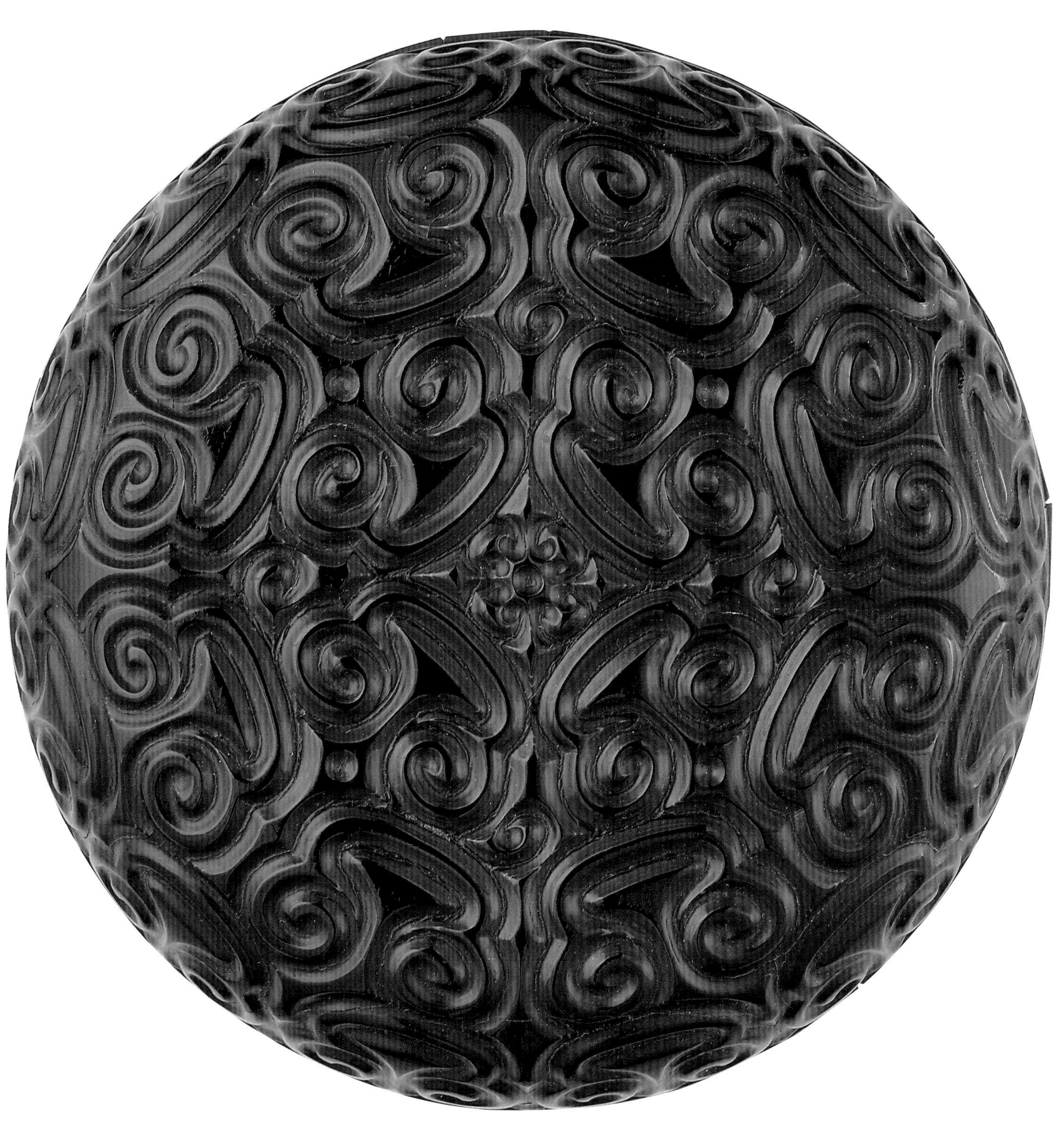

12

Round, Straight-edged Box

Ming dynasty, 15th century
Carved red and black lacquer *(tixi)*
H. 3 in. DIAM. 9¼ in.
L37,913

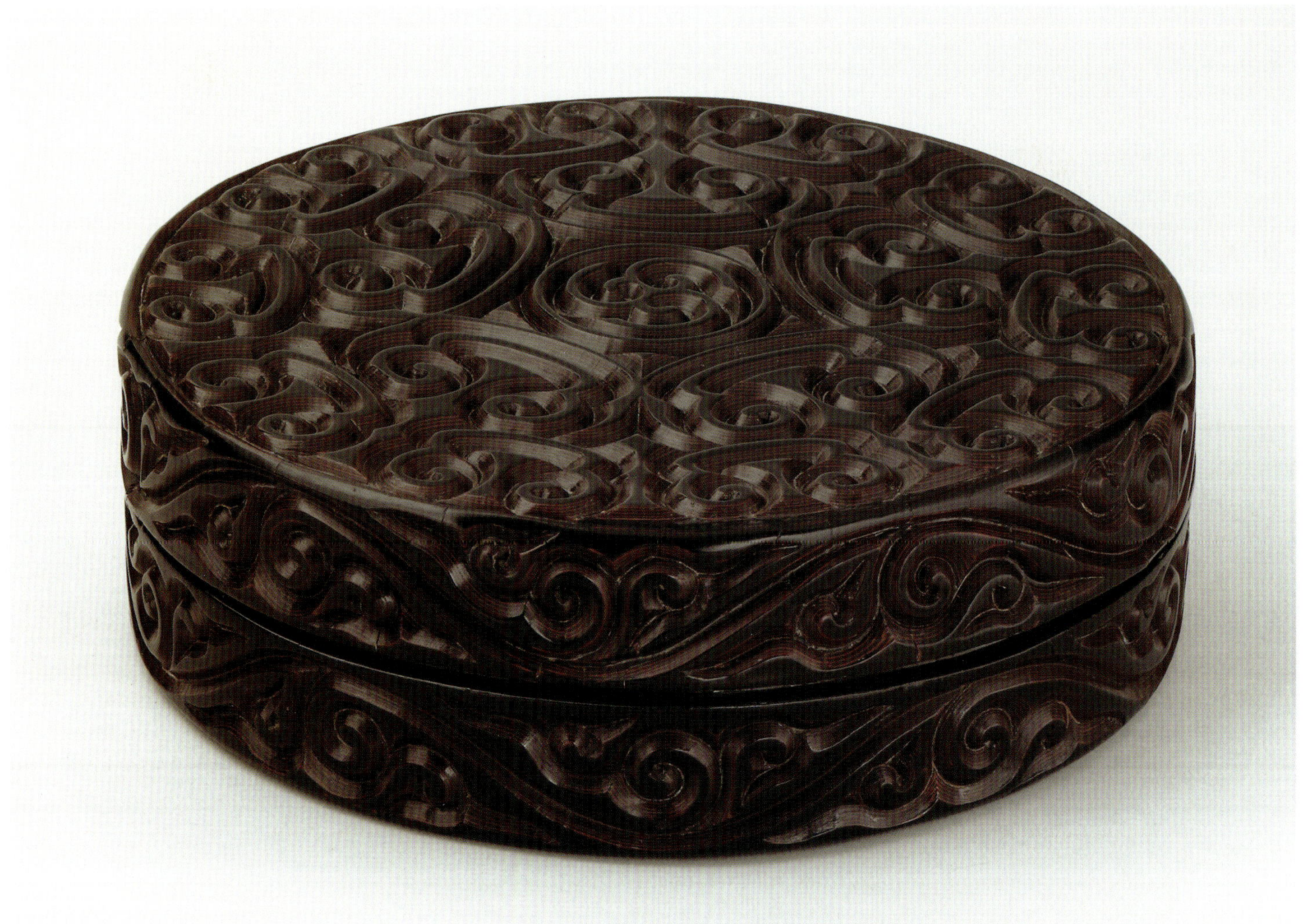

The very sharp and deeply cut surface of this box permits an ideal view of the repeated layers of red and black lacquer. The design is a central swirl surrounded by two bands of sword-pommel patterns, typical of the style favored for these *tixi* boxes and plates. The sides of the box are decorated with a flowing spiral design.

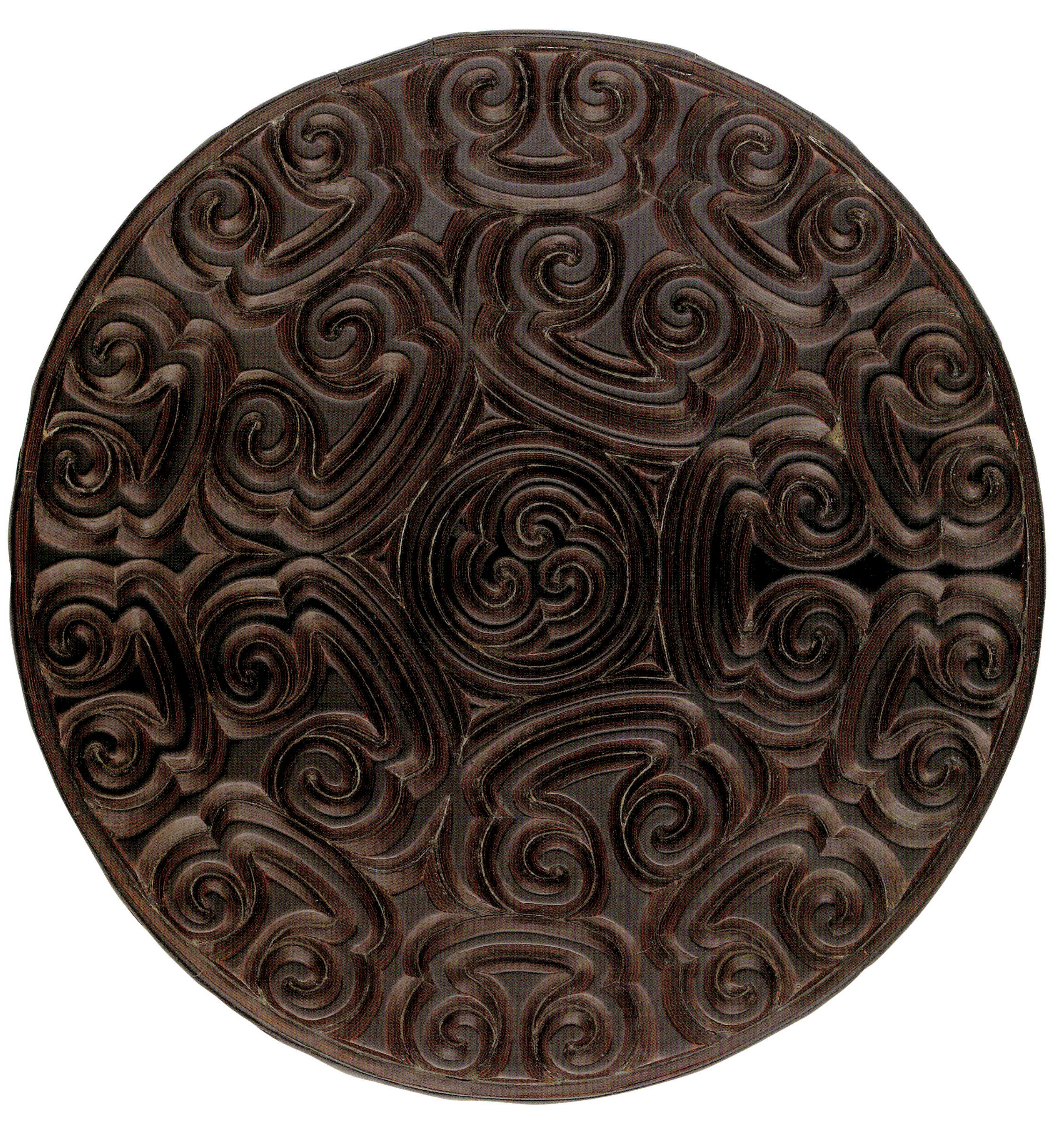

13

Covered Box

Ming dynasty, 15th century
Carved red and black lacquer *(tixi)*
H. 5⅛ in. DIAM. 8⅞ in.
L37,915

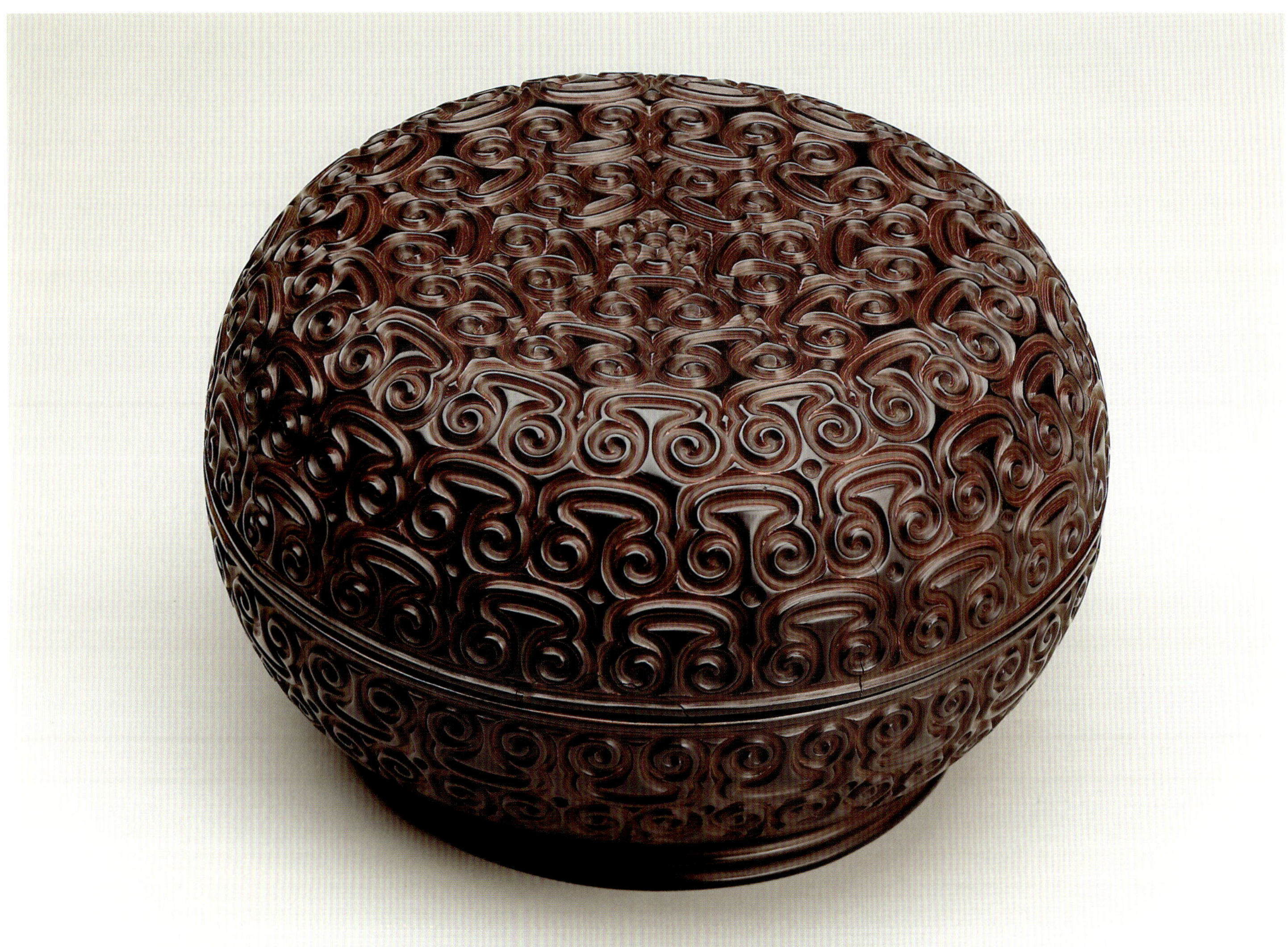

A robust form with high, sloping shoulder, this box of *tixi*, or layered and carved lacquer, demonstrates a slightly more ornate sword-pommel design than the ones illustrated in cat. nos. 10–12. Here the bands radiate in five rows outward from a starlike central medallion on the top. Three red layers alternating with black bands can be discerned. The box shows a high degree of craftsmanship in design and execution and has a lustrous sheen.

Like the other *tixi* carved lacquers shown here, this one was constructed by layering many coats of lacquer in alternating bands of color, then cutting through them to expose the bands in a subtle and refined pattern.

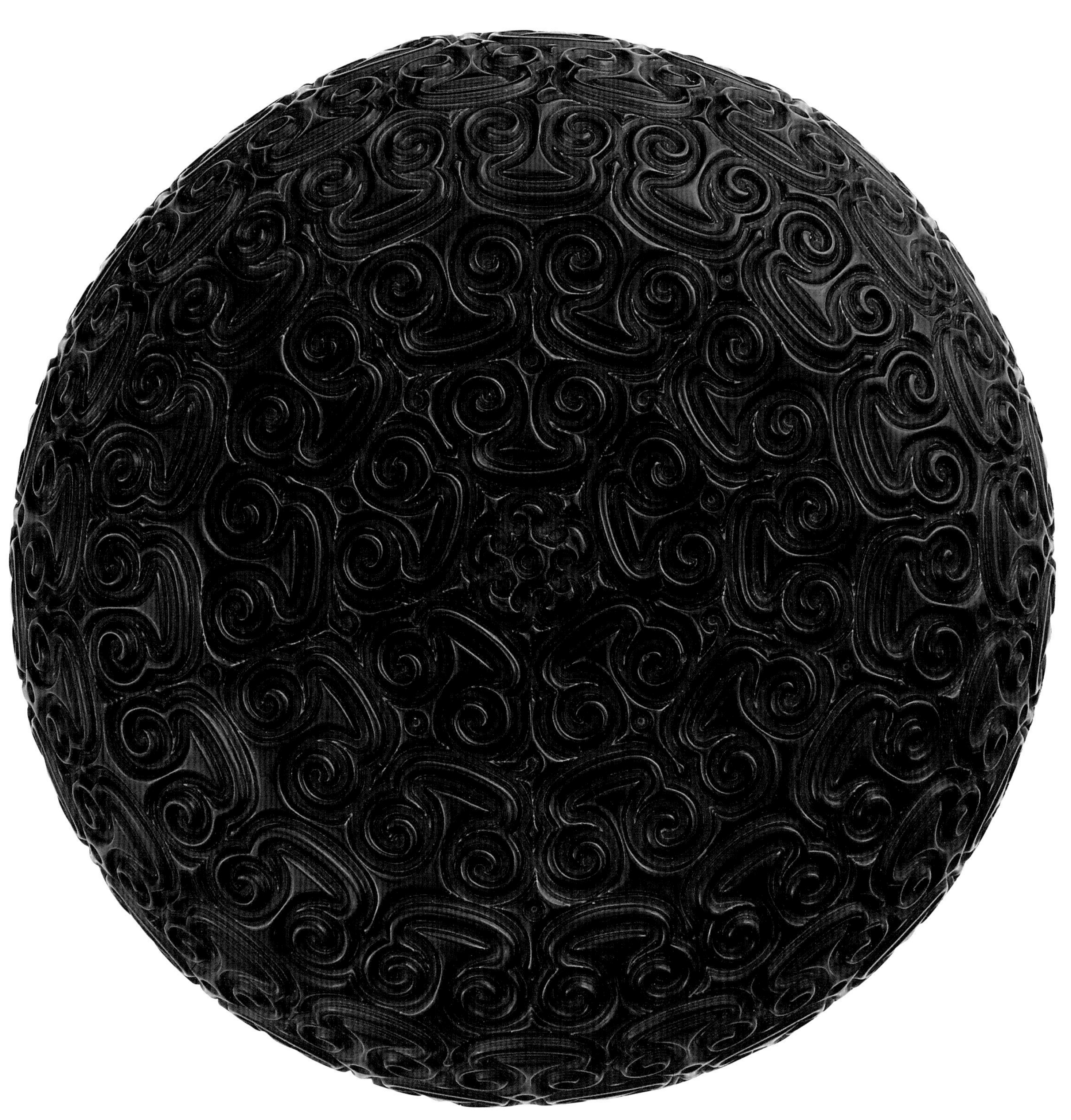

14

Oblong Plate

Early Ming dynasty, ca. 1400
Carved red and black lacquer *(tixi)*
H. 1 in. L. 7¾ in. W. 6¼ in.
L38,011

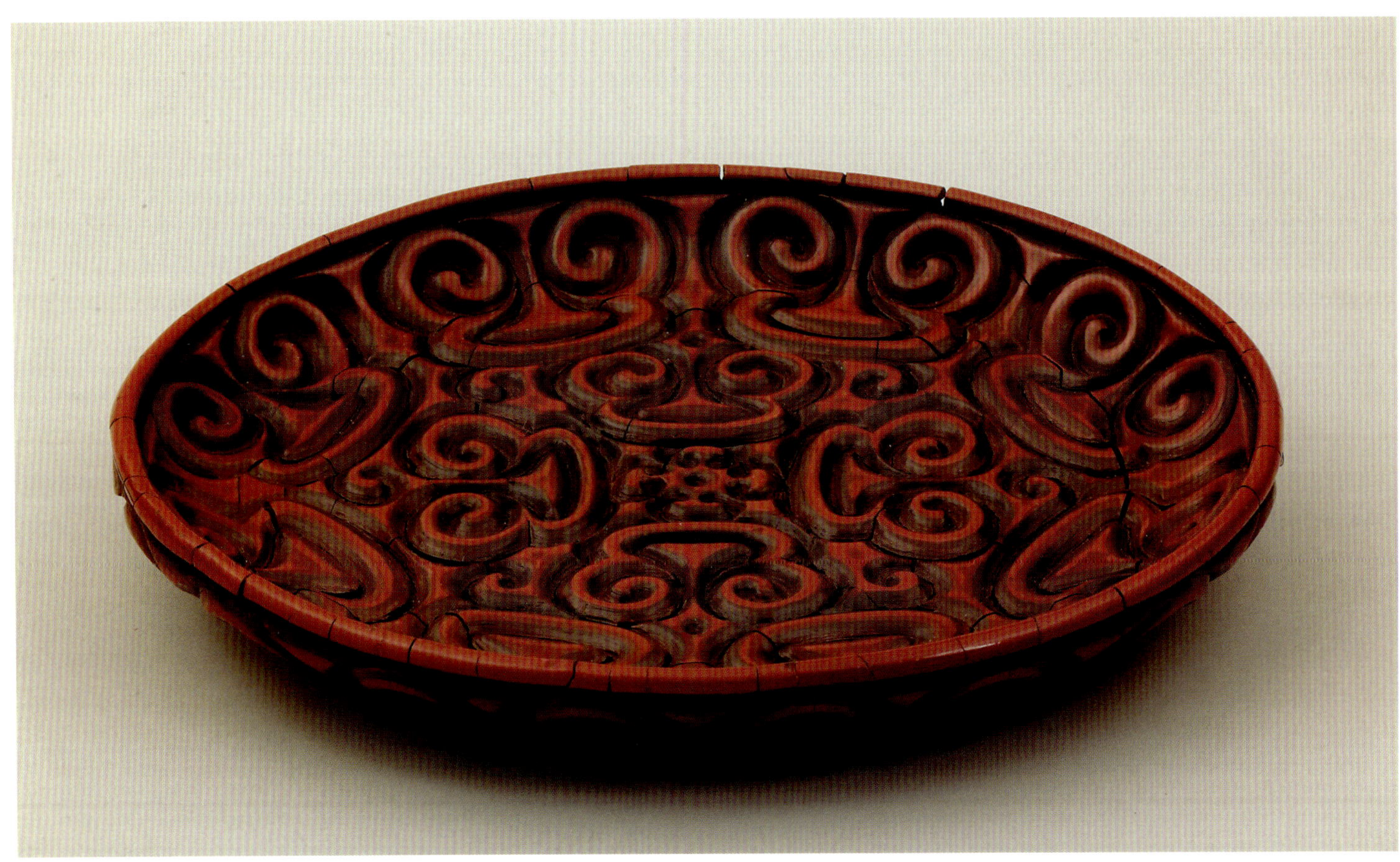

The patina between the larger design elements of this carved *tixi* plate somewhat obscures the layers of the carving. Additionally, the final coat is red, rather than the usual black, giving the plate a much different overall appearance from the more common black plates. The pattern is a familiar one for *tixi* carved lacquer design: a radiant star pattern in the center of the plate is surrounded by a band of four and then eight robust sword-pommel designs. The exterior rim is decorated with a flattened pommel design. A similar oval dish is in the Irving Collection at the Metropolitan Museum of Art; another is in the Lee Family Collection.[1]

Early large *tixi* plates were made by alternating layers of different colors of lacquer, usually red and black, over a core. They were laid on relatively thickly, creating a robust shape. The commonly seen sword-pommel pattern has a roundness and fullness that lend a three-dimensional quality to the design.

Occasionally, the heavier layers of lacquer pull away from the core and cracking occurs. Warping of the core further compromises the surface. The bottom of the tray is heavily crackled. This type of large, elegantly decorated plate was probably used as a tray.

Note

1. James C. Y. Watt and Barbara Brennan Ford, *East Asian Lacquer: The Florence and Herbert Irving Collection* (New York: Metropolitan Museum of Art, 1991), cat. no. 7, p. 51. See Lee King Tsi and Hu Shih Chang, *Drache und Phoenix: Lackarbeiten aus China: Sammlung der Familie Lee, Tokyo/Dragon and Phoenix: Chinese Lacquer Ware: The Lee Family Collection, Tokyo* (Cologne, Germany: Museum of East Asian Art, 1990), no. 5, p. 40. While very similar in size and style, neither of these plates has the radiant star pattern in the center of the plate.

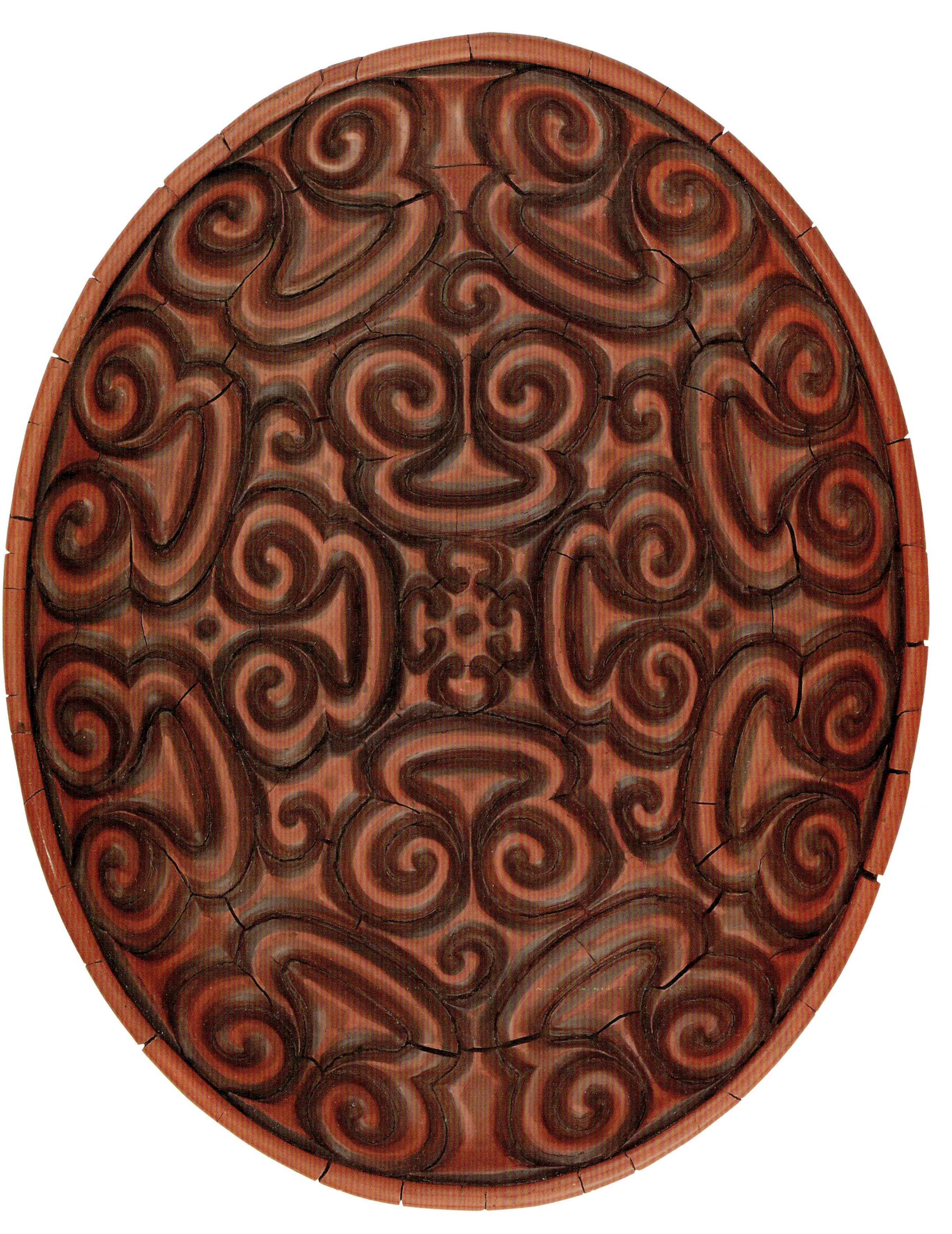

15

Octagonal Plate

Yuan dynasty, 14th century
Carved red lacquer
H. 1 in. DIAM. 12 in.
Signed Zhang Cheng
L38,010

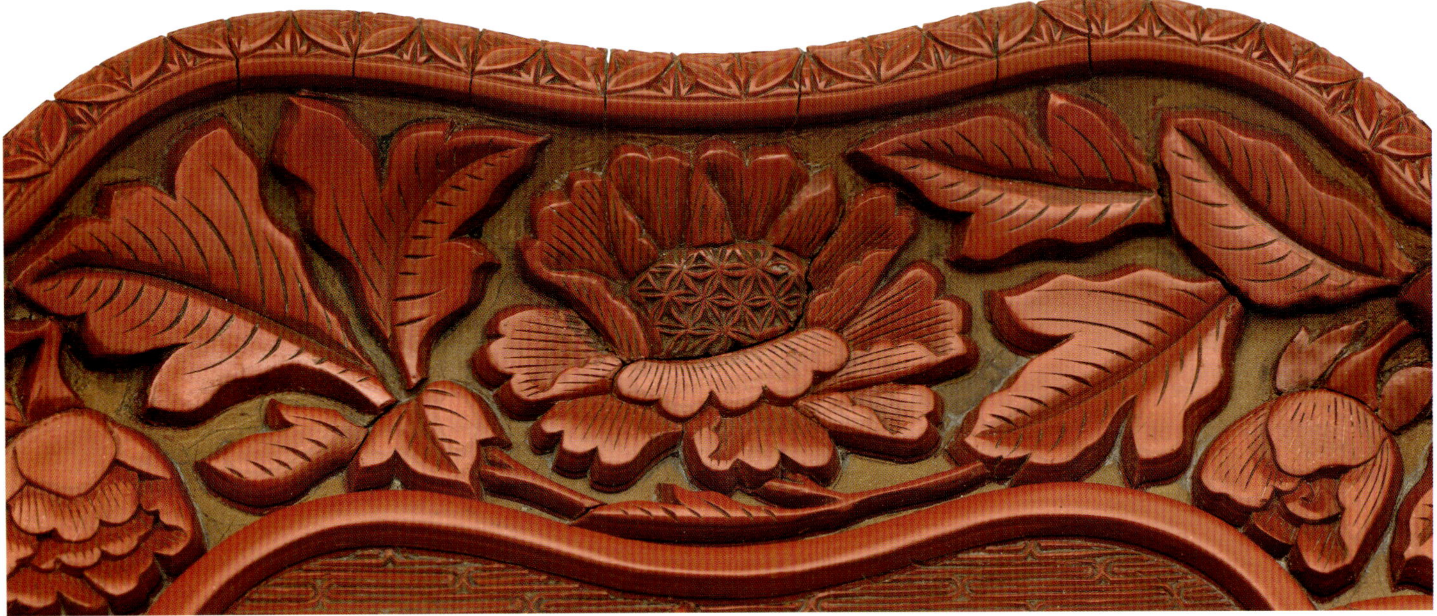

An exquisite example of carved red lacquer, this plate with a paired-bird design is characteristic of the finest Yuan lacquer.[1] The petal border, a popular motif, softens its overall octagonal shape; the motif is also found in ceramics and on stone carvings.

The band of naturalistically executed seasonal flowers around the principal design appears against an unusual background of yellow lacquer. This yellow ground is actually the layer that signals the depth of the carving; it is used here as a decorative device as well as a practical one. The same combination also appears on the plate's exterior rim. Floral decoration on lacquer derives from the densely patterned naturalistic examples that appear on both textiles and ceramics. As that pattern expanded in lacquer, the same colored background was replaced by a contrasting color, in this case yellow.

The central image, paired, long-tailed birds on a rock and tree branch, is accompanied by maple and bamboo set onto an "air diaper" pattern seen commonly on Yuan and early Ming-period lacquer. The air diaper was a convention utilizing repetitive patterns to add a sense of depth to the overall scene.[2] The background red color of the central design is consistent with the rest of the bird-and-rock design.

The plate is inscribed on the black lacquer base with the characters "Zhang Cheng," the name of one of the finest lacquer makers of the Yuan period. Zhang was from Yanghui in Xietang, Zhejiang Province. His name is recorded in documents pertaining to lacquer masters, but we know little else about him.[3] An additional mark, perhaps of ownership, appears in the middle of the plate's base. A plate in the Irving Collection (now at the Metropolitan Museum of Art, New York), also regarded as Yuan to early Ming and featuring two birds among flowers and leaves, is inscribed with the same mark.[4] The Healy plate certainly carries some of the same detailed characteristics, and the quality of carving appears to be equally accomplished.

Zhang may have died early in the Ming period, as it is recorded that the Yongle emperor wanted to appoint him to the court workshop. On learning of Zhang's death, the emperor chose his son Zhang Degang to be director of lacquer production. Other lacquer pieces with Zhang Cheng's signature are known, but it is extremely difficult to determine if it is authentic, as no excavated examples have been found.

Notes

1. The Healy plate has more in common with plates bearing landscape and garden-scene designs, such as the foliated dish in the British Museum (see Harry M. Garner, *Chinese Lacquer* [London: Faber and Faber, 1979], pl. 30) or the seven-lobed platter in the Irving Collection (see James C. Y. Watt and Barbara Brennan Ford, *East Asian Lacquer: The Florence and Herbert Irving Collection* [New York: Metropolitan Museum of Art, 1991], cat. no. 23) than with the more heavily decorated two-bird plates on which the entire plate has a continuous design of birds in flight (see p. 11, fig. 1). These more densely composed plates appear to date slightly later than those with narratives.

2. Harry M. Garner, "Diaper Backgrounds on Chinese Carved Lacquer," *Ars Orientalis: The Arts of Islam and the East* 6 (1966): 165–89.

3. Garner, *Chinese Lacquer*, pp. 61, 79 n. Garner remains skeptical about the attribution of works to this artist, though he agrees on a fourteenth-century date for some pieces bearing Zhang's name. See also Tokyo National Museum, *Tōyō no shikkōgei: Tokubetsuten* (Far Eastern lacquer arts: Special exhibition), glossary and object list in English (Tokyo: Tokyo National Museum, 1977), pls. 447–49, and p. 248.

4. Watt and Ford, *East Asian Lacquer*, cat. no. 19, pp. 68–69. The catalogue entry refers to a plate with a similar mark in the Tokugawa Art Museum, Nagoya, Japan.

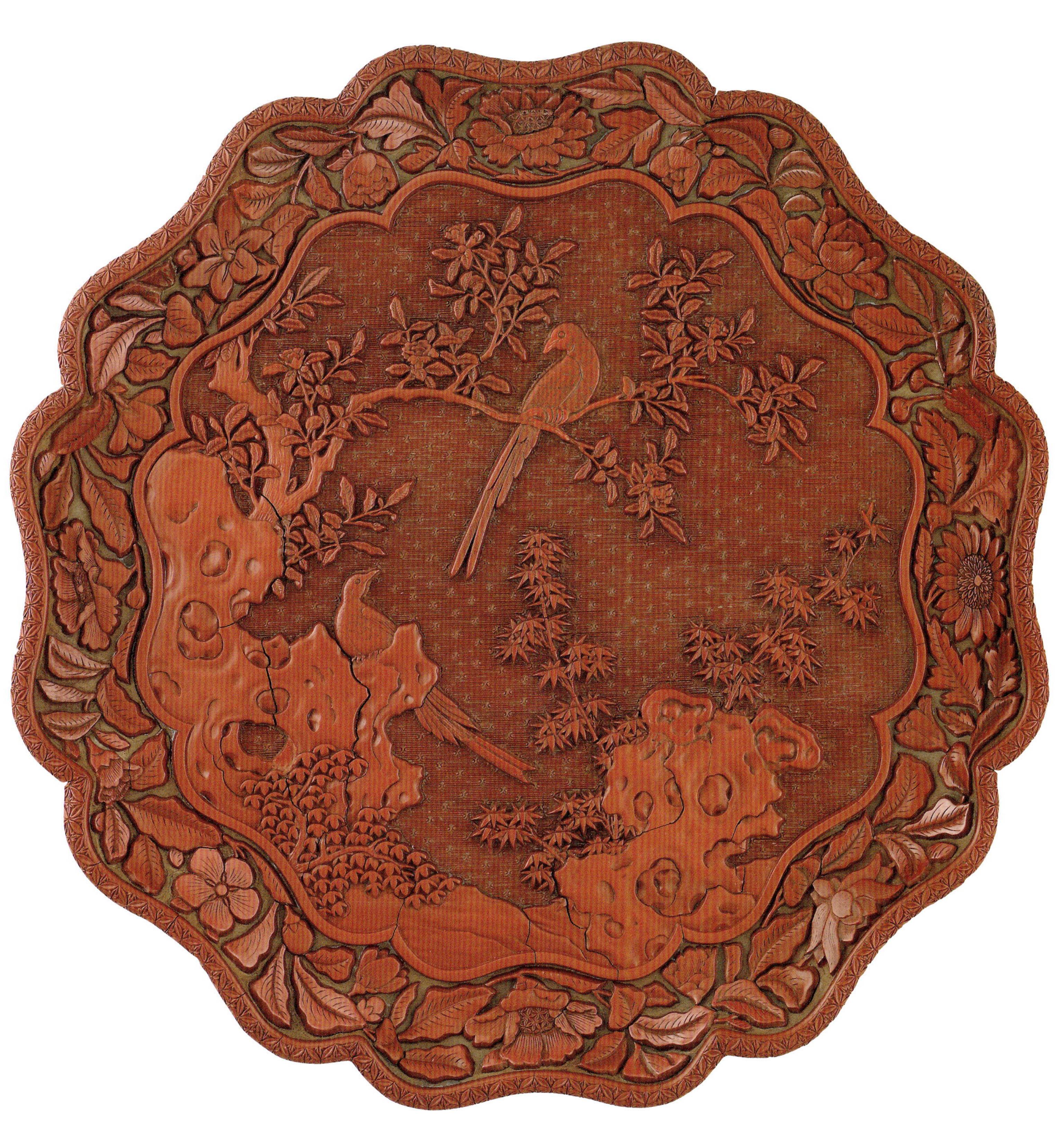

16

Plate with Chrysanthemum Pattern

Ming dynasty, 14th–15th century;
possibly late Yuan dynasty (1260–1368)
Carved red lacquer
H. 1½ in. DIAM. 11½ in.
L37,935

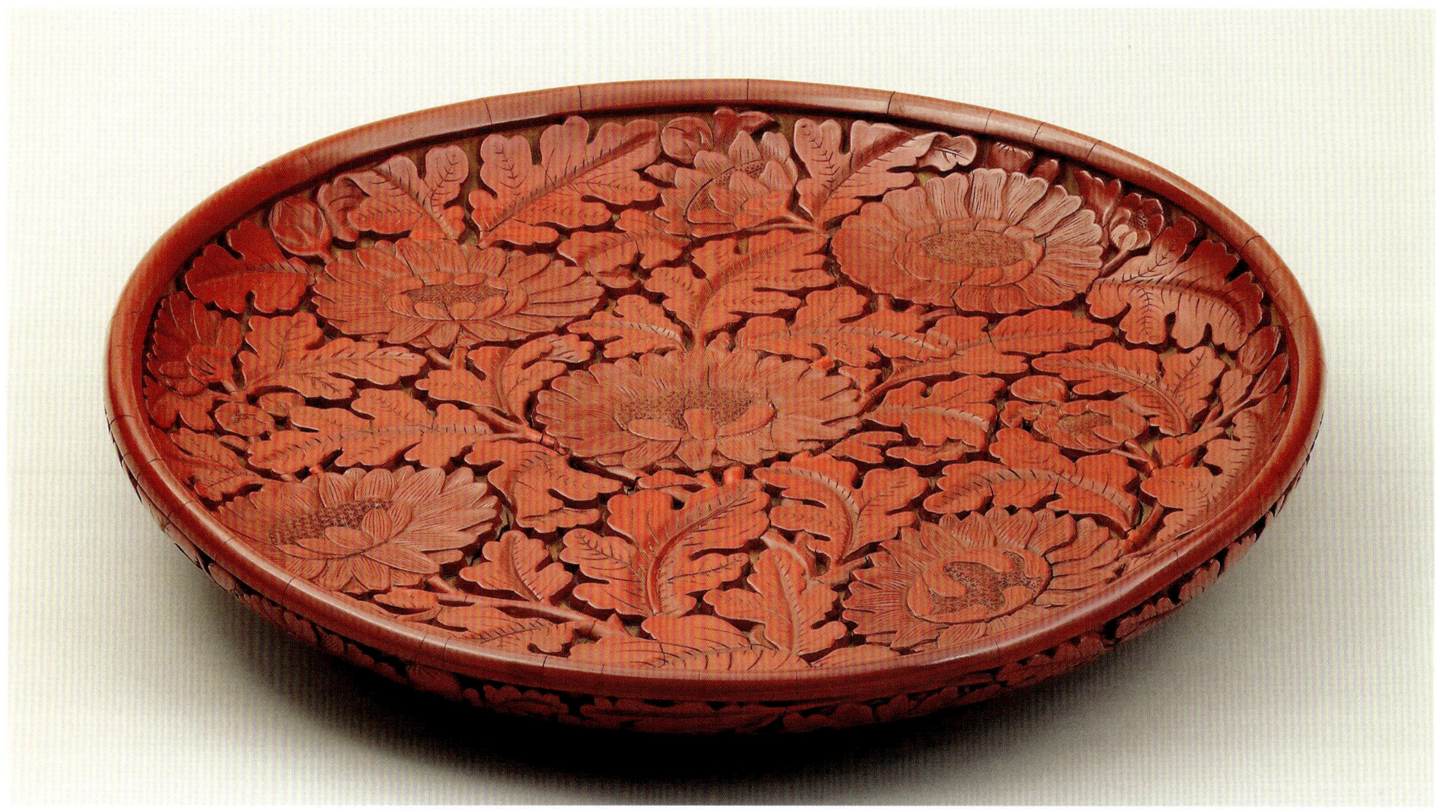

Five fully formed chrysanthemum blossoms are depicted against a background of carefully and densely carved leaves. The entire design is enclosed in a flat band of red lacquer, and the outside edge is decorated with a design of similarly shaped chrysanthemums. The background is a pale brownish yellow. A sharp vertical quality distinguishes the crisply and finely carved surface of the plate. The carving's even depth indicates a design striving for a consistent surface with neither protruding nor sunken areas.

Although it is known that some plates of this size were used either as trays or as plates, this example shows little wear. A plate of similar quality but slightly larger in diameter, bearing a Yongle mark on its base, is in the Aso Collection in Japan. It appears that it, and perhaps the Healy plate, belong to the type and quality exported to Japan as early as the fifteenth century.[1] The high quality of this plate points to its manufacture in a period when lacquer arts were closely regulated.

The Yongle emperor (the fifteenth-century usurper of the throne who moved the imperial capital from Nanjing in the south to Beijing in the north) is credited with strong support for the arts. Lacquerwares made during his reign were of singularly high quality, and special care was given to the surface treatment.

Marked pieces in today's formerly imperial collection have traits very similar to those of this plate, including the yellowish background.[2] Certain characteristics belonging to the earlier Yuan-period lacquers are present, including the delicately rendered veins of the lower leaves and the equally marked, incised veins of other leaves.[3]

Notes

1. See John Figgess, "Ming and Pre-Ming Lacquer in the Japanese Tea Ceremony," *Transactions of the Oriental Ceramic Society* 37 (1967–68, 1968–69): pp. 37–51. An illustration of the plate in the Aso Collection appears on p. 51.

2. See examples in Zhu Jiajin and Xia Gengqi, eds., *Zhongguo qiji quanji* (Lacquer treasures from China), vol. 5: *Ming* (Ming) (Fujian, China: Fujian Publishing House, 1998). See a box of similar design in pl. 27, p. 24.

3. *Chūgoku no urushi-kōgei* (Exhibition of Chinese lacquer) (Tokyo: Bijutsu Club, 1970), illus. no. 40, p. 79, in a private collection.

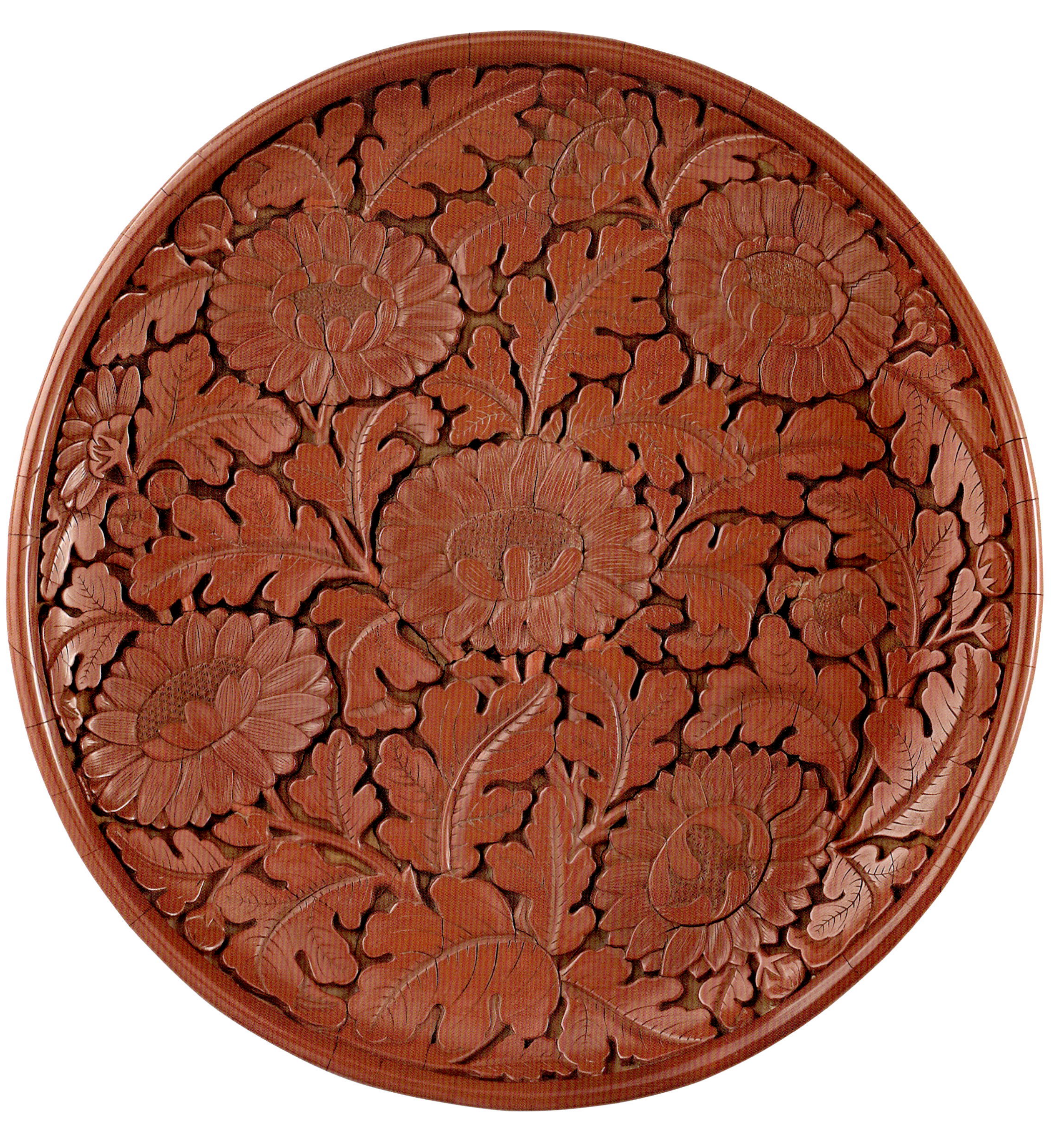

17

Peony Plate

Yuan–early Ming dynasty,
14th century
Carved red lacquer
H. 1 in. DIAM. 7⅛ in.
L37,934

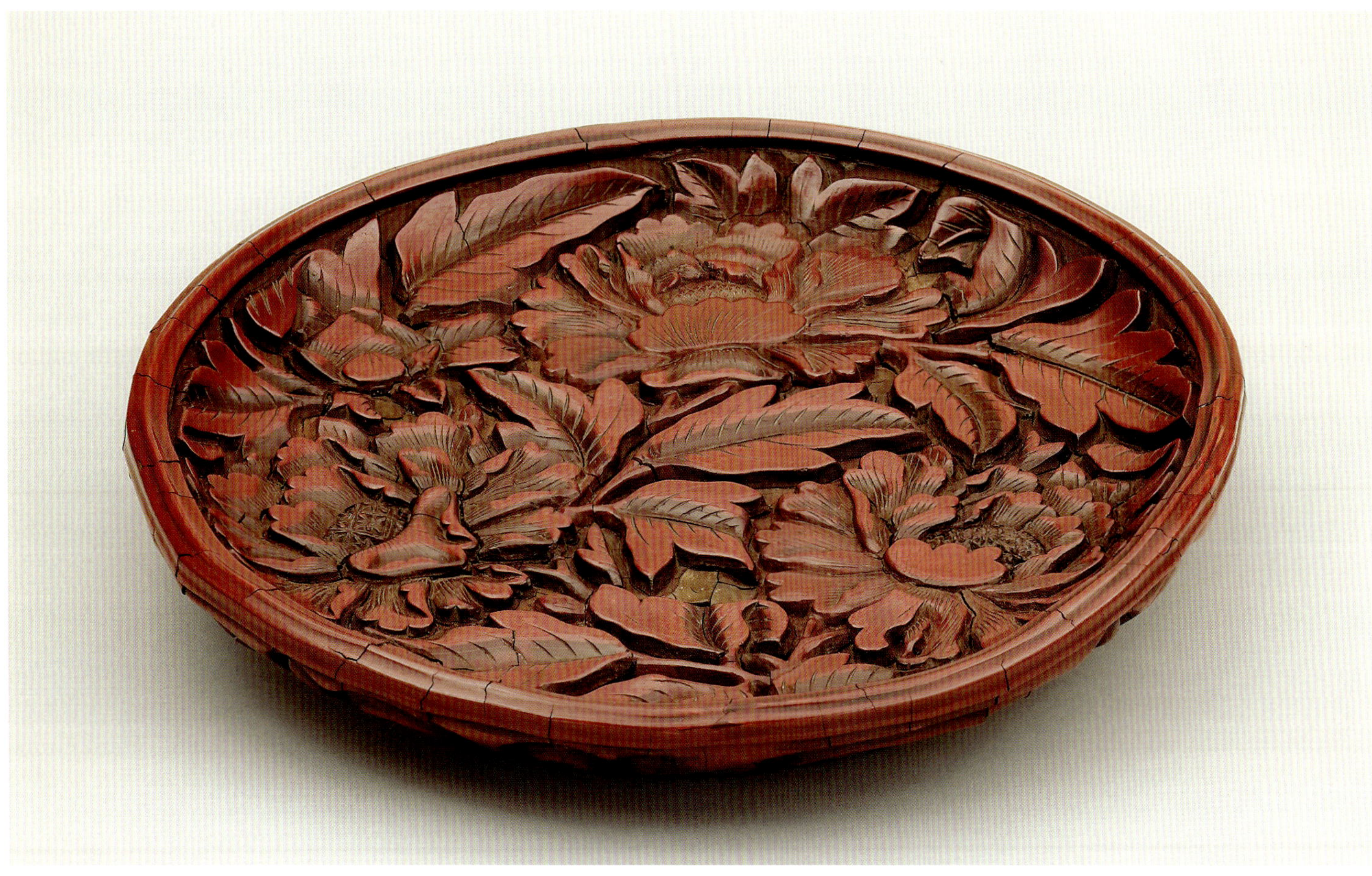

The exuberant design displayed on this small plate attests the vigorous tradition already in place in Chinese lacquer manufacture by the fourteenth century. The design's plasticity is enhanced by the varied depth of the carving that creates strongly organic forms. Leaves surround three peonies in full bloom, with strongly serrated edges covering the surface of the plate. The petals of the flowers turn on themselves and overlap, creating greater depth and visual interest.

This red-lacquered, carved plate has characteristics consistent with Yuan-period lacquer in its density of design and lack of patterning within the composition, which is more typical of later pieces.[1] The plate's exterior is decorated with a linked scroll pattern, which the lacquer expert Harry Garner has called "a feature which is associated with fourteenth-century rather than fifteenth-century lacquer."[2]

Its rarely seen inventiveness and spontaneity in design mark this plate as one of only a handful of red lacquer pieces from the period. Most lacquer production at the time was done in the Yangzi River basin, around the same area where porcelain production thrived, near the old Song capital of Hangzhou.

Surely porcelain production and lacquer manufacture shared some of the same principles of design, although it has been pointed out that decoration on Yuan and early Ming porcelain was largely a painted art form. Still, the decorations do have similarities. The patronage that supported both art forms was probably quite similar, consisting of wealthy patrons with a love of fine and beautiful objects. This size of plate might have been quite useful as a small tray for incense or merely as a decorative object.

Notes

1. Chen Chang, ed., *Zhongguo qiji quanji* (Lacquer treasures from China), vol. 4: *Sanguo–Yuan* (Three Kingdoms–Yuan dynasty) (Fujian, China: Fujian Publishing House, 1998). See no. 159, illustrated on p. 175, described on p. 65.

2. Harry M. Garner, "Two Chinese Carved Lacquer Boxes of the Fifteenth Century in the Freer Gallery of Art," *Ars Orientalis: The Arts of Islam and the East* 9 (1973): 46.

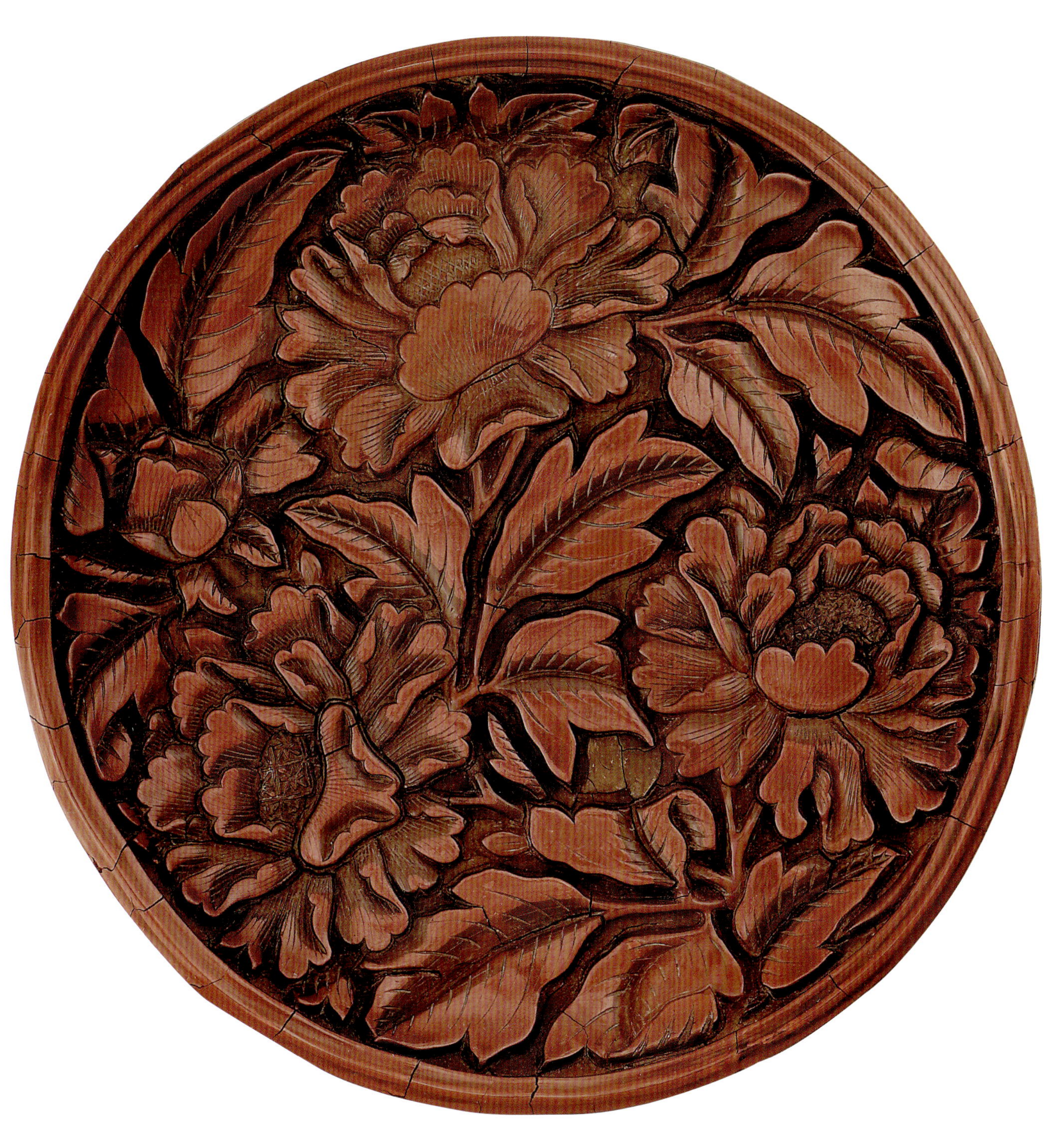

18

Round Plate

Late Yuan–early Ming dynasty,
14th–15th century
Carved red lacquer
H. ¾ in. DIAM. 7⅛ in.
L37,917

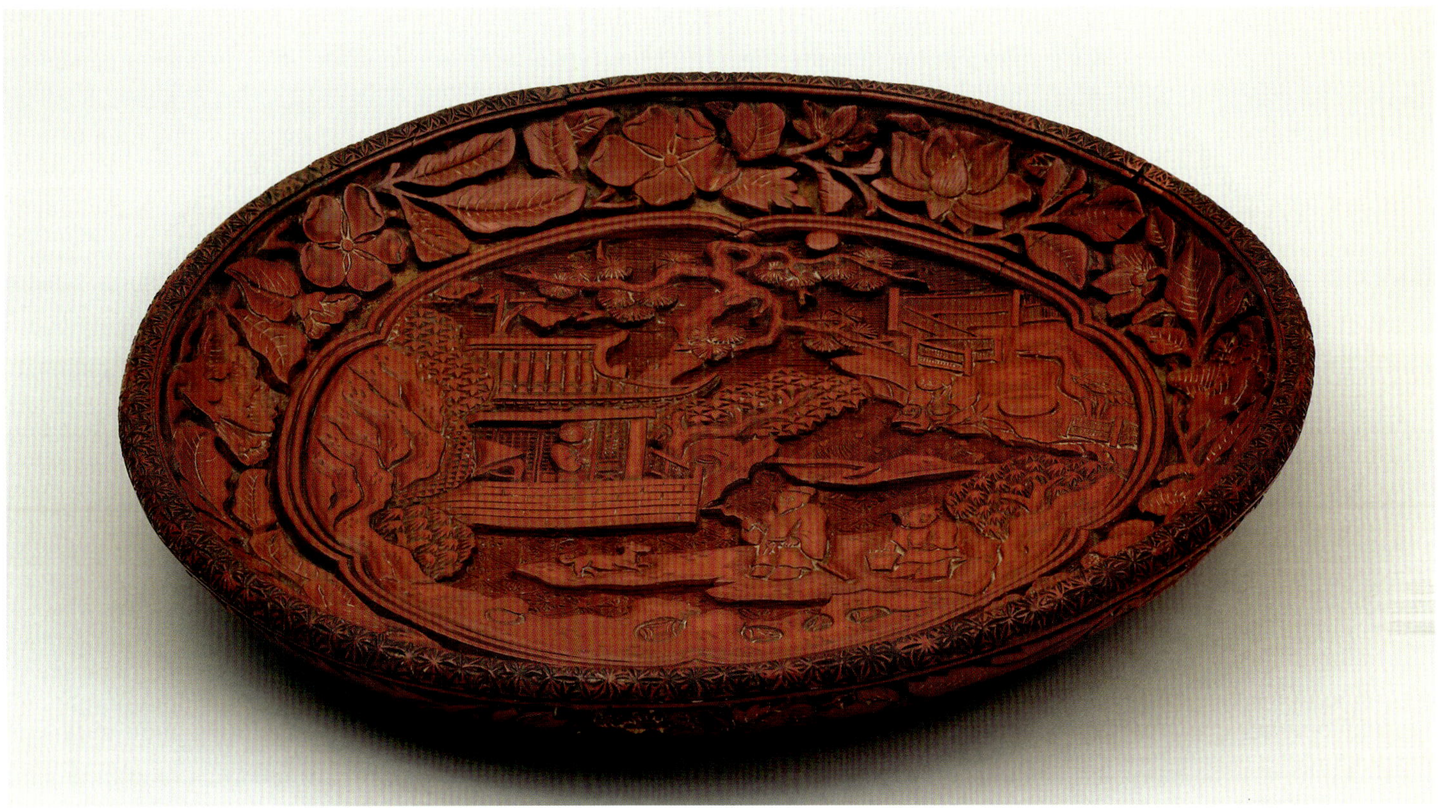

The narrative decoration on this carved red plate is of a type popular in the late Yuan and early Ming dynasties. In the narrative, under a moonlit, starry night, a gentleman with a long staff and young boy approach a wineshop, where a dog greets them. The details of this scene include the typical "air diaper" and "ground diaper," standardized repetitive patterns that serve as a backdrop for the decoration and help to establish depth within the scene.[1] A unique wave pattern defines the water, where a servant washes utensils from the shop. A hexagonal double-lined, smooth frame surrounds the scene.

A band of flowers carved in red against a yellow background includes plum, tree peony, camellia, and pomegranate,[2] which decorate the interior and exterior rim of the plate. The outer rim of the small plate has a unique crosshatched pattern carved into the surface.

The combination of the aged central figure with a pine tree branching out under a full moon may make reference to the painting genre of depicting "birthday" images. In addition, a crane, another symbol of longevity, is depicted to the side of the servant.

Carved red lacquer plates with similar details are in collections in China and the United States.[3] A lozenge-shaped dish in the Irving Collection at the Metropolitan Museum of Art shares many of the same attributes of carving style, polish, and subject matter as the Healy plate.[4] The rocks in both are depicted with long smooth surfaces, and the diaper patterns are regular and distinctive. Moreover, in both plates the exterior rim banding has a distinctive hatched pattern, and the band of seasonal flowers points to an early Ming date.[5]

Notes

1. Harry M. Garner, *Chinese Lacquer* (London: Faber and Faber, 1979), p. 111. Garner discusses the beginning of diaper patterns that describe the air, land, and water backgrounds in red carved lacquer as beginning in the fourteenth century and continuing into the eighteenth. In his article "Diaper Backgrounds on Chinese Carved Lacquer," *Ars Orientalis: The Arts of Islam and the East* 6 (1966): 165–89, Garner describes the use of diaper backgrounds at length.

2. See cat. no. 15 for a similar rendering of the banded seasonal motif on yellow ground.

3. Chen Chang, ed., *Zhongguo qiji quanji* (Lacquer treasures from China), vol. 4: *Sanguo–Yuan* (Three Kingdoms–Yuan dynasty) (Fujian, China: Fujian Publishing House, 1998). See cat. no. 153, p. 168, a hexagonal, carved red lacquer plate dated to the Yuan period, in the Beijing Palace Museum collection.

4. James C. Y. Watt, *East Asian Lacquer* (New York: Metropolitan Museum of Art, 2004), cat. no. 24, p. 79.

5. Watt also notes that the Irving dish "answers well to descriptions of the carved red lacquerware sent to Japan during the reign of Yongle." Watt, *China*, p. 79.

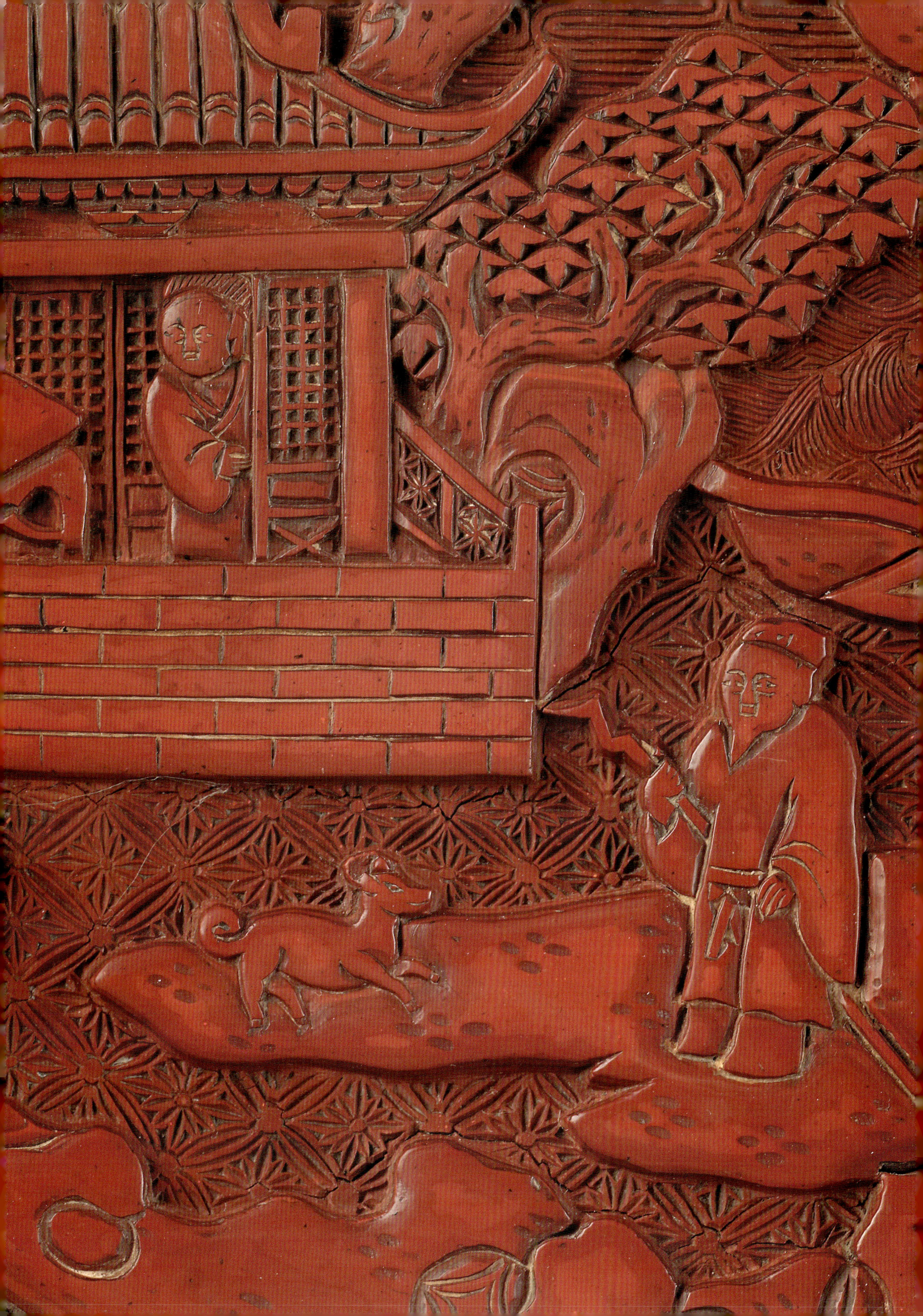

19

Round Box with Figures in the Landscape

Late Yuan–early Ming dynasty, 14th–15th century
Carved red lacquer
H. 5½ in. DIAM. 13¾ in.
L37,925

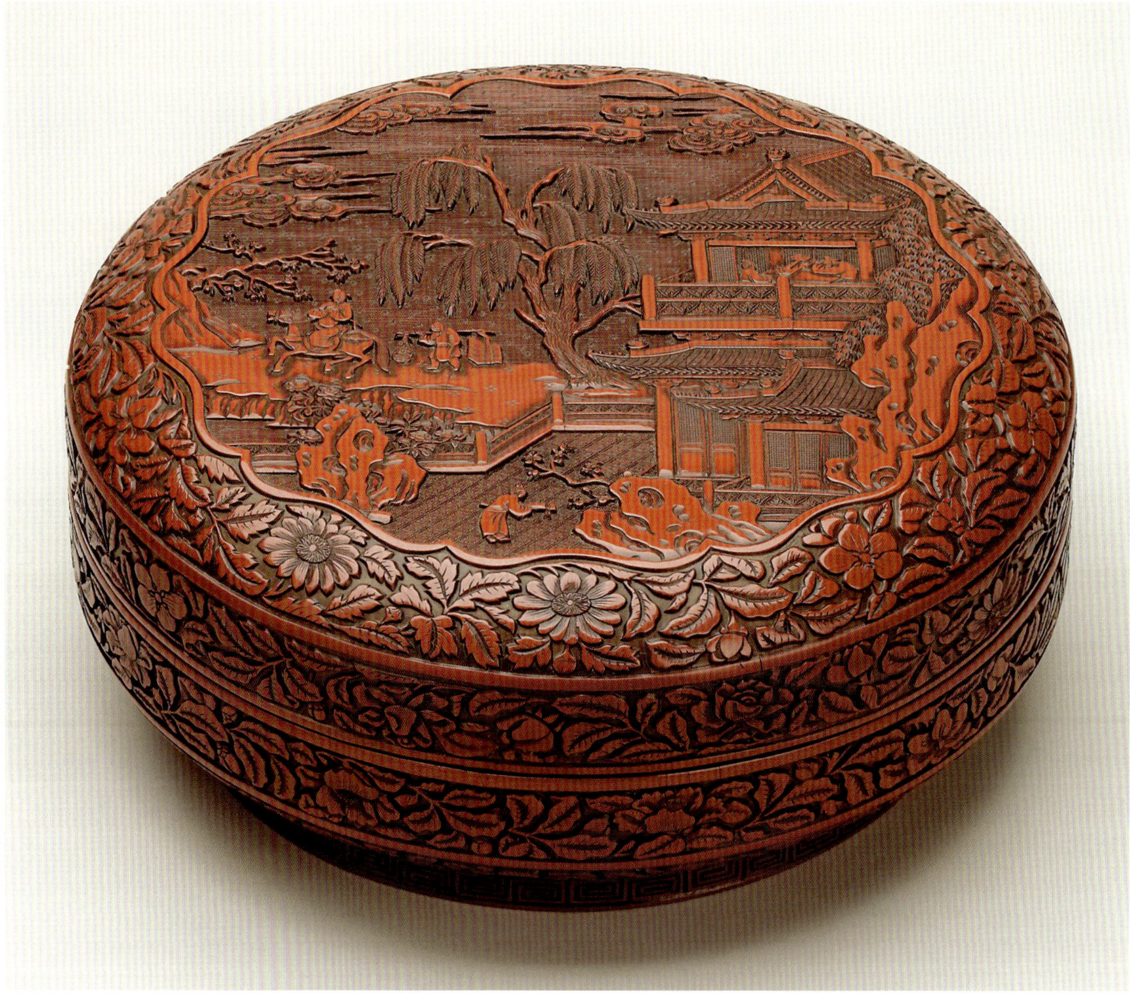

Carved lacquer pieces with narrative scenes began to appear in the fourteenth century, continuing as a popular motif well into the Qing dynasty. Here a two-storied country pavilion and garden setting are depicted with distinctive "air diaper" and "ground diaper" patterns, whereas the garden rail and pavilion are shown as architecturally viable with overlapping rooflines. The narrative is surrounded by a smooth, ten-petaled band followed by pairings of auspicious flowers of the four seasons: tree peony, chrysanthemum, plum, and pomegranate. The plum and tree peonies are also visible in the garden area, along with a tall willow, central to the composition. The sides of the lid and base are also decorated with carved lacquer flowers in a continuous but repeating pattern.[1]

In the midst of the garden is a servant carrying a *qin* (zither), an instrument often associated with the scholar-literati gentleman. In a sophisticated pictorial composition, a whole scene of architecture, landscape, and figures is played out. Three men are visible through a window in the upstairs pavilion. One appears asleep at a table, another lounges on one elbow, and the third has his back to the viewer. On a raised platform (above the garden), a small boy carries packages, perhaps the belongings of a gentleman on horseback riding away from the group.[2]

Although scenes like these frequently are associated with Daoist or literary themes, this one does not present a clear reference. It may be a scene of nighttime departure after an evening of music, or simply a depiction of a gentleman's villa, but might also have literary meaning.

The Japanese wooden storage box for this object has an inscription on the top, which indicates it is a food container, with a relief of a Chinese-style building and figures.

Notes

1. Noted as an indication of dating by Garner, *Chinese Lacquer* (London: Faber and Faber, 1979), p. 83. Some debate which flowers are depicted because the design somewhat compromises the botanical characteristics. In some instances, the flowers alternate in series of four; in others, they are paired; but variation in types of flowers is the most important factor in differentiating late fourteenth- and fifteenth-century floral patterns from earlier ones. Earlier pieces, especially the inlaid examples, have one repetitive floral motif in edge bands.

2. A box of much less complex overall design but with the same attention to architectural and landscape details in the Beijing Gugong Boyuyuan dates to the Yuan period. See Chen Chang, ed., *Zhongguo qiji quanji* (Lacquer treasures from China), vol. 4: *Sanguo–Yuan* (Three Kingdoms–Yuan dynasty) (Fujian, China: Fujian Publishing House, 1998), no. 154, p. 169.

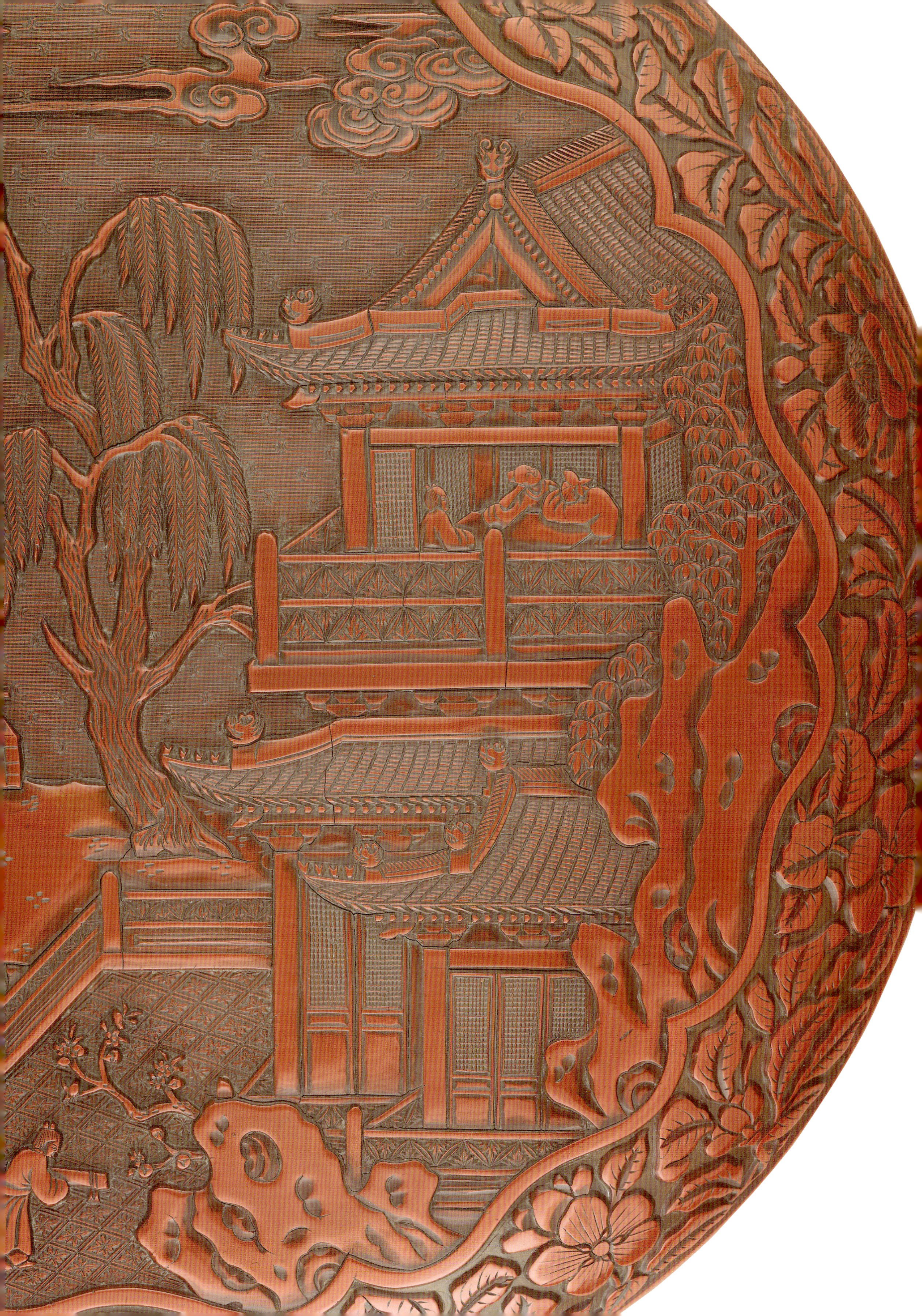

20

Peony Box

Late Yuan–early Ming dynasty,
14th–15th centuries
Carved red lacquer
H. 2½ in. DIAM. 7⅜ in.
L37,927

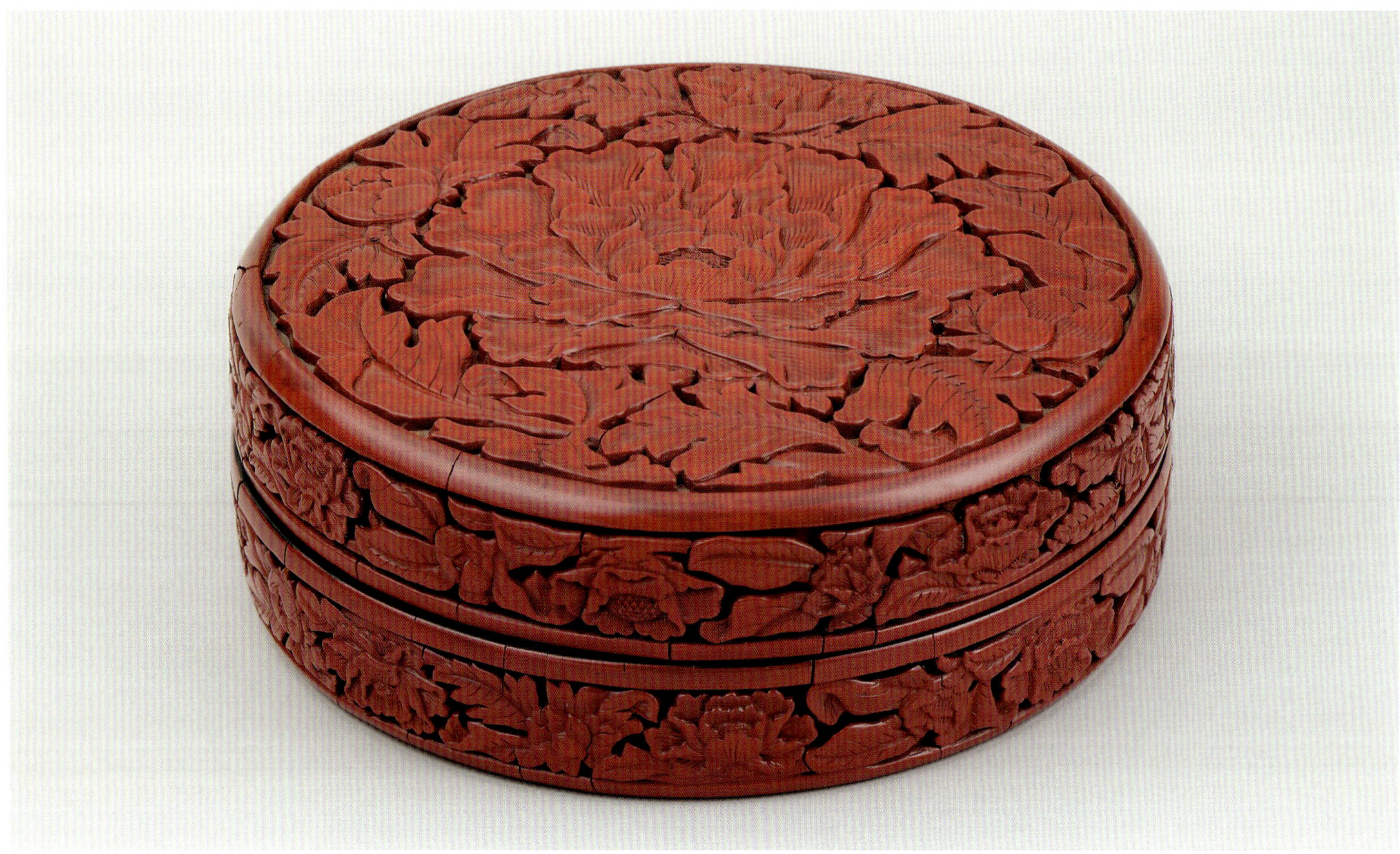

Boxes and plates decorated with densely carved images of flower motifs were a distinctive achievement of the late Yuan and early Ming periods. Although some experts look to their relationship with blue-and-white ceramics for their painted patterns, others point to the three-dimensional quality of the works and the possibility of association with carved ceramics.

Either way, it is their lively expression of intricate space that makes them compelling visual images. True to period, this elegant, straight-sided box has a densely executed, single open peony with tendrils of leaves around the central flower. The edges of the box's top and bottom are decorated with a folding leaf pattern interspersed with peony and chrysanthemum flowers. The peony is usually associated with rank and the chrysanthemum with longevity. The background, where visible, is a dull brown color.

This box shares several interesting traits with lacquer objects in the imperial collection at the Palace Museum, Beijing.[1] A tendency toward a full and somewhat crowded design is noted in the Yuan pieces housed there, as is a tendency toward an overlapping and folded leaf design, both characteristics noted on this peony box. A seldom seen, raised rib on one or two leaves (as seen here on the lower left and upper central areas) is pointed to as being a characteristic of the earlier Yuan-period types, particularly when paired with an evenly marked secondary veining.

The base of this box contains a partially obscured inscription of the Yongle period (1403–1424), but that is not wholly reliable for dating the piece. Evidence suggests that even though some of these intricate lacquers carry imperial inscriptions of the Hongwu (1368–1398) and Yongle periods, these are not reliable, and more concrete evidence of dating should come through comparative analysis. The judgment to base the date on the inscription should be outweighed by the fact that this box demonstrates characteristics found only on slightly earlier boxes, plates, and vases from the Palace Museum in Beijing.

Note

1. Chen Chang, ed., *Zhongguo qiji quanji* (Lacquer treasures from China), vol. 4: *Sanguo–Yuan* (Three Kingdoms–Yuan dynasty) (Fujian, China: Fujian Publishing House, 1998). See Yuan examples, especially no. 157, p. 173, and cat. no. 159, p. 175.

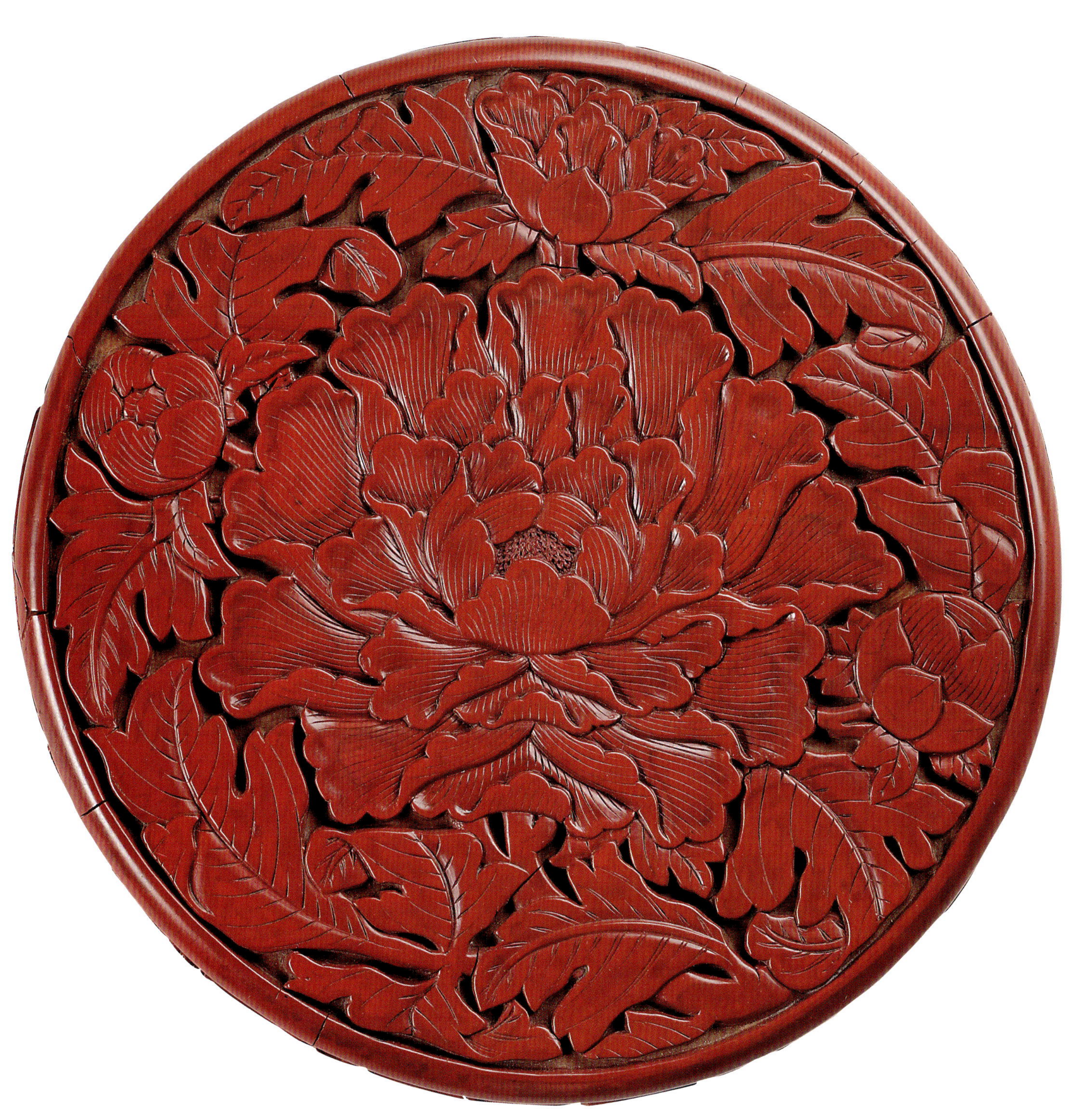

21

Phoenix Box

Early Ming dynasty,
15th century
Carved red lacquer
H. 2¼ in. DIAM. 3 in.
L37,921

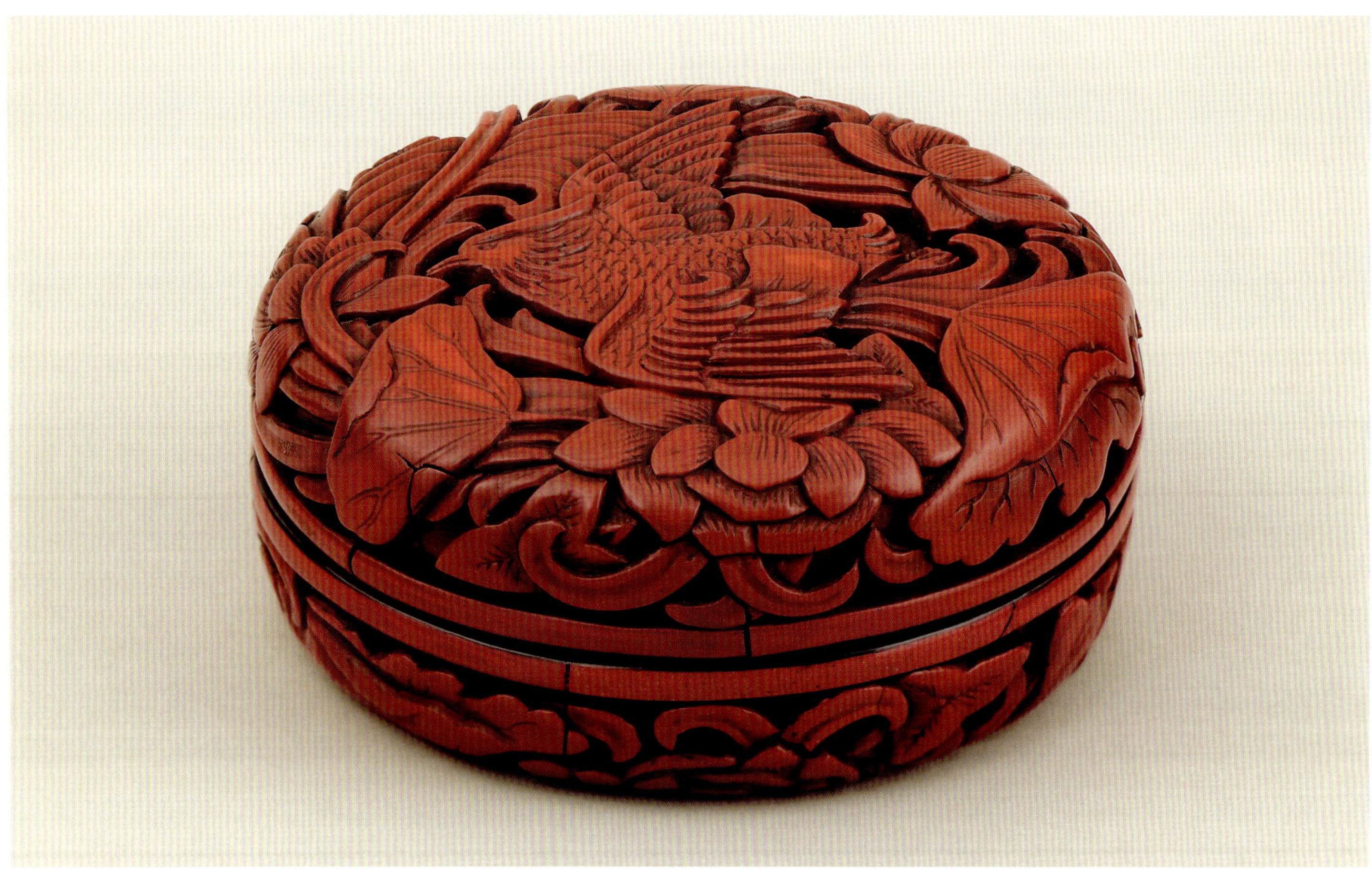

A long-tailed phoenix is set against a design of lotus leaves and flowers on both the top and bottom of the box. The minutely detailed patterns of feathers on the bird and the crisp details of veining in the lotus leaves and flowers enhance the deep, rich red color of the lacquer. The overall surface is quite consistent and even, with a deeply cut, straight-edged design typical of early Ming-period lacquers.

The phoenix is associated with the empress and with beauty. Along with the dragon, *qilin*, and tortoise, it is one of the four great mythological animals. In China it is associated with positive human qualities.[1] The lotus is associated with Buddhism and has been called "the flower of purity and integrity since it emerges from the mud and remains unstained."[2]

Larger plates with a similar bird-and-lotus pattern are found in collections in China, including one in the Shandong Provincial Museum.[3] This type of small box was sometimes used in China as a container for a small mirror. Many made their way into Japanese collections, where, much admired, they were adapted for use as small incense boxes in the tea ceremony.

A large group of what are now considered to be late Yuan or early Ming lacquers was sent to Japan in the early fifteenth century, whereas others were later exports.[4] For the most part these early entries into Japan were much-coveted items and became treasures of the wealthy and privileged, just as they did in China.

Notes

1. Fang Jing Pei, *Symbols and Rebuses in Chinese Art: Figures, Bugs, Beasts, and Flowers* (Berkeley, Calif.: Ten Speed Press, 2004). See pp. 149–50, entry for Phoenix.

2. Asian Art Museum, Choong Moon Lee Center for Asian Art and Culture, *Botanical Symbols in Chinese Art: Knowledge Cards*, text by Therese Tse Bartholomew (San Francisco: Pomegranate Communications, 2004).

3. Zhu Jiajin and Xia Gengqi, eds., *Zhongguo qiji quanji* (Lacquer treasures from China), vol. 5: *Ming* (Ming) (Fujian, China: Fujian Publishing House, 1998). See no. 4, p. 4, for description, and also p. 2, where an early Ming date is suggested.

4. John Figgess, "Ming and Pre-Ming Lacquer in the Japanese Tea Ceremony," *Transactions of the Oriental Ceramic Society* 37 (1967–68, 1968–69): 37–51. Figures 56b–c illustrate boxes of approximately the same size.

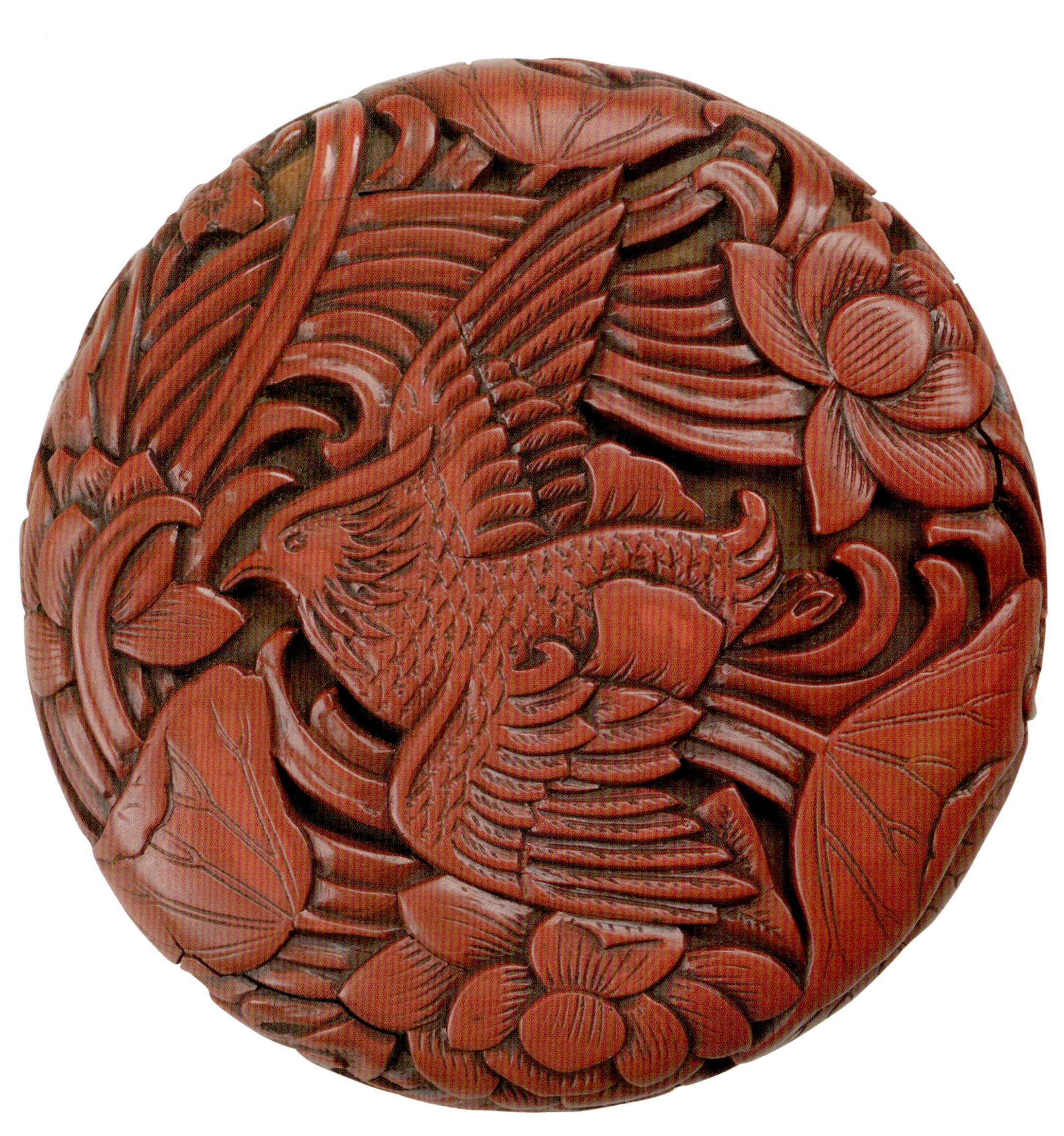

22

Lobed Plate

Late Yuan–early Ming dynasty,
14th–15th century
Carved red lacquer
H. ¾ in. DIAM. 6⅞ in.
L38,009

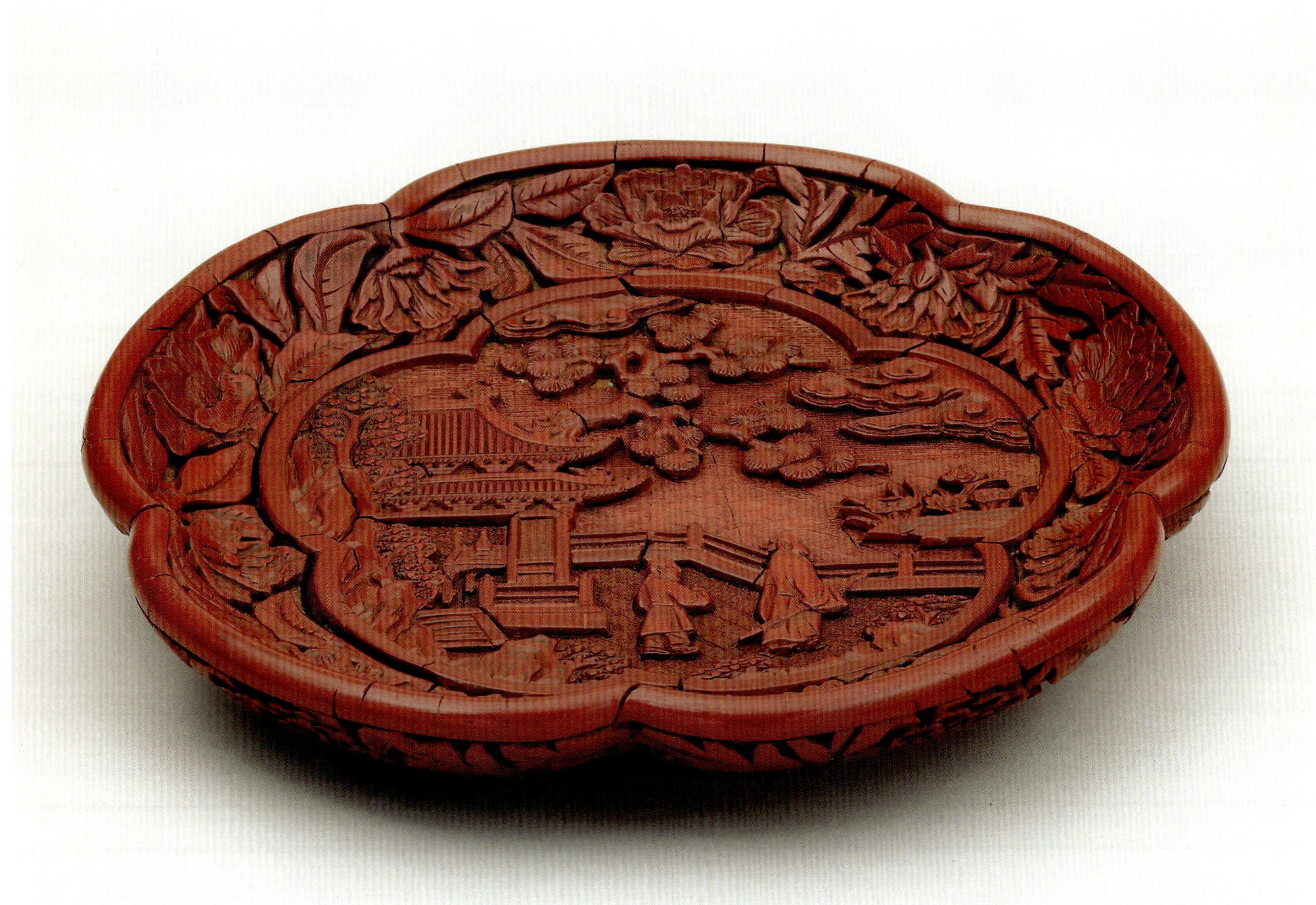

The gentleman's appreciation for the natural world is depicted on this five-lobed plate. Standing on a terrace, staff in hand, the gentleman gazes across the railing at a cluster of flowering lotus amid a wave-patterned surface. Frequently seen in carved lacquer from this period, the figure is said to be Zhou Dunyi, a Neoconfucian philosopher of the Song dynasty. The pavilion door remains open, allowing a glimpse of the so-called horse-hoof-footed table with a vase on top. The rim of the plate is composed of carved seasonal flowers.

The table depicted inside the pavilion resembles one on a box in the Irving Collection (now at the Metropolitan Museum of Art) that dates by inscription to the early Ming period.[1] Another point of similarity in both pieces is a spreading pine tree that canopies the pavilion and gentlemen. A hexagonal plate with a related composition is in the Palace Museum in Beijing.[2] It is regarded as a product of the late Yuan period and is signed "Yang Mao." Since a box with similar furnishings in the Palace Museum in Beijing carries the signature of lacquer artist Zhang Minde (the son of Zhang Cheng), it seems plausible that this plate may be from the same workshop.[3]

Notes

1. James C. Y. Watt and Barbara Brennan Ford, *East Asian Lacquer: The Florence and Herbert Irving Collection* (New York: Metropolitan Museum of Art, 1991), cat. no. 27, pp. 84–85.

2. Chen Chang, ed., *Zhongguo qiji quanji* (Lacquer treasures from China), vol. 4: *Sanguo–Yuan* (Three Kingdoms–Yuan dynasty) (Fujian, China: Fujian Publishing House, 1998), cat. no. 153, illus. p. 168, description p. 62. The scene on this plate is very similar, though the scholar appears to gaze at a rock face rather than at a lotus pond, as in the Healy plate. In addition, the Beijing plate is octagonal rather than lobed.

3. Chen, ed., *Zhongguo qiji quanji*, cat. no. 154, illus. p. 169, description p. 63.

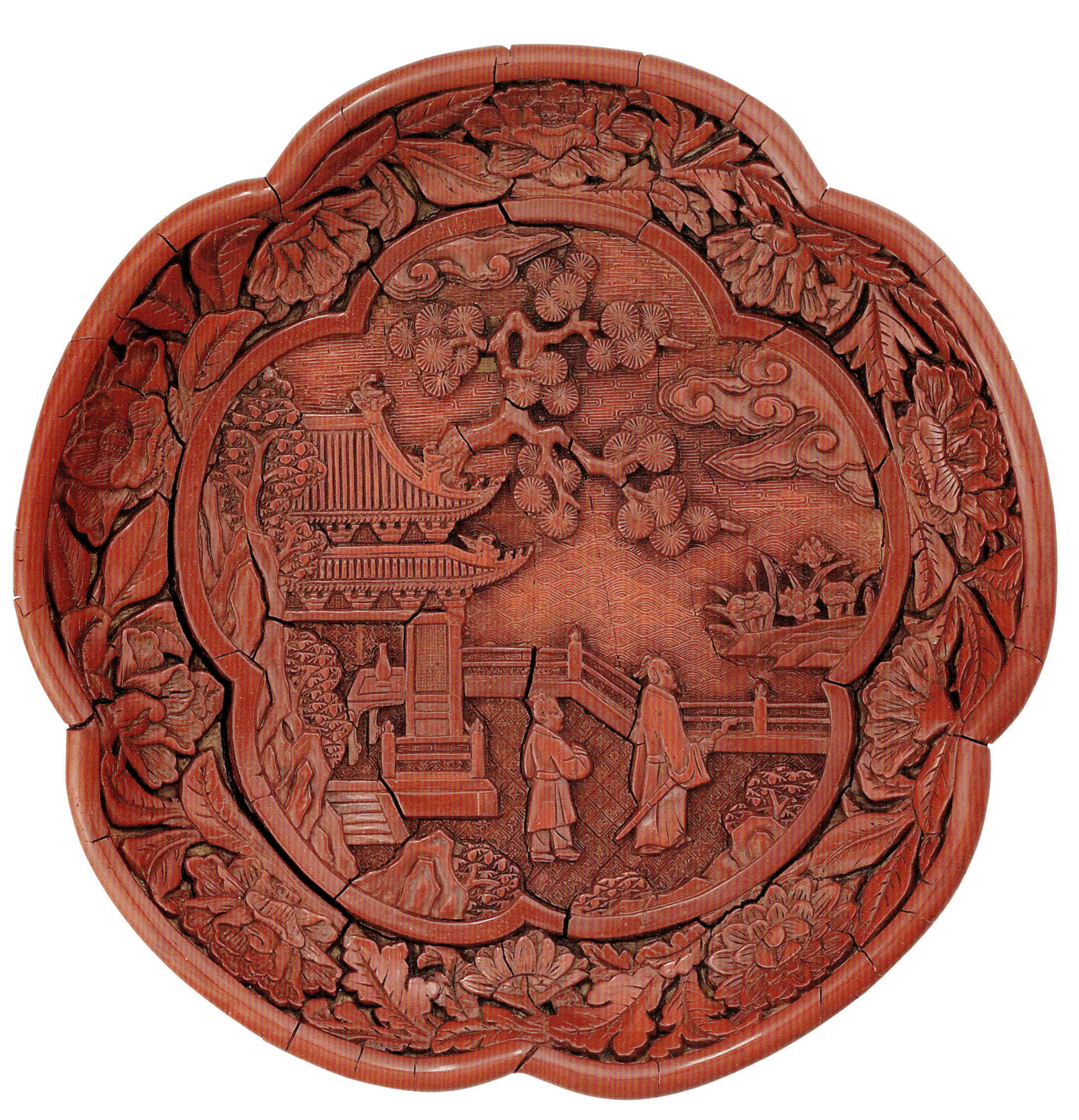

23

Plate with Horse and Rider

Late Yuan or early Ming dynasty, 14th–15th century
Carved red lacquer
H. 1 in. DIAM. 12⅝ in.
L37,926

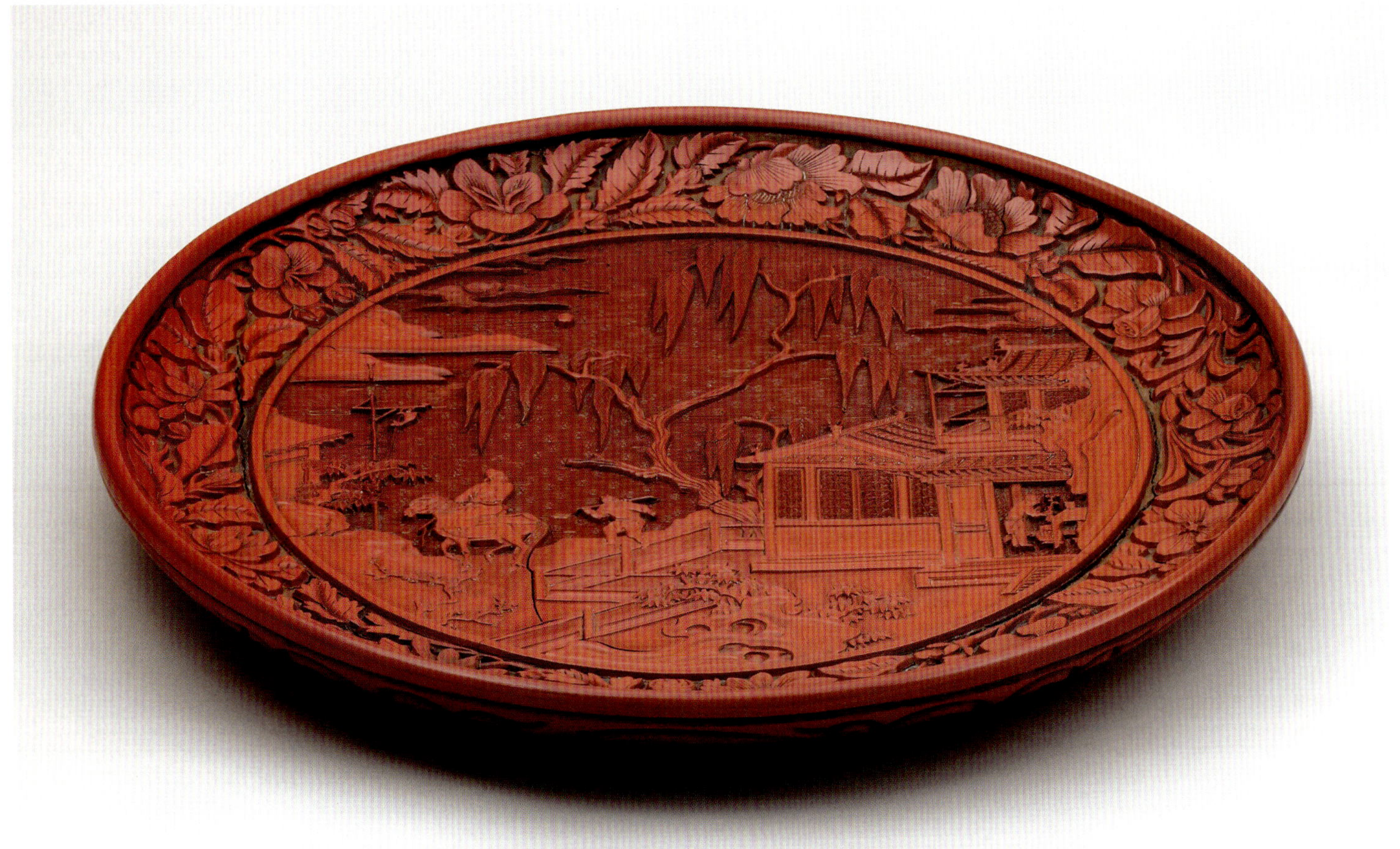

This plate resembles other narrative-type red lacquer plates from the late Yuan or early Ming period. It takes a standard format, with a horse and rider attended by a figure on foot set against a garden, rock, and architectural setting. The narrative scene is surrounded by a ring of six paired flowers: plum, lily, peony, pomegranate, magnolia, and chrysanthemum.

When details of the design are carefully examined, however, some unusual points can be observed. The faces of the figures seem distorted and animal-like, such as that of the figure inside one of the buildings. The structures have odd architectural elements, especially the second-floor roofline, which is supported illogically by listing columns. Other elements, such as the flag over the wineshop at the left and the moon represented in an "evening diaper" pattern, are represented more rationally.

The plate is finely made, displaying the technical skill expected in a late Yuan or early Ming piece. In every way it appears genuine. So what do the discrepancies noted above mean? It seems quite likely that this narrative is a scene from a mythological tale, perhaps the *Xiyouji*, a popular legend about the world of the Monkey King. The realm of the mythological animal would not have the same logic as that of humans, and this may explain why the artist purposefully exaggerated certain features of the scene. It may also be that the model or cartoon used for the design had some unusual or misunderstood elements.

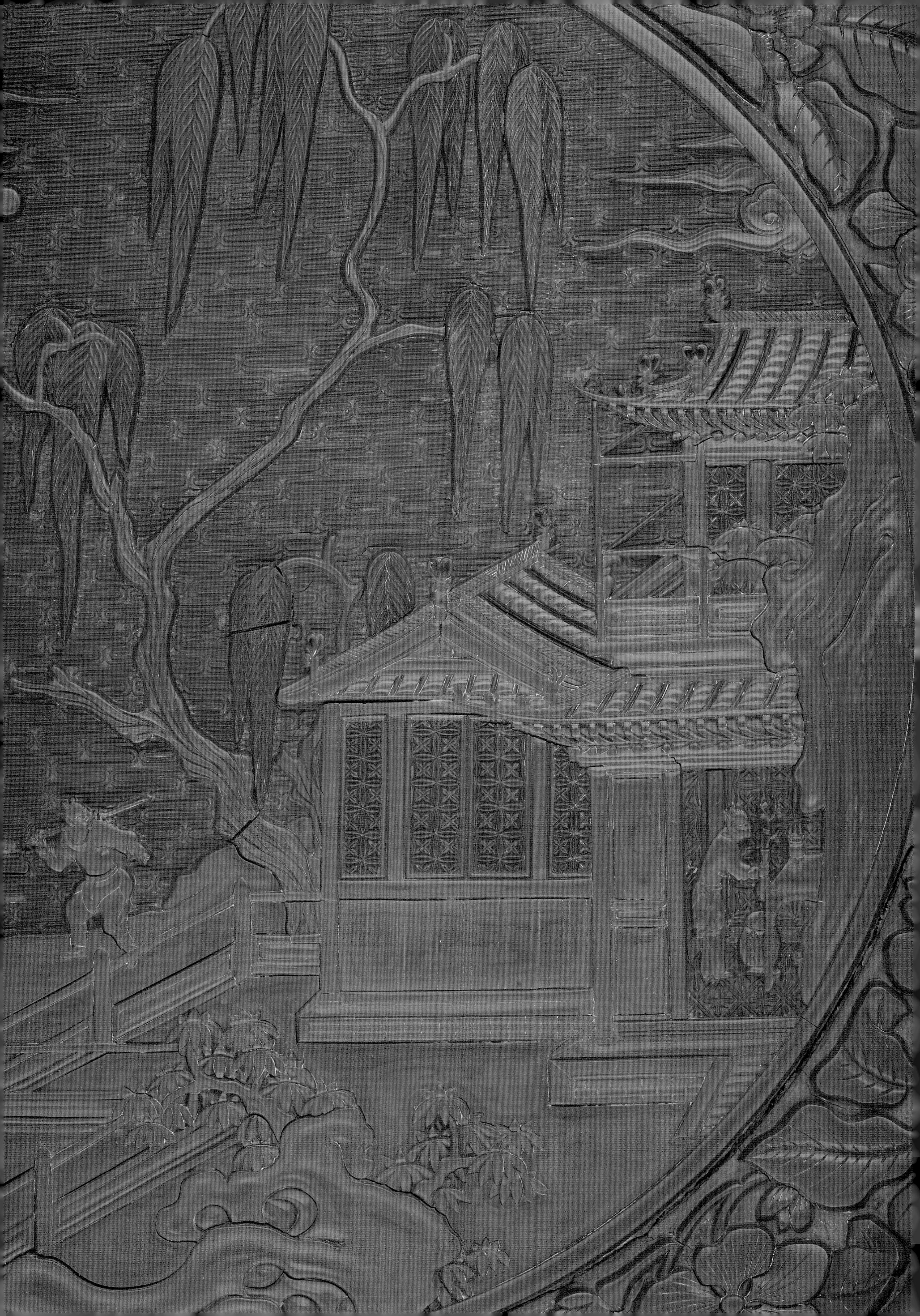

24

Round Box

Ming dynasty, Jiajing mark and period, 1522–1566
Carved red lacquer
H. 4⅜ in. DIAM. 7¼ in.
L38,012

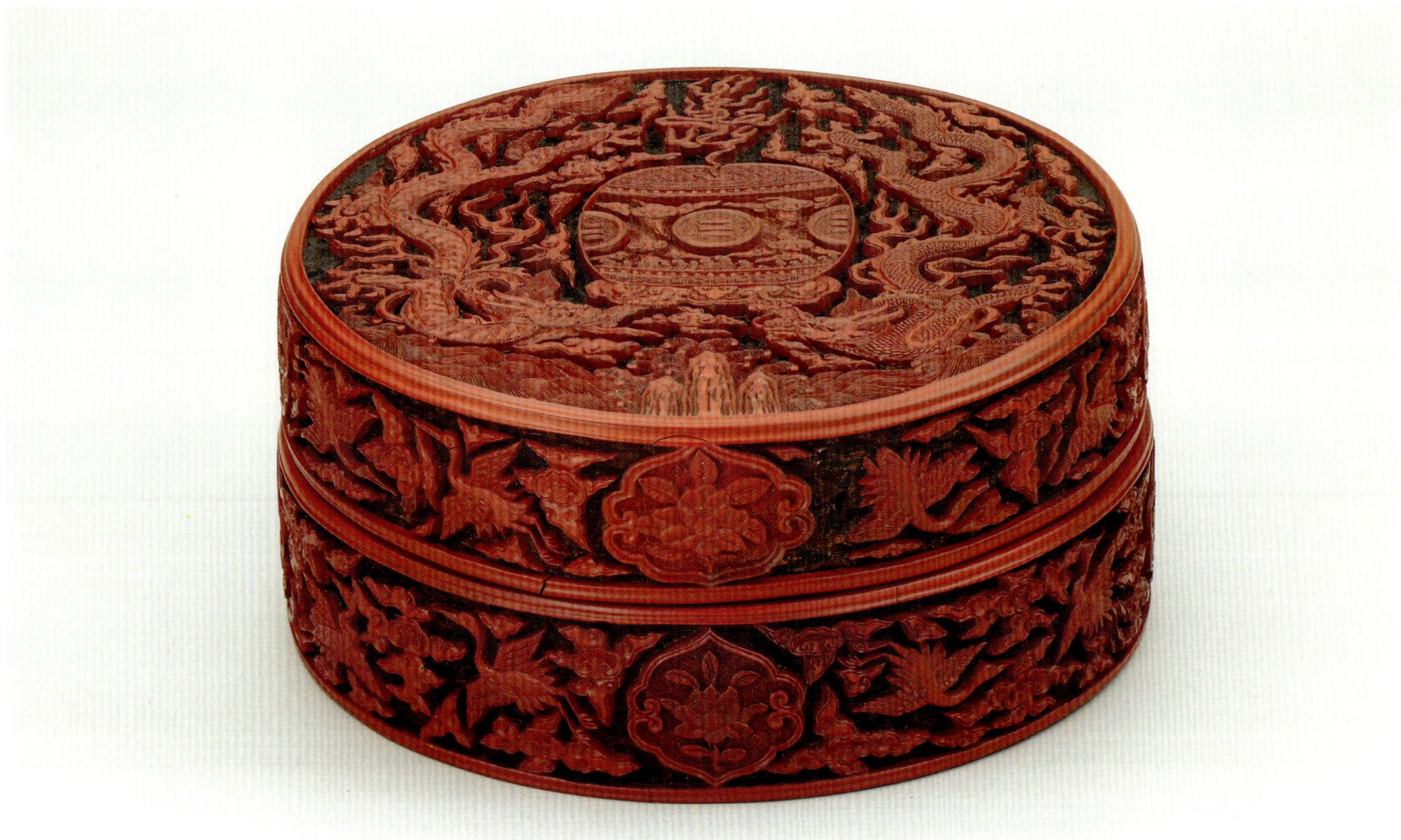

A pair of five-clawed dragons swirls across the top of this box, floating amid the clouds and holding up an object decorated with auspicious trigrams. This object is probably a Daoist alchemical reaction vessel, used for creating and refining elixirs. The character *shou* (longevity) emerges as a vapor out of the top of the vessel, much like the decoration seen on blue-and-white porcelains of the Jiajing period. The central trigram is *qian*, the left is *kan*, and the right, *kun*. The dragons are curiously sinuous and display different heads. The one on the right has a long snout, and the left dragon sports a tigerlike head. The design is decidedly vertically oriented, with the bottom firmly established by a classic design of three rocks vertically placed between crashing waves. The sides of the box are decorated with stylized cranes interspersed with clouds and further decorated with lobed panels filled with decorative flowers.

The overall design of red lacquer is deeply carved from a richly patterned background of black diaper patterns and is rimmed with a raised and thick band of red lacquer.

The Jiajing emperor was particularly interested in Daoist pursuits, including the search for immortality, which may have ended his life prematurely; he died after having consumed an elixir to promote long life. Lacquer art during his reign thrived, and those objects that remain show a high level of skill, both in application and in carving. Thus it is not surprising to find strong Daoist designs on this box.

The designs on lacquer of this mid-Ming-period box are consistent with others of the period, of which many carry Jiajing marks.[1] New compositions emphasizing Daoist over Buddhist subject matter and following distinctive patterns, such as the three-rock motif at the base of the design, are hallmarks of lacquerwares of this period.

Note

1. James C. Y. Watt and Barbara Brennan Ford, *East Asian Lacquer: The Florence and Herbert Irving Collection* (New York: Metropolitan Museum of Art, 1991). See nos. 32–35, pp. 92–99. See also the Lee Family Collection in Lee King Tsi and Hu Shih Chang, *Drache und Phoenix: Lackarbeiten aus China, Sammlung der Familie Lee, Tokyo / Dragon and Phoenix: Chinese Lacquerware from the Sammy Lee Family Collection, Tokyo* (Cologne, Germany: Museum of East Asian Art, 1990). The lacquer mirror box illustrated in cat. no. 60, pp. 146–47, has much the same spirit and flow in its overall design.

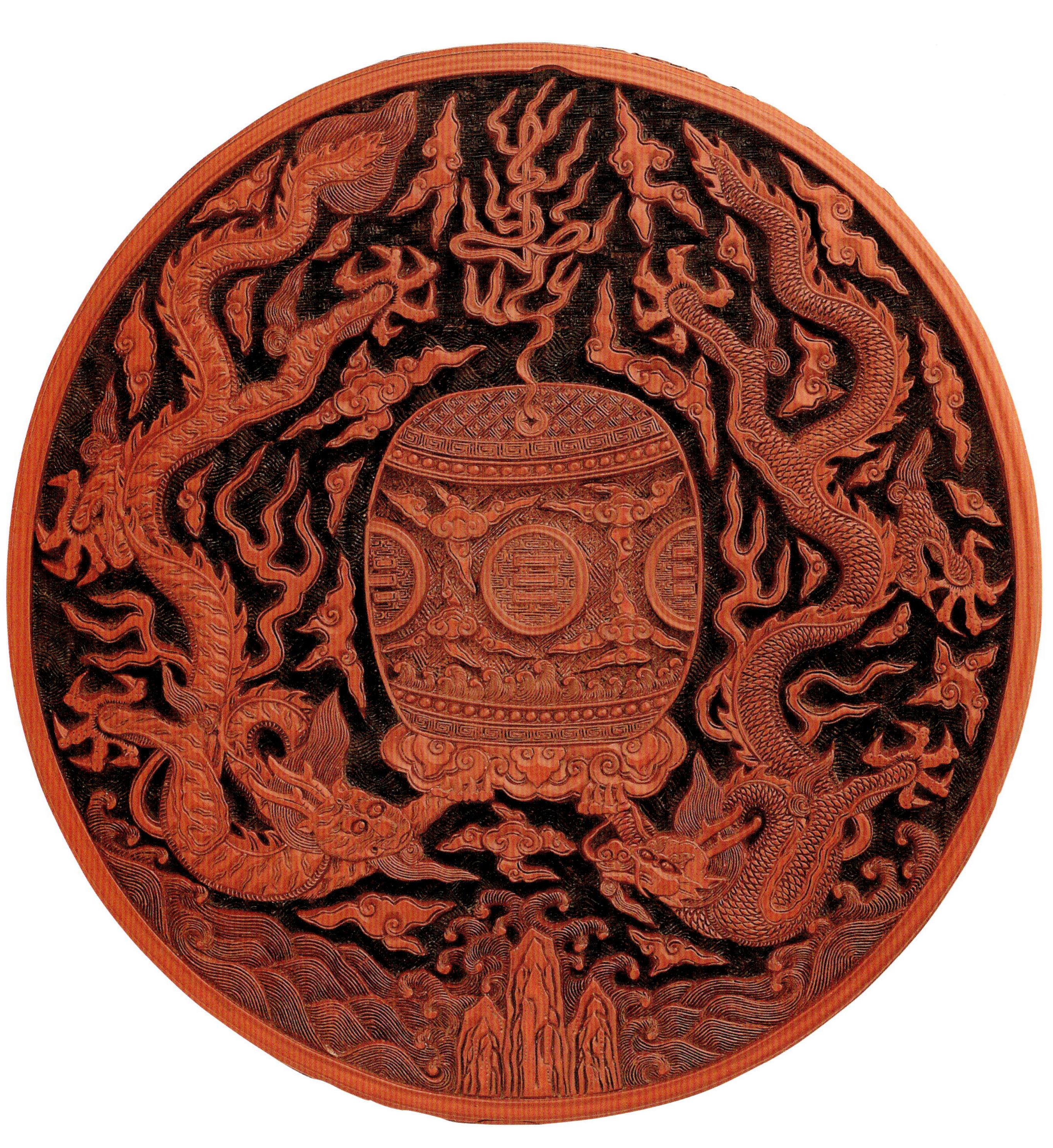

25

Box with Cranes in Flight

Ming dynasty, Jiajing period, 1522–1566
Carved red, black, and brown lacquer *(ticai)*
H. 4½ in. DIAM. 10 in.
L 38,245

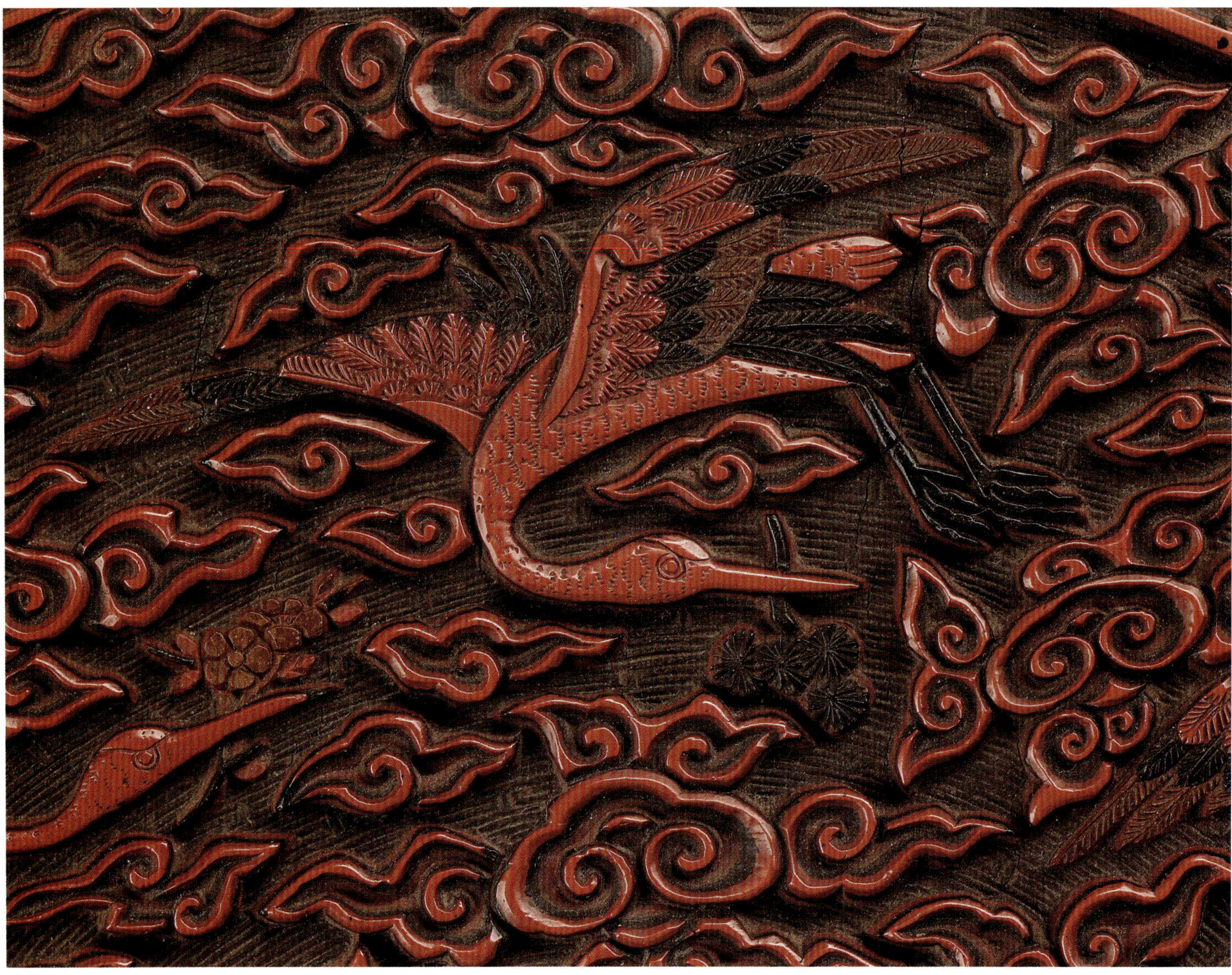

A robust design of eight cranes in flight encircling a raised roundel containing the single character *shou* (longevity) in a simplified seal script decorates the top of this large box. The straight sides are further embellished with cranes amid clouds. Cranes are associated with both official status and longevity, and therefore this box may have conveyed wishes of longevity for a civil official.

The cranes are surrounded by stylized clouds set onto a stylized "air diaper" pattern of black lines. The overall impression of the box is similar to that of imperial red lacquerware from the mid-sixteenth century, with a very fine and precise method of carving. It also demonstrates the technical mastery of the lacquerer, who combined red, black, and small sections of brown lacquer in the detailing of the birds' feathers.

As in the other Jiajing-period box (cat. no. 24), this elegant round box has the fine, pronounced detailing of carving we expect to see in lacquer of the period.

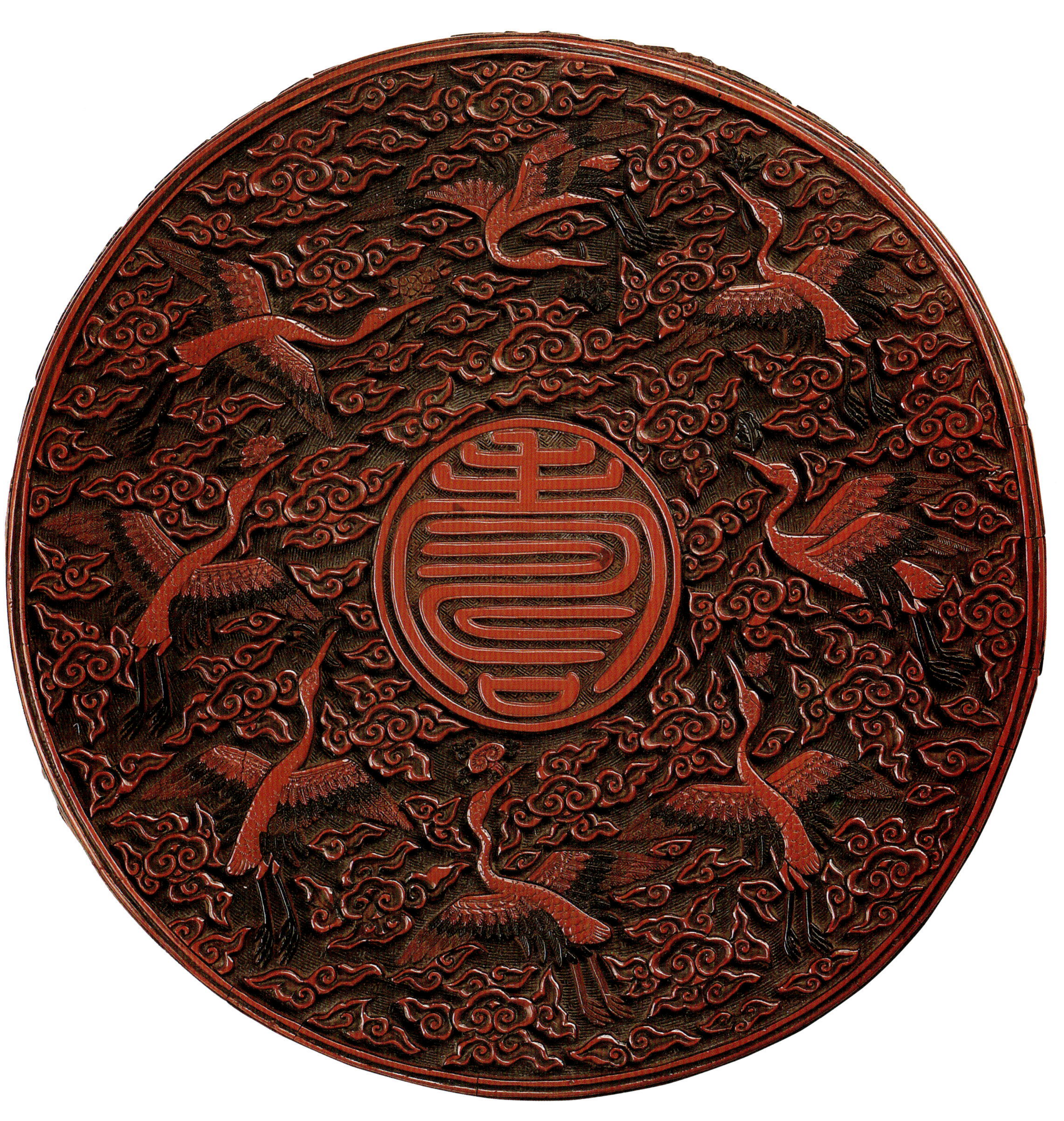

26

Large Lidded Box

Ming dynasty, possibly Wanli period (1573–1620)
Carved red lacquer
H. 4 in. W. 7 in. L. 29⅜ in.
L37,932

This type of large, rectangular box was frequently used to hold various kinds of official and marriage documents. The box is unusual in that it is decorated on the top and bottom as well as all four sides. The bottom of the box depicts three phoenixes in flight against a background of peony-motif decoration. Both the top and bottom of the box are rimmed with carved flowers, including plum, pomegranate, peony, camellia, and hibiscus.

The top of the box is decorated with three distinct garden scenes. The top one shows a deer (associated with officialdom and with Daoism in China) in a garden setting with an old bearded man, attendants, and a woman and child. In a moonlit sky, a crane descends upon the group. The visual references here seem to pertain to longevity and age. The middle scene is the largest and contains numerous figures within and outside an architectural setting. A band of horizontal clouds helps to distinguish it from the scene above. An older man is arriving at the scene in a two-horse carriage. His retinue includes military officials and attendants carrying two fans, which indicate the passenger's high rank. The figure within the pavilion also wears a cap that indicates rank. The lower scene is also that of an older male figure wearing a cap of rank, this time seated and with ladies and attendants. Because these garden scenes include imagery known to be indicators of rank, we may assume that this was an official's document box, and he might have used it to transport his official symbol of authority to and from court.

top

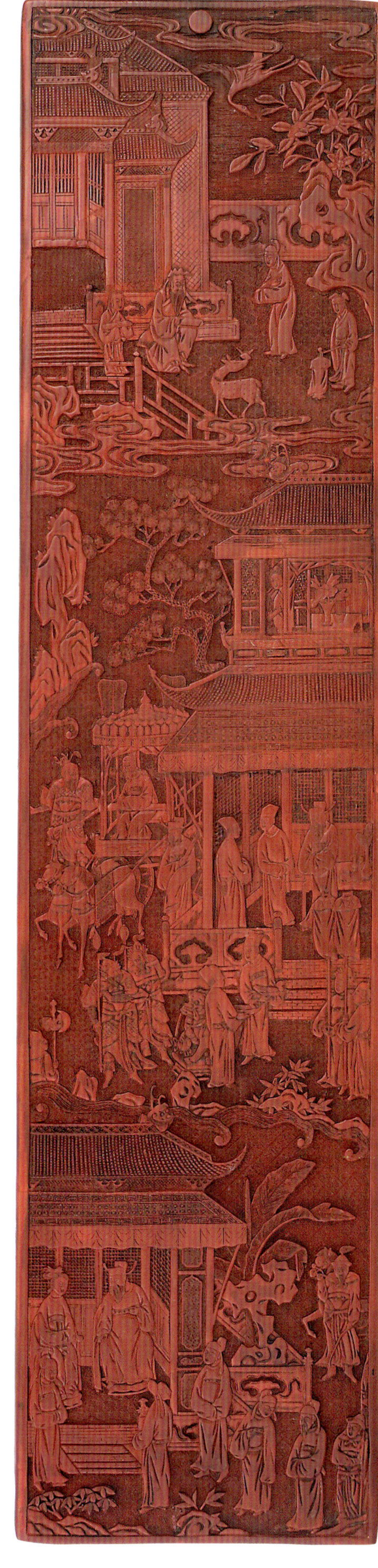

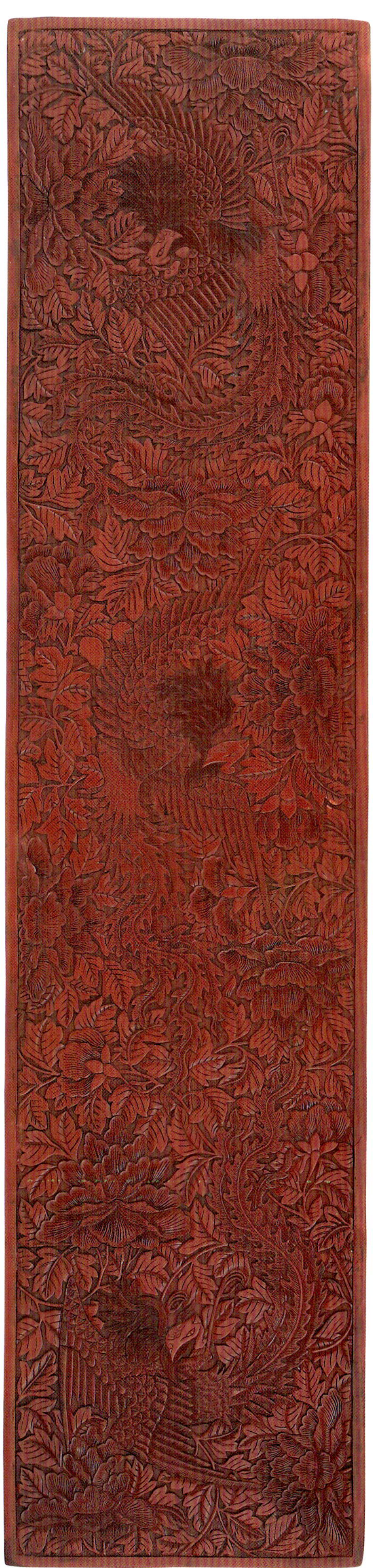

bottom

27

Cup Stand

Ming dynasty,
Yongle mark and period (1403–1424)
Carved red lacquer
H. 3 in. DIAM. (of plate) 6¾ in.
L37,928

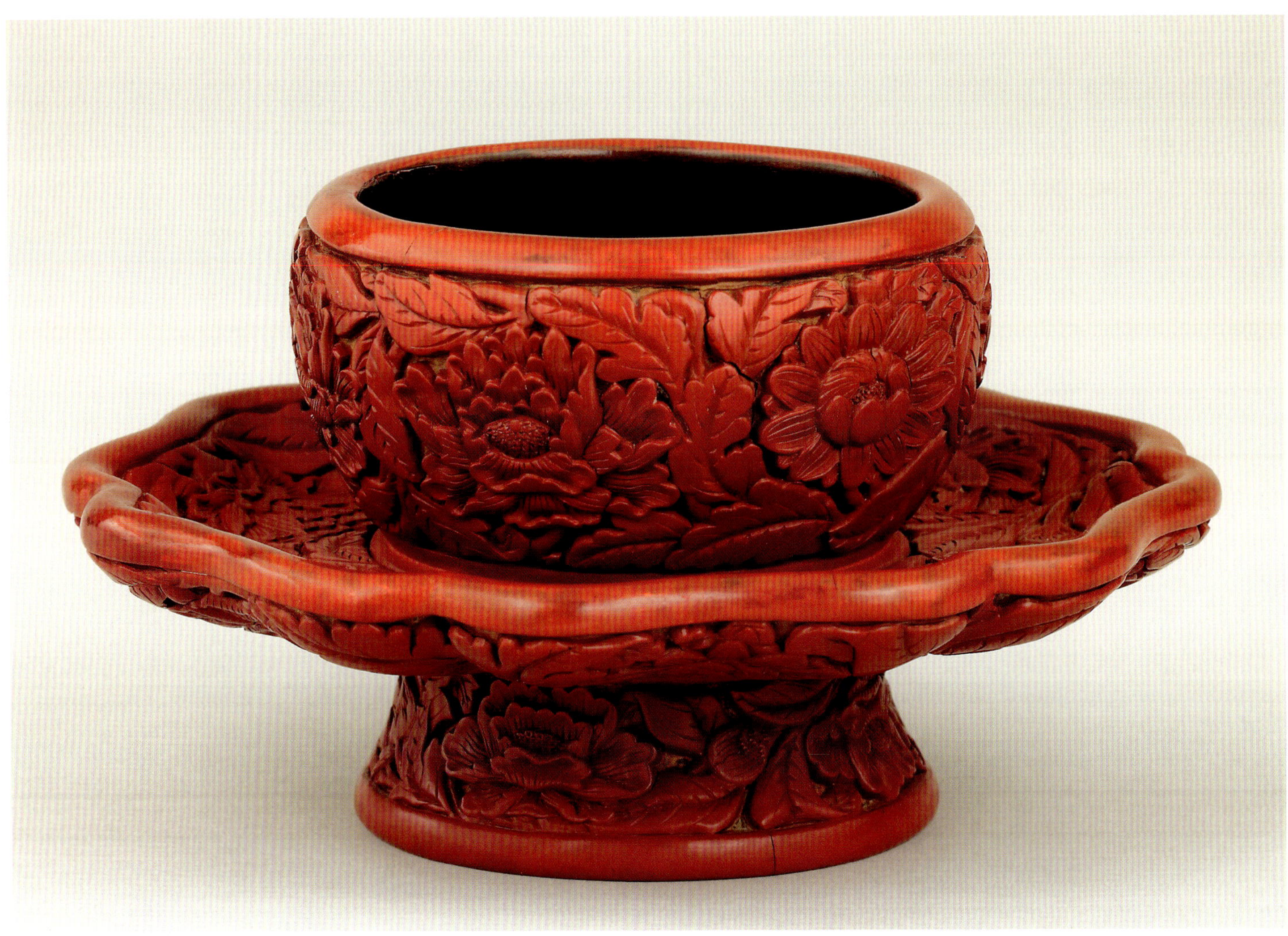

Lacquer objects were expressly designed for functional use in the tea ceremony and in association with other leisure activities of the privileged class. This round cup stand, its exterior decorated with a densely filled floral pattern of peonies and chrysanthemums, and its interior of plain black lacquer, is just such an item. The bowl is attached to a mallow-shaped plate and then to a stand that is slightly flared at the base. A similar cup stand with a Yongle mark and floral decoration is in the Palace Museum collection in Beijing.[1]

Cup, plate, and base all have thick red lacquer bands on their edges, capturing the full design. There is no background diaper pattern in the densely executed design, but the background is a pale yellowish-brown color. It is interesting to note that each band of decoration on the cup, the plate, and the stand is embellished with a single chrysanthemum surrounded by peony blossoms. The peony is associated with rank and the chrysanthemum with longevity, so the imagery may have been created for a special occasion.

Cup stands of lacquer were not made as drinking vessels themselves but as stands for a ceramic bowl that would be placed directly onto the stand's wide bowl. An elaborately decorated stand such as this fine piece might have been paired with a bowl of plain white porcelain, brown-glazed stoneware, or a more ornamental piece of fine celadon. The mallow shape of the plate is one seen frequently in earlier ceramics.[2]

Cup stands with imperial marks of the Yongle period (1403–1424), with pronounced phoenix designs but otherwise similar shape, are in the Irving Collection at the Metropolitan Museum of Art and in the Lee Family Collection.[3]

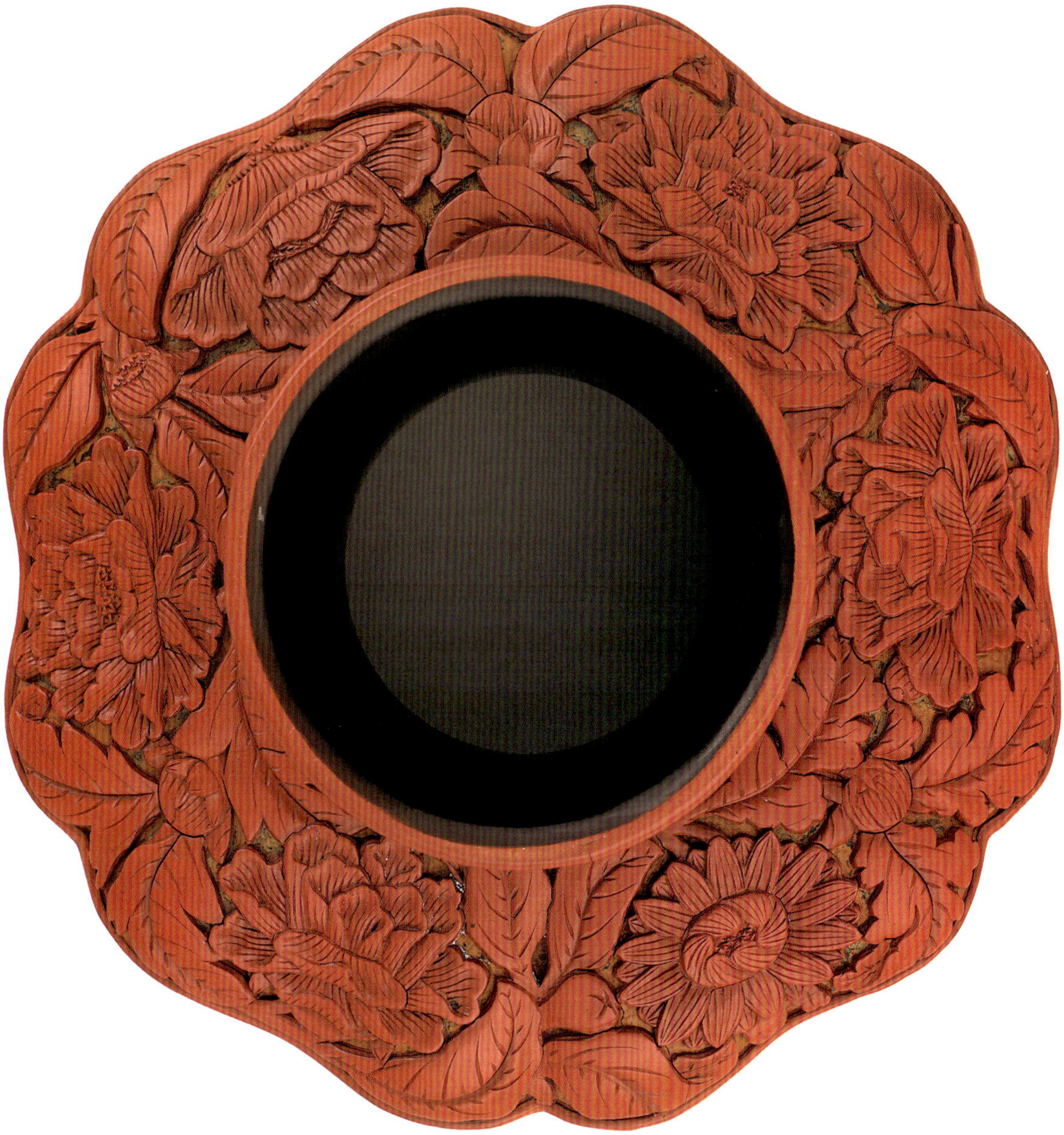

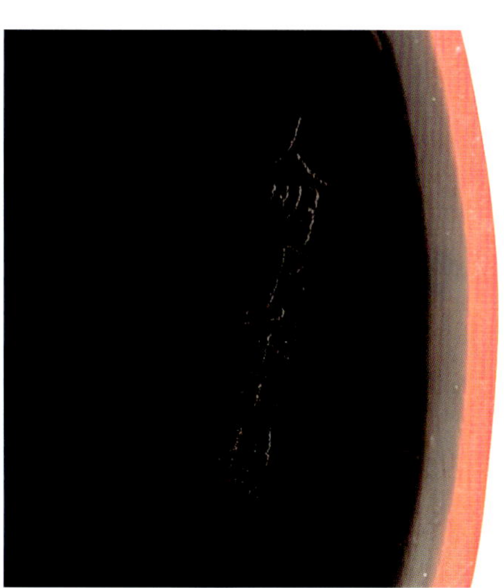

Notes

1. Zhu Jiajin and Xia Gengqi, eds., *Zhongguo qiji quanji* (Lacquer treasures from China), vol. 5: *Ming* (Ming) (Fujian, China: Fujian Publishing House, 1998), no. 26, p. 23. Another is illustrated in a Hong Kong exhibition catalogue; see Peter Lam, ed., *2000 Years of Chinese Lacquer* (Hong Kong: Oriental Ceramic Society of Hong Kong and Art Gallery, The Chinese University of Hong Kong, 1993), cat. no. 46, pp. 98–99.

2. Hin-Cheung Lovell, "Sung and Yuan Monochrome Lacquers in the Freer Gallery," *Ars Orientalis: The Arts of Islam and the East* 9 (1973): 121–30, discusses the mallow-shaped ceramics in relationship to Song-period ceramics.

3. James C. Y. Watt and Barbara Brennan Ford, *East Asian Lacquer: The Florence and Herbert Irving Collection* (New York: Metropolitan Museum of Art, 1991), no. 28, pp. 86–87. See also Lee King Tsi and Hu Shih Chang, *Drache und Phoenix: Lackarbeiten aus China, Sammlung der Familie Lee, Tokyo/Dragon and Phoenix: Chinese Lacquerware from the Sammy Lee Family Collection, Tokyo* (Cologne, Germany: Museum of East Asian Art, 1990), cat. no. 46, pp. 120–21.

28

Brush and Cover

Late Ming dynasty,
16th–17th century
Carved red lacquer
H. 8½ in. DIAM. ½ in.
L37, 924

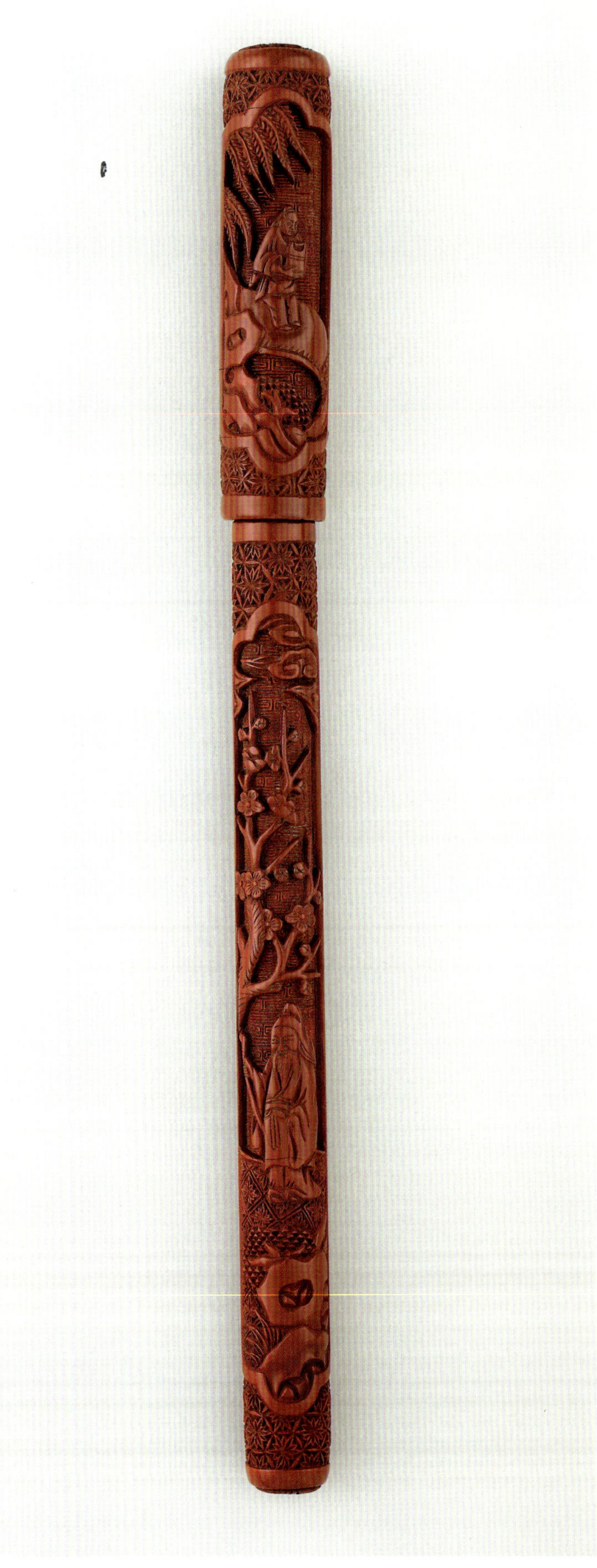

Chinese brushes made from hollow bamboo or reed tubes have been common writing utensils for thousands of years. Elaborately decorated, red-lacquered brushes of this type are much rarer.[1] The delicacy of the carving of this brush, with its foliated scenes of a scholar with staff, combined with the plum branch depicted on the cap, makes it such a treasure. It was probably cherished by a well-educated man, perhaps an official.

Note

1. There is a red-lacquered writing brush in the Los Angeles County Museum of Art. See George Kuwayama, *Far Eastern Lacquer* (Los Angeles: Los Angeles County Museum of Art, 1982), cat. no. 24, p. 83.

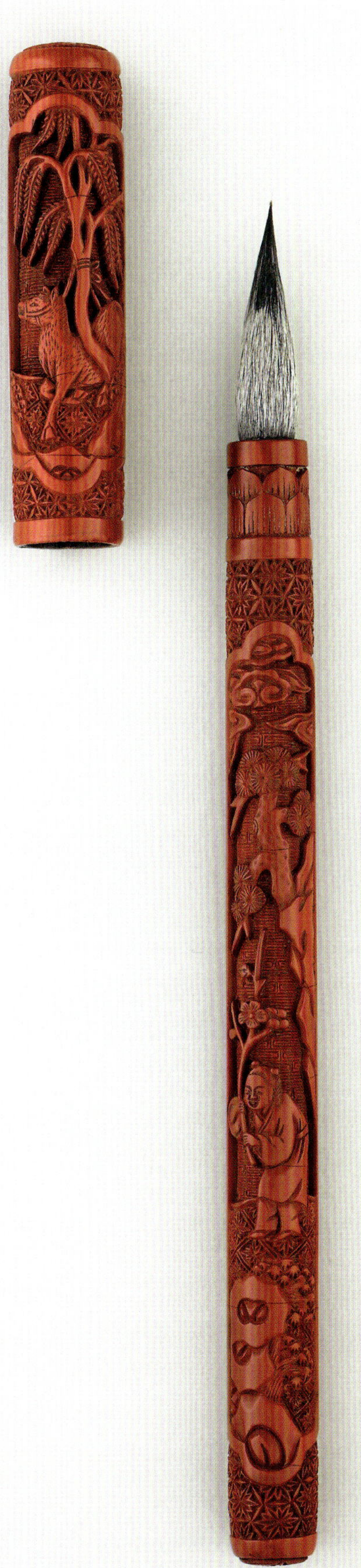

29

Lychee Box

Late Ming dynasty,
16th–17th century
Carved red lacquer
H. 1½ in. DIAM. 3¼ in.
L37,919

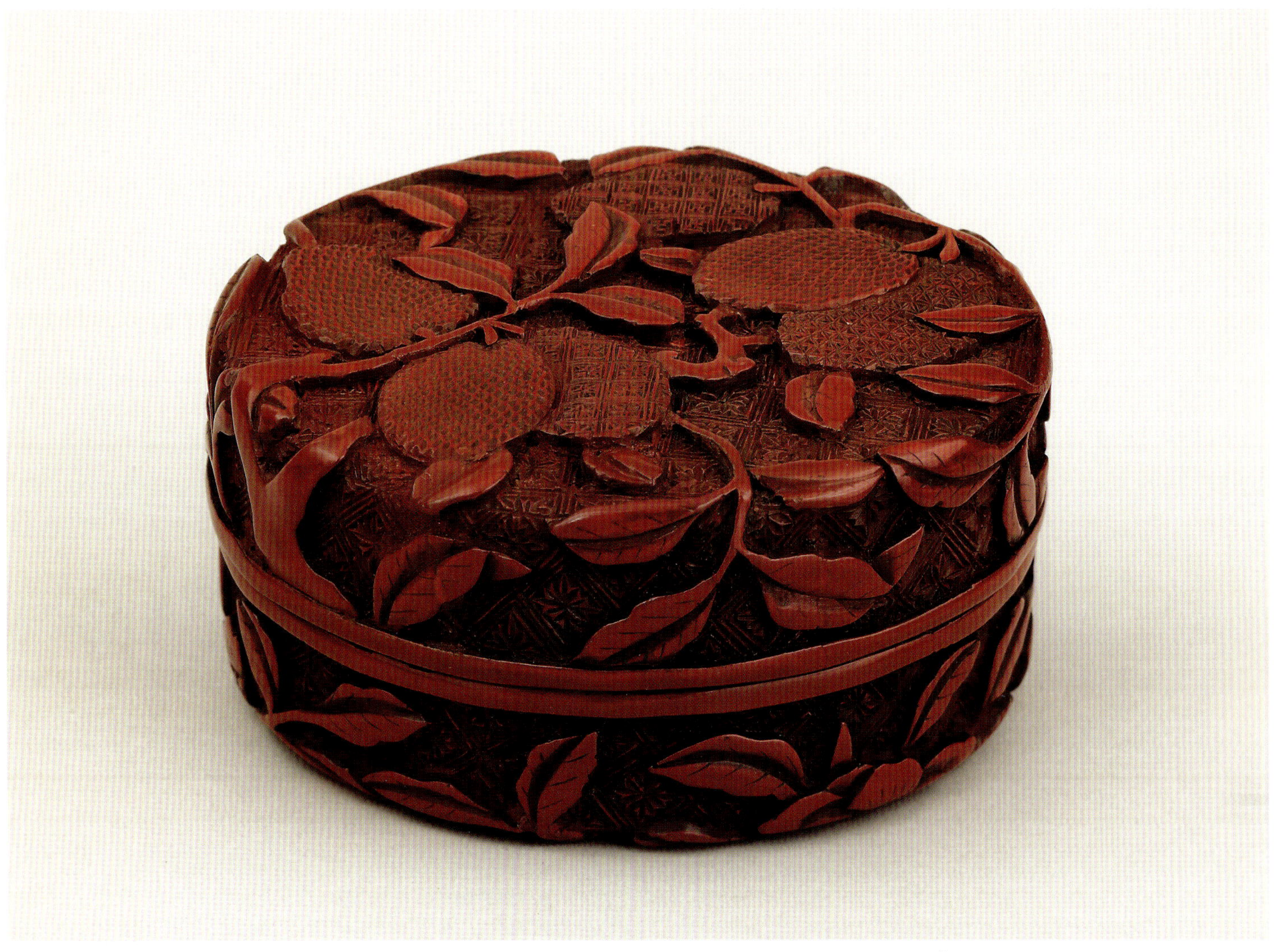

Both the top and bottom of this box are decorated; lychee designs appear on the top, and pomegranate flowers on the bottom. The fruits are realistically depicted, their rough skins set against a background of intricate patterning. Some fruits have a raised and bumpy surface; two are depicted with a stylized diaper pattern. The leaves of the lychee plant spread diagonally across the surface and continue onto the sides of the box. There is no hint of a top rim, as is seen on earlier boxes of similar size. The pomegranate flower and leaves are also generously placed on a background pattern.

Similar boxes found in European and Chinese collections generally date to the late Ming period; among them is a very similar box in the Metropolitan Museum of Art, New York.[1] This type of small box was made to store valuables, perhaps a small mirror or other precious items. In both China and Japan, this type of box may have been used to hold incense and may have had a role in the Japanese tea ceremony. The surface sheen indicates that it was a treasured item and probably belonged to a wealthy individual.

Note

1. See James C. Y. Watt and Barbara Brennan Ford, *East Asian Lacquer: The Florence and Herbert Irving Collection* (New York: Metropolitan Museum of Art, 1991), no. 40, p. 105.

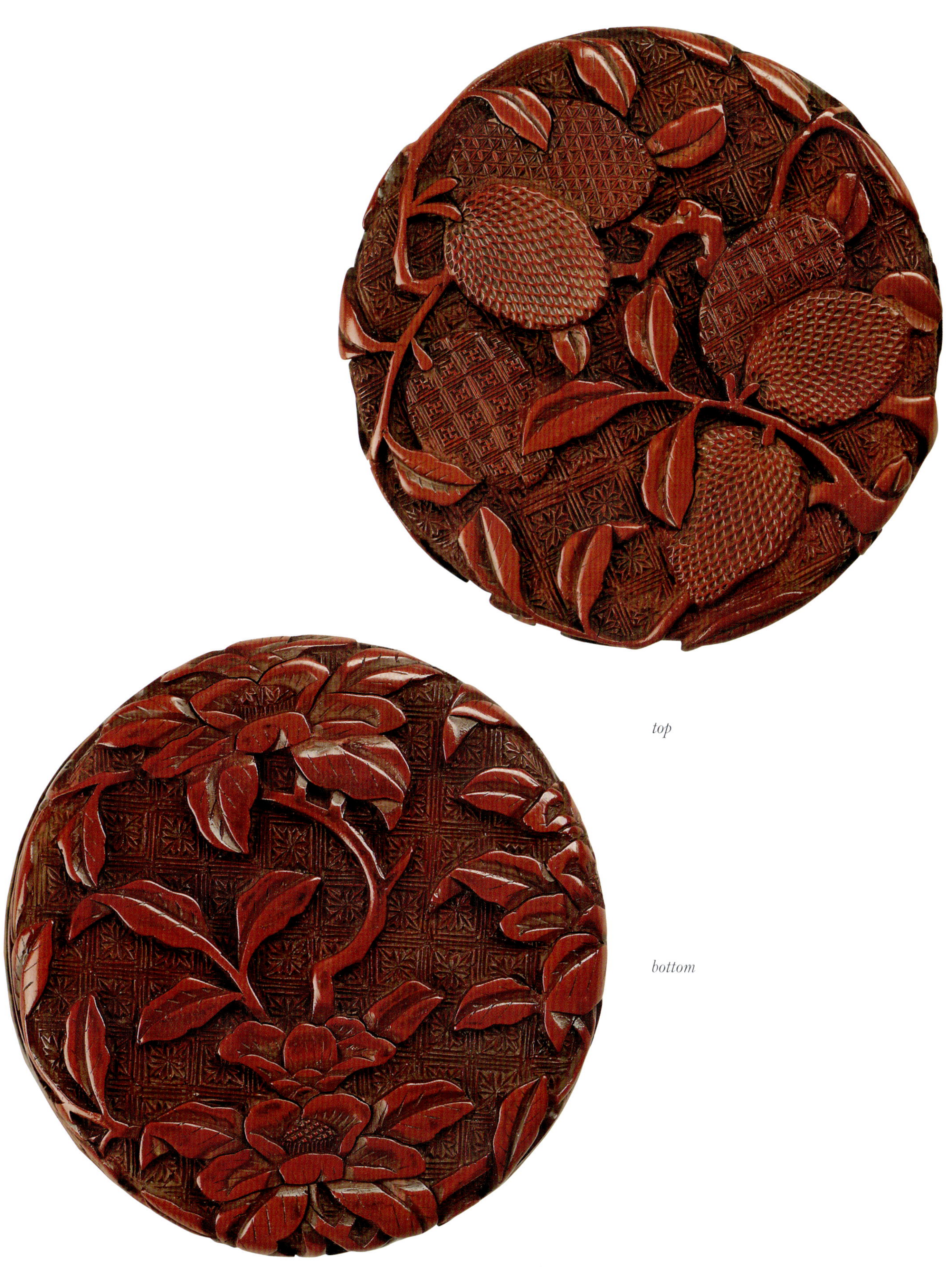

top

bottom

30

Double Dragon Plate

Ming dynasty, Wanli mark and period, 1595
Polychrome lacquer
H. 1 in. DIAM. 6¼ in.
L37,938

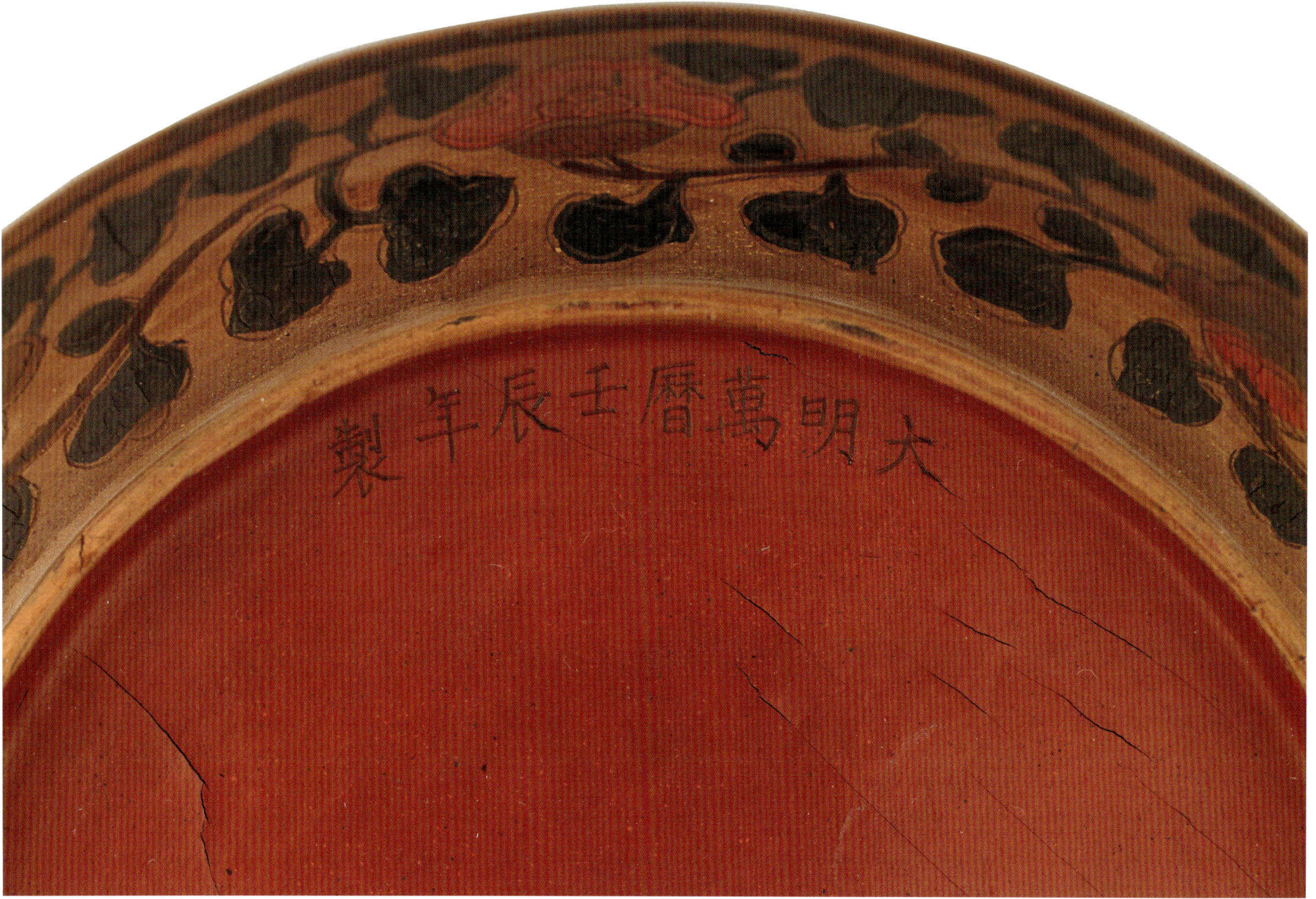

The lively design on this small plate, of two writhing dragons, one red-bodied with a black mane, the other black with a red mane, is consistent with the finest *tianqi*, or filled-in, lacquer. The overall ground is a warm, yellowish brown lacquer, but details of the dragons, flowers, and background design are sharply rendered in an outline filled in with a saturated lacquer of black and red.

The background of repeated reverse swastikas (a Buddhist symbol of infinity and a Chinese character meaning 10,000) is executed in minute red characters encased in black boxes. The interior of the rim is separated from the central design by a black band defined by fine trim. A floral pattern with buds of chrysanthemum, plum, and peony flowers set amid tendrils of leaves surrounds the rim.

The fine detail in the plate could only have been achieved with the *tianqi* technique, which allowed the artist sufficient control of his material to render both a clear design and deep color. Creating such an elegant piece required skillful initial design, provided perhaps by another artisan working from a preliminary drawing. The core body of such lacquerware was probably saturated cloth, which was susceptible to changes in humidity and temperature, perhaps explaining the cracking on the surface of this plate. Nonetheless, the pictorial decoration and variety of lacquer colors create a very pleasing design.

A rectangular tray with a double dragon design, also from the reign of Wanli, is in the Irving Collection at the Metropolitan Museum of Art.[1]

Note

1. Illustrated in James C. Y. Watt and Barbara Brennan Ford, *East Asian Lacquer: The Florence and Herbert Irving Collection* (New York: Metropolitan Museum of Art, 1991), cat. no. 51, pp. 120–21.

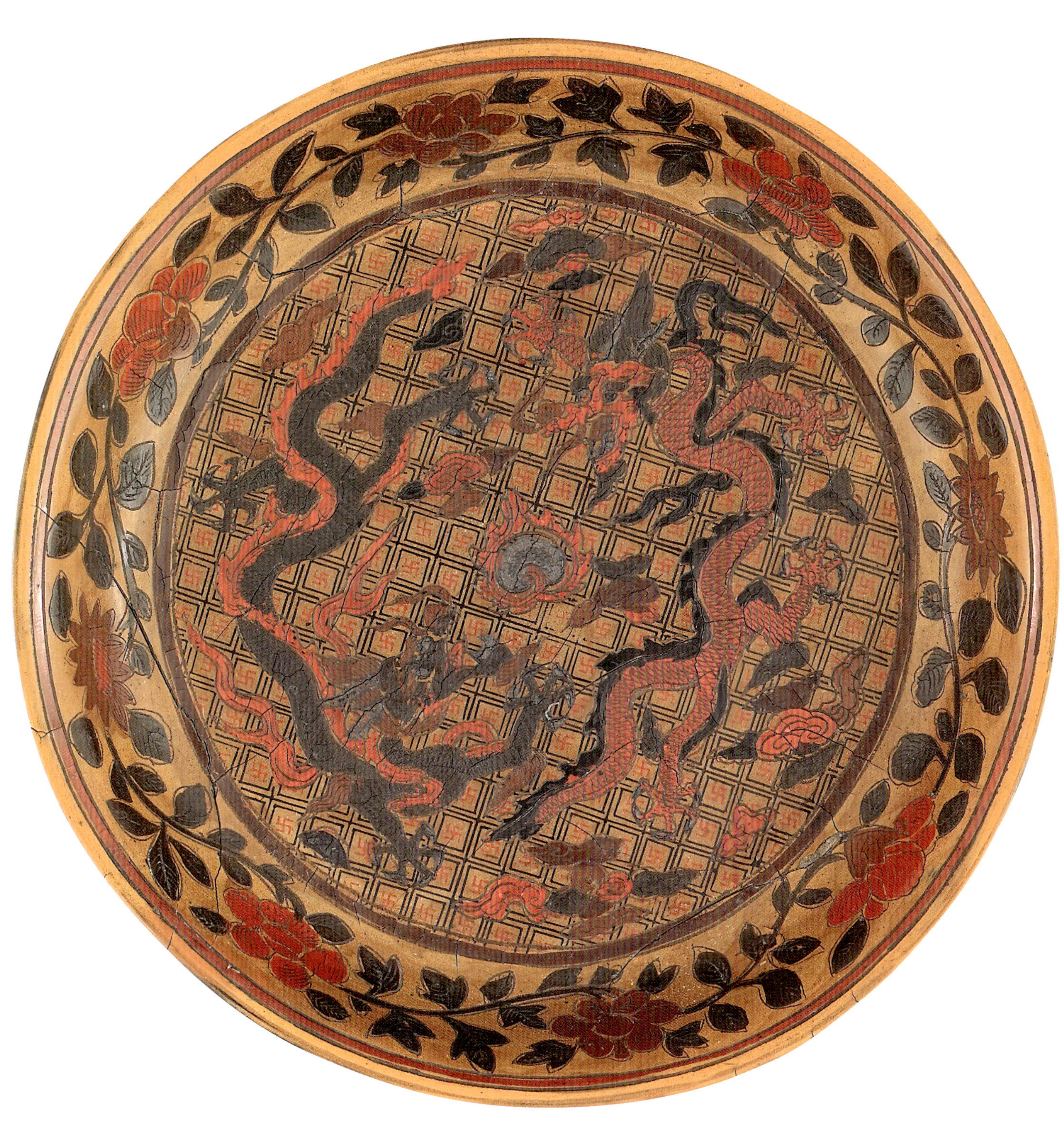

31

Dragon Plate

Ming dynasty, Wanli mark and period, dated 1592
Polychrome lacquer with silver wire
H. ¾ in. DIAM. 8¼ in.
L37,918

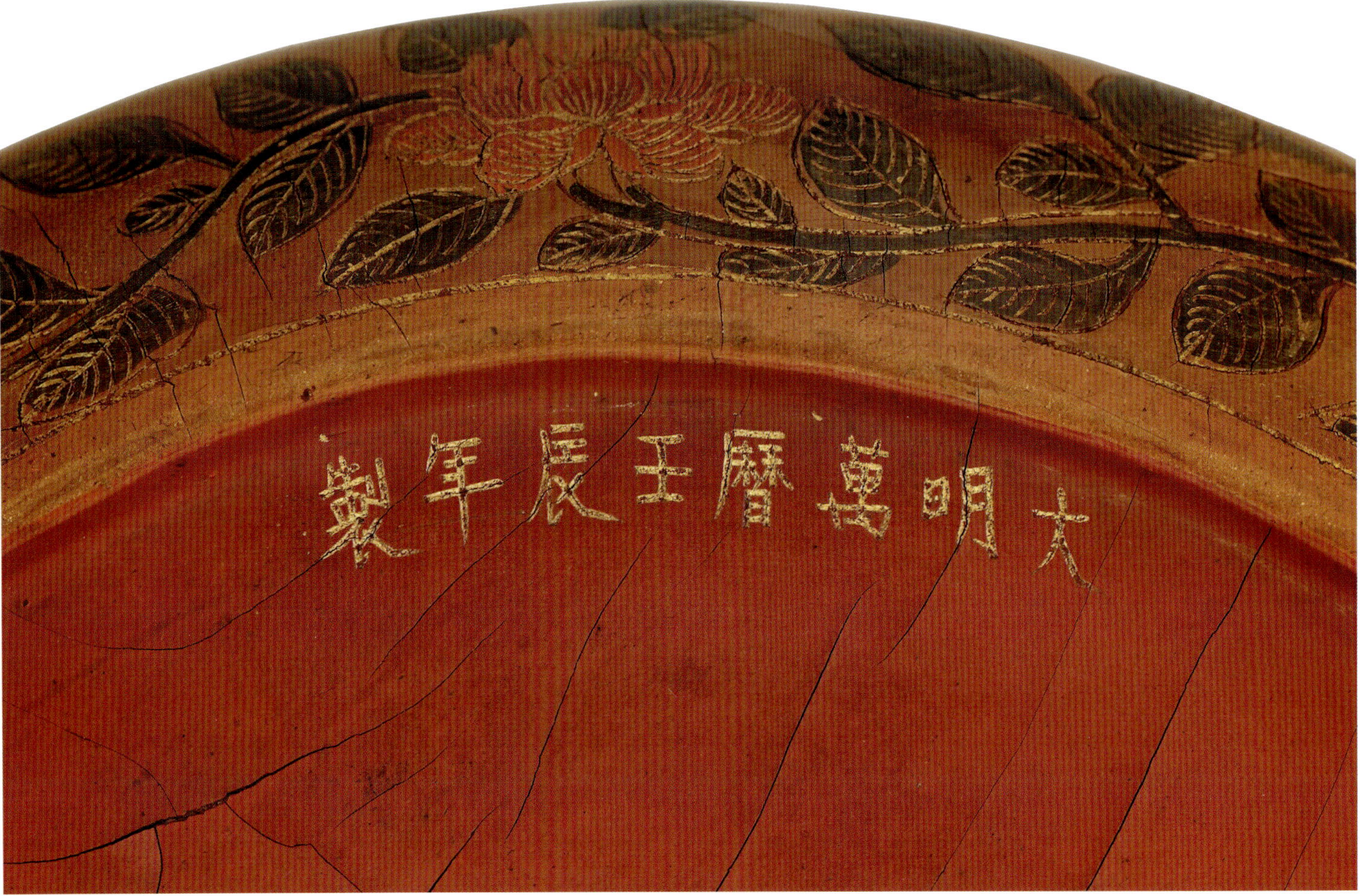

Inlaid lacquers, in which the design is carved into the surface and then filled in with color, are known as *tianqi* in Chinese. They are some of the most elaborately decorated wares of the Ming period. Sometimes called polychrome lacquer, this type was probably first produced in the fifteenth century. This sixteenth-century example, decorated with a single five-clawed dragon pursuing a flaming pearl, employs red, black, silver, and subtle golden brown and yellow lacquers to render the robust design. Golden-colored scales, silvery claws and hair, and a wide, gaping red mouth elaborately define the dragon's body. Tendrils of silver-colored wire extend from the head of the dragon; the artist filled the spaces between the wire with rich black lacquer.[1]

The dragon motif is encircled by a quatrefoil, lobed band, with stylized wave patterns along the bottom border and a stylized *ruyi* at the top left. The band itself is created by sharply differentiated black and yellow bands on a paler red. The quatrefoil is edged by a tightly patterned band of reverse swastikas in black set against a yellow-brown background. The reverse swastika is a Buddhist symbol of infinity and a Chinese character meaning 10,000.

The eight Buddhist symbols are depicted around the interior edge of the plate. A band of red, defined by a thin, metal wirelike line, captures the central design and delineates the final border of meandering lotus stalks and leaves interspersed with distinctly outlined red lotus flowers.

The sum of the decoration points to a Buddhist theme, which, when considered with the technical mastery and complex patterning, indicates that the plate was made for imperial use. Lacquer artists of this high caliber typically worked in hereditary ateliers and enjoyed considerable imperial support.

Note

1. A dish and a box from the Irving Collection are dated 1595 and illustrated in James C. Y. Watt and Barbara Brennan Ford, *East Asian Lacquer: The Florence and Herbert Irving Collection* (New York: Metropolitan Museum of Art, 1991), pp. 119 and 121.

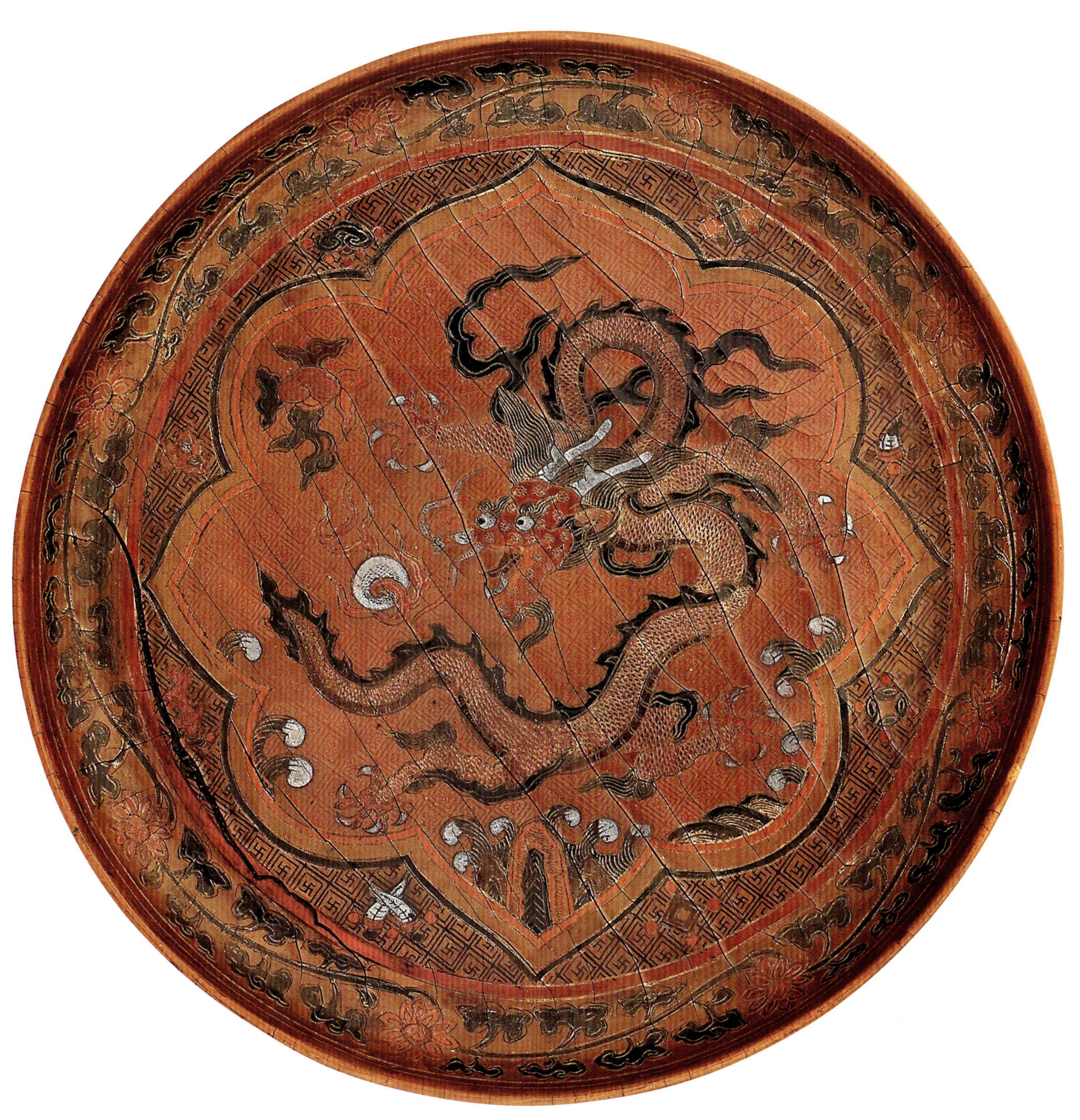

Bibliography

Asian Art Museum, Choong Moon Lee Center for Asian Art and Culture. *Botanical Symbols in Chinese Art: Knowledge Cards.* Text by Therese Tse Bartholomew. San Francisco: Pomegranate Communications, 2004.

Bai, Qianshen. "Inscriptions, Calligraphy, and Seals on Jingdezhen Porcelains from the Shunzhi Era." In *Treasures from an Unknown Reign: Shunzhi Porcelain 1644–1661*, by Michael Butler, Julia B. Curtis, and Stephen Little. Alexandria, Va.: Art Services International, 2002.

Chen Chang, ed. *Zhongguo qiji quanji* (Lacquer treasures from China). Vol. 4: *Sanguo–Yuan* (Three Kingdoms–Yuan dynasty). Fujian, China: Fujian Publishing House, 1998.

Chūgoku no urushi-kōgei (Exhibition of Chinese lacquer). Tokyo: Bijutsu Club, 1970.

Clifford, Derek. *Chinese Carved Lacquer.* London: Bamboo Publishing, 1992.

The Colors and Forms of Song and Yuan China: Lacquerwares, Ceramics, and Metalwares (Tokyo: Nezu Museum of Fine Arts, 2004).

David, Sir Percival, trans. and ed. *Chinese Connoisseurship: The Ko Ku Yao Lun, The Essential Criteria of Antiquities.* New York: Praeger, 1971.

Fang Jing Pei. *Symbols and Rebuses in Chinese Art: Figures, Bugs, Beasts, and Flowers.* Berkeley, Calif.: Ten Speed Press, 2004.

Figgess, John. "A Letter from the Court of Yung Lo." *Transactions of the Oriental Ceramic Society* 34 (1962–63): 97–101.

———. "Ming and Pre-Ming Lacquer in the Japanese Tea Ceremony." *Transactions of the Oriental Ceramic Society* 37 (1967–68, 1968–69): 37–51.

Garner, Harry M. *Chinese Lacquer.* London: Faber and Faber, 1979.

———. "Diaper Backgrounds on Chinese Carved Lacquer." *Ars Orientalis: The Arts of Islam and the East* 6 (1966): 165–89.

———. "The Export of Chinese Lacquer to Japan in the Yuan and Early Ming Dynasties." *Archives of Asian Art* 25 (1972): 6–28.

———. Introduction. *Ming Lacquer: An Exhibition Arranged by Bluett & Sons.* London: 1960.

———. "Two Chinese Carved Lacquer Boxes of the Fifteenth Century in the Freer Gallery of Art." *Ars Orientalis: The Arts of Islam and the East* 9 (1973): 41–50.

Honolulu Academy of Arts: Selected Works. Honolulu: Honolulu Academy of Arts, 1990.

Hu Shih-chang and Jane Wilkinson. *Chinese Lacquer.* Edinburgh: National Museums of Scotland, 1998.

Hubei Provincial Museum. *Lacquerware from the Warring States to the Han Periods Excavated in Hubei Province.* Hong Kong: Art Gallery, The Chinese University of Hong Kong, 1994.

Japan: An Illustrated Encyclopedia. Tokyo: Kodansha International, 1993.

Knight, Michael. *East Asian Lacquers in the Collection of the Seattle Art Museum.* Seattle: Seattle Art Museum, 1992.

Kuwayama, George. *Far Eastern Lacquer.* Los Angeles: Los Angeles County Museum of Art, 1982.

Lam, Peter, ed. *2000 Years of Chinese Lacquer.* Hong Kong: Oriental Ceramic Society of Hong Kong and Art Gallery, The Chinese University of Hong Kong, 1993.

Lee King Tsi and Hu Shih Chang. *Drache und Phoenix: Lackarbeiten aus China, Sammlung der Familie Lee, Tokyo/Dragon and Phoenix: Chinese Lacquerware from the Sammy Lee Family Collection, Tokyo.* Cologne, Germany: Museum of East Asian Art, 1990.

Lee Yu-kuan. *Oriental Lacquer Art.* New York: Weatherhill, 1972.

Lovell, Hin-Cheung. "Sung and Yüan Monochrome Lacquers in the Freer Gallery." *Ars Orientalis: The Arts of Islam and the East* 9 (1973): 121–30.

Low-Beer, Fritz. "Chinese Lacquer of the Middle and Late Ming Period." *Museum of Far Eastern Antiquities Bulletin*, no. 24 (1952): 27–137.

Suo Yuming, ed. *Zhongguo wenwu* (Chinese art treasures). Vol. 3, *Qipin* (Lacquer). Taipei: Guangfu Publishing, 1983.

Tokyo National Museum. *Chūgoku no raden* (Mother-of-pearl inlay in Chinese lacquer art). Tokyo: Benridō, 1981.

———. *Tōyō no shikkōgei: Tokubetsu-ten* (Oriental lacquer arts: Special exhibition). Glossary and object list in English. Tokyo: Tokyo National Museum, 1977.

Urushi Study Group. *Urushi: Proceedings of the Urushi Study Group, June 10–27, 1985.* Edited by N.S. Brommelle and Perry Smith. Marina del Rey, Calif.: Getty Conservation Institute, 1988.

Varley, Paul. *Japanese Culture.* 4th ed. Honolulu: University of Hawaii Press, 2000.

Wang Shixiang and Zhu Jiajin, eds. *Zhongguo meishu quanji* (Anthology of Chinese Art), Vol. 8, *Gongyi meishubian* (Decorative arts). Beijing: Wenwu Chubanshe, 1989.

Watson, William, ed. *Lacquerwork in Asia and Beyond.* Colloquies on Art and Archaeology in Asia, no. 11. London: Percival David Foundation, 1982.

Watt, James C. Y. *China: Dawn of a Golden Age, 200–750 A.D.* New York: Metropolitan Museum of Art, 2004.

Watt, James C. Y., and Barbara Brennan Ford. *East Asian Lacquer: The Florence and Herbert Irving Collection.* New York: Metropolitan Museum of Art, 1991.

Wirgin, Jan. "Some Chinese Carved Lacquer of the Yuan and Ming Periods." *Museum of Far Eastern Antiquities Bulletin*, no. 44 (1972): 93–114.

Wu Tung. *Masterpieces of Chinese Painting from the Museum of Fine Arts, Boston: Tang through Yuan Dynasties.* Boston: Museum of Fine Arts, Boston; Tokyo: Ōtsuka Kōgeisha, 1996.

Zhu Jiajin and Xia Gengqi, eds. *Zhongguo qiji quanji* (Lacquer treasures from China). Vol. 5, *Ming* (Ming). Fujian, China: Fujian Publishing House, 1998.

Chronology

221–206 BCE	QIN DYNASTY
206 BCE–220 CE	HAN DYNASTY
	Western (Former) Han Dynasty 206 BCE–9 CE
	Xin Dynasty (Wang Meng Interregnum) 9–23 CE
	Eastern (Later) Han Dynasty 25–220 CE
220–265	THREE KINGDOMS
265–420	JIN DYNASTY
317–589	SOUTHERN DYNASTIES
386–581	NORTHERN DYNASTIES
581–618	SUI DYNASTY
618–907	TANG DYNASTY
907–960	FIVE DYNASTIES (in the north)
907–979	TEN KINGDOMS (in the south)
907–1125	LIAO DYNASTY
960–1279	SONG DYNASTY
	Northern Song 960–1127
	Southern Song 1127–1279
1115–1234	JIN DYNASTY
1260–1368	YUAN DYNASTY
1368–1644	MING DYNASTY

Emperor's Reign Title and Dates

Hongwu	1368–1398
Jianwen	1399–1402
Yongle	1403–1424
Hongxi	1425
Xuande	1426–1435
Zhentong	1436–1449
Jingtai	1450–1456
Tianshun	1457–1464
Chenghua	1465–1487
Hongzhi	1488–1505
Zhengde	1506–1521
Jiajing	1522–1566
Longqing	1567–1572
Wanli	1573–1620
Taichang	1620
Tianqi	1621–1627
Chongzhen	1628–1644

1644–1911	QING DYNASTY

Index

Page numbers in *italics* refer to supporting illustrations. Numbers in parentheses refer to catalogue entry numbers; all entries are illustrated.

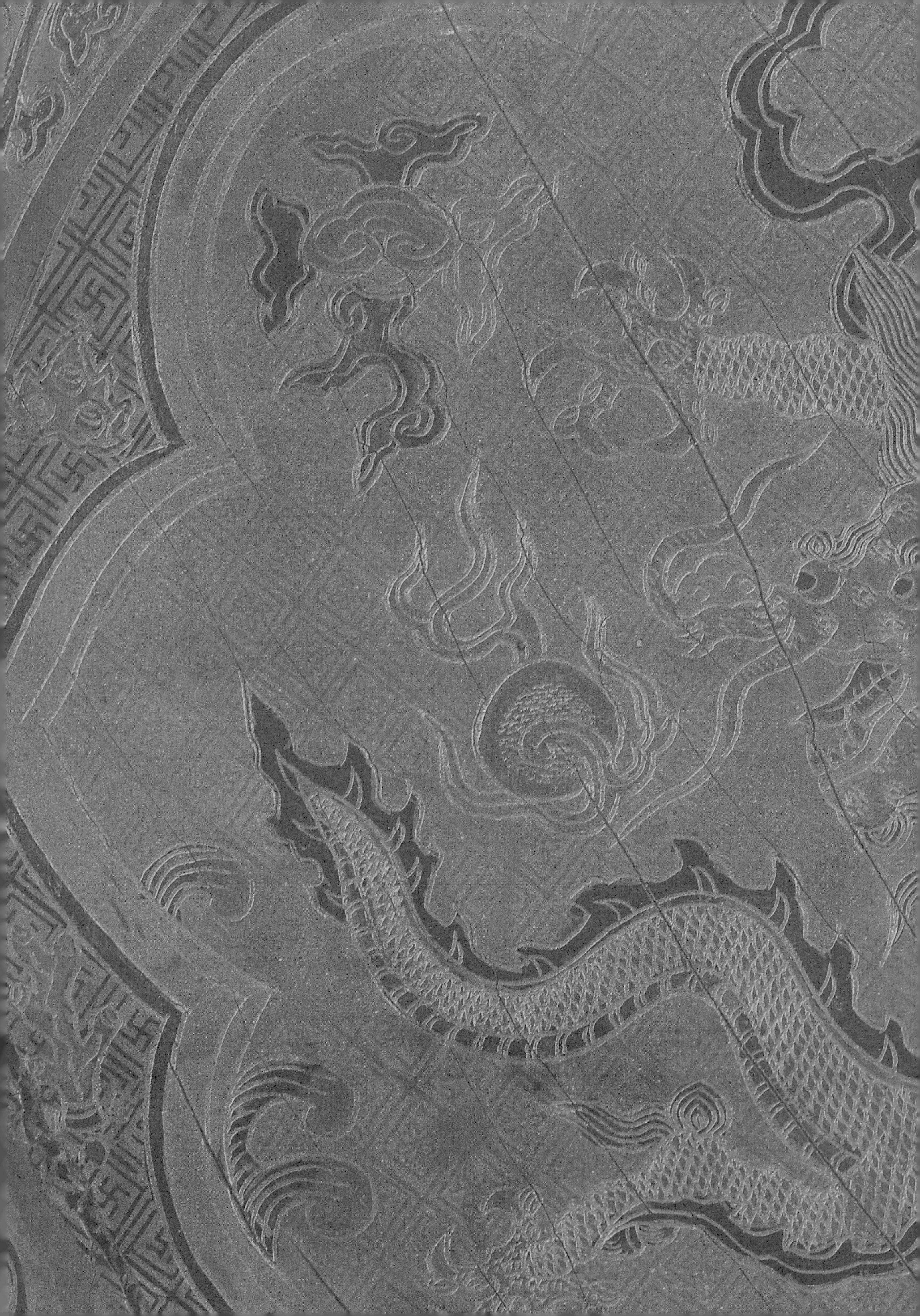